GENERATION Z
GOES TO COLLEGE

GENERATION Z GOES TO COLLEGE

Corey Seemiller
Meghan Grace

A Wiley Brand

Published by Jossey-Bass
A Wiley Brand
One Montgomery Street, Suite 1000, San Francisco, CA 94104-4594 — www.josseybass.com

Jossey-Bass books and products are available through most bookstores. To contact Jossey-Bass directly call our Customer Care Department within the U.S. at 800-956-7739, outside the U.S. at 317-572-3986, or fax 317-572-4002.

Wiley publishes in a variety of print and electronic formats and by print-on-demand. Some material included with standard print versions of this book may not be included in e-books or in print-on-demand. If this book refers to media such as a CD or DVD that is not included in the version you purchased, you may download this material at http://booksupport.wiley.com. For more information about Wiley products, visit www.wiley.com.

Library of Congress Cataloging-in-Publication Data

Names: Seemiller, Corey, author. | Grace, Meghan, author.
Title: Generation Z goes to college / Corey Seemiller, Meghan Grace.
Description: San Francisco, CA : Jossey-Bass, 2016. | Includes
    bibliographical references and index.
Identifiers: LCCN 2015036096 (print) | LCCN 2015041434 (ebook) | ISBN
    9781119143451 (cloth) | ISBN 9781118143529 (ePDF) |
    ISBN 9781118143482 (ePub)
Subjects: LCSH: College students – Attitudes.
Classification: LCC LB3605 .S3828 2016 (print) | LCC LB3605 (ebook) | DDC
    378.1/98 – dc23
LC record available at http://lccn.loc.gov/2015036096

Cover design by: Wiley

Printed in the United States of America

FIRST EDITION

HB Printing   10 9 8 7 6 5 4 3 2

I dedicate this book to the most important Generation Z person I know–my daughter, Kacey.

— Corey

To my grandparents, for supporting my love for learning. To my parents, for being my best friends and biggest fans.

— Meghan

CONTENTS

About this Book   ix

About the Authors   xi

Acknowledgments   xiii

Preface   xv

Introduction   xxi

CHAPTER 1: Who Is Generation Z?   1

CHAPTER 2: Beliefs and Perspectives   25

CHAPTER 3: Communication Platforms and Preferences   57

CHAPTER 4: Social Media Use   65

CHAPTER 5: Friends, Family, and Romance   87

CHAPTER 6: Cares and Concerns   97

CHAPTER 7: Engagement and Social Change   129

CHAPTER 8: Leadership Styles and Capacities   151

CHAPTER 9: Maximizing Learning   173

CHAPTER 10: Working with Generation Z   191

References   229

Index   267

ABOUT THIS BOOK

WE WROTE THIS BOOK BECAUSE WE WANTED TO SHARE findings from our study, Generation Z Goes to College and other studies that would help educators, parents, employers, and students themselves understand Generation Z better. We wanted specifically to frame this book in the context of higher education because Generation Z is already in college. As programs, courses, processes, environments, and initiatives adapted to Millennials in higher education, we must be prepared to do the same for this next generation of students.

This book reports data from 295 sources, and incorporates findings from the Generation Z Goes to College study, for which both of us served as the primary investigators. A great deal of the findings presented in this book are from this study, yet we heavily supplement them with work from other scholars whom we cite throughout the book. The statistics, charts, graphs, and quotations of student perspectives that we do not explicitly cite come from our study.

ABOUT THE AUTHORS

Corey Seemiller has worked in higher education for more than twenty years in faculty and administrative positions. She has both taught and directed programs related to her areas of expertise, which include leadership, civic engagement, career development, and social justice. She currently serves as an assistant professor in the organizational leadership program at Wright State University and previously held roles including director of leadership, learning, and assessment at OrgSync, a campus management technology platform, and director of leadership programs at the University of Arizona. In 2008, Seemiller cofounded the Sonoran Center for Leadership Development, a 501(c)(3) organization that offers affordable and accessible leadership development training for individuals and groups in southern Arizona. She is the author of *The Student Leadership Competencies Guidebook,* to help educators design intentional curriculum aimed to develop students' leadership competencies. She also designed evaluation measurements for each competency, an online database that outlines leadership competencies needed by each academically accredited industry, a workbook, online competency self-inventory, and an iOS app. Seemiller received her bachelor's degree in communication from Arizona State University, master's degree in educational leadership from Northern Arizona University, and Ph.D. in higher education from the University of Arizona. She is a member of Generation X.

Meghan Grace received her undergraduate degree in communication studies from Chapman University. After receiving her master's degree in higher education from the University of Arizona, she pursued a career in student affairs. She worked in leadership programs at the University of Arizona, where she taught courses in social entrepreneurship, event planning, leadership, and career readiness. She currently serves as the new member orientation director for Sigma Phi Epsilon fraternity, where she coordinates orientation events and educational programs. Meghan is a Millennial.

ACKNOWLEDGMENTS

WE ACKNOWLEDGE THE MANY SCHOLARS AND AUTHORS WHO have put forth seminal research that has contributed to the dialogue on generations, including Neil Howe and William Strauss, Arthur Levine and Diane Dean, Ron Zemke, Haydn Shaw, Chuck Underwood, and Tim Elmore. Generation Z authors, including Chole Combi who compiled stories of Generation Z as well as Tom Koulopoulos and Dan Keldsen who highlight how to work with Generation Z in the business world, have contributed greatly to our understanding of this generation.

PREFACE

WE STARTED OUR JOURNEY WITH GENERATION Z IN summer 2013, right before the oldest in this generation were about to start college. Both of us at the time were working in a university leadership programs office, putting together programs, events, and courses for thousands of students each year. We were fascinated with the new generation of students before us. No one in higher education was talking about them yet. We knew if we did not pay attention to changing demographics, the leadership experiences we designed for these students might not be relevant.

Thus began our quest of trying to find information about Generation Z, a task that was quite challenging at the time. For one thing, very little research was available about Generation Z in general, with the exception of a handful of resources from market research agencies. And since this group of students was just entering college, there was not a base of research about them in the context of higher education. We decided in May 2014 that it was time to conduct our own study. We spent months fine-tuning our research design and filling out paperwork. And as with all other studies involving human subjects, our project required review and approval. We also logged many hours reaching out to create institutional partnerships to gather participants. We launched the study in August 2014.

Our goal was to learn the styles, motivations, and perspectives of Generation Z students to better work with them. Our plan was to analyze the data we collected and see what patterns emerged. Because of our role in supporting students, we hoped our data would help us answer a number of questions—for example: What social issues do students in Generation Z care most about? What motivates them? How do they prefer to learn? What technology do they use? If our study could shed some light on these and other issues, we would be better able to design programs, develop curriculum, set up administrative processes, create marketing and outreach plans, and advise these students.

We have written this book as a way to share our findings and those from other studies to help educators, parents, employers, students, and anyone else interested in preparing for this generation as they enter college and adulthood. As with any other book, keep in mind that here you will get information from a specific viewpoint. Our perspective is that of two former student affairs professionals who not only have studied this generation but also have worked with Generation Z students directly. We designed the research and looked at the data we collected in a way that reflects our personal and professional experiences—and in a way that we hope will be constructive to others who wish to bring out the best in today's teens and college students. Corey is a seasoned professional with twenty years of experience in higher education, and Meghan is a new professional coming into the field shortly after graduate school.

We decided to share some thoughts on our respective generations separately to give readers a better idea of how each of us approached Generation Z initially and how we feel about them now after conducting our research.

Corey

I am a member of Generation X. Growing up, I had to figure out if I wanted to watch VHF or UHF television channels, my phones all had cords (some had dials too), and I learned to type on a typewriter. I was not very informed about world issues, although I was in high school during the Gulf War. We watched Channel 1 in homeroom class, and that is about the only place I got the news.

Technology is not the only thing that has changed. Relationships seemed different then as well. I would stay up all night talking to my best friend on the phone because texting and social media had yet to be invented. Dating meant being asked out by someone in person or on the phone or taking the chance of a blind date set up by a friend. There were no online dating sites or matchmaking services to screen potential dates, and being able to search someone online before the date was not an option. As diversity seems the norm today, in the 1980s and 1990s, we were taught that diversity was something to tolerate rather than celebrate. During my coming of age, most gay people were in the closet, and the Women's National Basketball Association was not even in existence.

College was exciting for me because computers were finally a bit more mainstream, and I had access to one in my residence hall computer lab. But we still had to go to the library to read a journal article, hoping that someone had not misfiled the volume and issue we needed. One of the starkest differences about college then and college today was that a public education was very affordable. My tuition was so low at my state institution that I could make enough money in a summer job to pay for tuition for both upcoming semesters. With my resident assistant job and summer work, I was able to leave college debt free.

Fast-forward twenty years. I have now worked at a number of colleges, public and private, four year and two year, in different capacities. I have witnessed the traditional-aged college population make the transition from Generation X to Millennials and now to Generation Z. I was just getting used to Millennials, and now there is another demographic culture I need to understand. I have to admit that with this new generation, it is sometimes frustrating to compete with their cell phones in class, be Google fact-checked during lectures, or get a very impersonal e-mail in text language the night before an assignment is due saying something like, "Am sick sorry have to turn in pper L8." But I have to check myself and think, "How can I capture this energy they have for learning?"

Yet it is refreshing to work with students who are informed and engaged in changing the world. I remember the chagrin I felt when I let students know about service hour requirements for our leadership program and a student asked if she could count the time she spends running her nonprofit toward the requirements. That day reframed my thinking about service and community engagement in ways I will always appreciate As I think about what this generation has to offer in college and afterward, I am excited and energized, and I feel that we are in good hands.

Meghan

Born and raised in the 1990s, I remember computer class being the best time of the school day and having to tear the perforated edges off printer paper. And while Mavis Beacon, the typewriting software, was supposed to be teaching me typing, there was nothing that helped me increase my words per minute more than staying up later than I was supposed to chatting with my friends on AOL Instant Messenger. Not having a cell phone until I started high school was pretty much the hardest fourteen years of my life, and today I'm not sure how I survived that long.

When I went to college, I was looking for the most beautiful setting I could possibly find and a school with a great reputation (so I could enjoy my four years and eventually get a great job after graduation). Eighteen-year-old me was pretty optimistic when I started at Chapman University in sunny Orange, California. But twenty-two-year-old me was astounded and overwhelmed by the thought of student loan payments and this strange land called "the real world" so many people spoke of. I knew that graduate school was the path for me to continue exploring my passions and to narrow in on what my career would hold.

Little did I know that as I finished my graduate work in higher education and started my career as a student affairs administrator, I would come face to face with a new generation of students: Generation Z. I started to see, and sometimes became frustrated with, the way they behaved on campus, in programs, in organizations, and in the classroom. They were so close in age to my own generation but also so different. They would attempt to be my friend on social media and message me about assignments or meetings, neither act that I would have ever thought to do as a college student. I found myself not only sending an e-mail reminder to my student staff about our meetings but following up with a text message as well to make sure they showed up. Some students did not understand why I did not call them back when they called my office and missed their call. I had to explain that my landline did not have caller ID, so I would know if they called only if they left a voice mail, which a majority of the time they did not.

While their frequent and informal communication took me by surprise, I also realized they are intelligent and motivated to make a change in the world. Along with that, I found that as the new cohort of students would soon become the majority in higher education, there was still much to know and understand. In my day-to-day work, I interact mainly with first-year students who are part of the first wave of Generation Z. The more I interact with Generation Z, the more thankful and hopeful I become, knowing this smart, savvy, innovative, driven, responsible, caring, and understanding group of young people will be taking on the real world soon.

INTRODUCTION

IN 1995, EXCITING THINGS WERE HAPPENING IN THE world. Pixar released *Toy Story,* the first completely computer-generated film.[1] George Foreman was still known for his boxing, not yet for his grilling devices.[2] Basketball superstar Michael Jordan returned to the National Basketball Association from retirement.[3] That year not only marks the time that the web had become worldwide,[4] it also serves as the beginning of Generation Z, the most recent generation to come of age. In 1995, they were making their first appearances in the world; today they are making their ways into the halls of colleges and universities across America.

Why Generation Z?

As Millennials end their reign as the majority in higher education, their parents, employers, educators, and advisors are just figuring out what makes them tick. But what worked for Millennials might not fit this new generation. To provide the most effective and beneficial experiences for Generation Z, it is crucial to know how these students think, what they are concerned with and care about, and how they prefer to be engaged.

Just as it took time to adapt to working with Millennials as they entered college (and some are still struggling to adapt), a whole new generation has shown up with a different set of needs. Levine and Dean's *Generation on a Tightrope* explored the Millennial generation and helped those in higher education be more effective in how they worked with and engaged these students.[5] Now, with the first wave of Generation Z students already in college, it is necessary to turn our attention to them.

Looking at Generation Z

Much of the buzz and conversation about Generation Z has focused on their teen years, not in the context of higher education. But it is now imperative to be prepared for what they bring to higher education.

In discussing Generation Z in this book, we have sought to interpret our data and the results of other social scientists' research in a way that will provide a better understanding of this cohort of students and capture their peer personality, which includes the common age range, common beliefs, attitudes, behaviors, and perceived membership of the group.[6] Our goal is to explain and explore trends and similarities within Generation Z. It is important, however, to keep in mind that age and time period have effects on generational trends.[7] As a group ages, they may grow in and out of trends and behaviors, and particular events occurring in their lifetimes can shift their outlook and experiences.

Not every Generation Z student will align with every finding or topic in this book, and thus it is important to recognize and validate the differences among individuals in this group. Just because an individual falls within this generation does not mean he or she will exhibit all the characteristics of the generation in its entirety. The trends and behaviors we discuss are what we see as tendencies of the group, not decrees that every individual will act in accordance with. Therefore, we discuss Generation Z in the aggregate to best explain the generation as a group. We recognize that there are outliers but do not focus on them. Our hope is to better understand what makes this generation unique and provide insight into how to best engage these students during their time in higher education.

Overview of the Generation Z Goes to College Study

Our Generation Z Goes to College study aimed to uncover characteristics, outlooks, and trends of current college students born 1995 or later as they relate to their experience in higher education. We examined:

· Their characteristics, styles, and motivations
· How they learn, engage, communicate, and form relationships
· Pertinent social issues and outlook on life

The study was approved by the University of Arizona Human Subjects Protection Program, which is aimed at protecting human subjects in research studies.

Institutional Partners

In order to include as many college students born in 1995 or later as possible, we cast a wide net to solicit institutional partners using three recruitment strategies during July and

August 2014. First, we sent an e-mail describing the study with a call for institutional partners over a number of professional e-mail lists in student affairs. These were:

- American College Personnel Association, Commission for Student Involvement
- National Clearinghouse for Leadership Programs
- National Association of Student Personnel Administrators, Student Leadership Programs Knowledge Community
- OrgSync, Administrator's Club
- 2014 National Collegiate Leadership Conference Advisor Listserv
- 2014 National Leadership Symposium Participant Listserv

These lists are connected to associations and events in which one or both of us are networked, which allowed us to easily access student affairs professionals at a number of institutions.

Second, we posted a call for institutional partners on social media, including the Student Affairs Professional Group on Facebook (16,300 members) and the National Association of Student Personnel Administrators Student Leadership Programs Knowledge Community Facebook (1,300 members).

Finally, we reached out directly through e-mail and LinkedIn messaging to connect with potential institutional partners based on our networks. This approach entailed sending personalized messages to fifty individuals.

Through this process, we secured fifteen institutional partners. For each contact person at our partner institutions, we provided e-mail content and the survey link to forward to students. Table I.1 lists each institutional partner we sent the survey link to and details on the population and the sample.

Participants

The Generation Z Goes to College study was conducted between August and October 2014 and solicited students from fifteen partner institutions. Students were sent an e-mail from an administrator in their own institution inviting them to complete the online survey. Each institutional contact determined which student populations would receive the survey link (in many cases, it was based on institutional permission or access). We began the survey with 1,223 students; 1,143 of those met the qualifications of being born in 1995 or later. Individual measurement responses ranged from 614 to 759 for quantitative measurements and 618 to 685 for qualitative measurements, and declined between earlier measurements and later ones. Table I.2. describes the number of responses analyzed in each measure.

Since demographic questions were included at the end of the survey, only those who completed the entire survey responded to the demographic questions, which was 613 participants. Table I.3. outlines the demographic data of those participants.

Instrument Design

Participants were asked to complete an online survey that included both quantitative measurements (multiple choice and

Table I.1 Institutional Partners for the Generation Z Goes to College Study

Institution	Four Year/ Two Year	Public/ Private	Enrollment	Geographic Location	Population	Population N	Sample N
Wingate	4	Private	2,163	North Carolina	All first-year students	500	31
University of Central Florida	4	Public	53,401	Florida	First-year LEAD scholars	262	44
Sacramento City College	2	Public	27,171	California	First-time students	3,375	24
University of Illinois	4	Public	43,881	Illinois	Residence life	2,220	41
Cal State-San Bernardino	4	Public	17,852	California	All first-year students	2,724	43
University of Connecticut*	4	Public	25,029	Connecticut	First-year program instructors	150	0

Institution		Type	Enrollment	State	Sample		
University of Arizona	4	Public	38,767	Arizona	First-year leadership students	579	116
Oklahoma State University	4	Public	23,033	Oklahoma	First-year students living on campus	4,000	230
Glenville State College	4	Public	1,721	West Virginia	Student support services students	185	1
Fairfield University	4	Private	5074	Connecticut	Random first-year students	100	9
Harper College	2	Public	15,711	Illinois	All students	2,600	32
Sonoma State University	4	Public	8,546	California	Students in freshman learning communities	300	3
Michigan State University	4	Public	47,071	Michigan	Study of the environment Living Learning Community	100	8

(continued)

Table I.1 (Continued)

Institution	Four Year/ Two Year	Public/ Private	Enrollment	Geographic Location	Population	Population N	Sample N
Winston-Salem State University	4	Public	64,27	North Carolina	First-year students living on campus	836	17
Oakton Community College**	2	Public	12,087	Illinois	NA	1	1
SUNY Brockport	4	Public	8,490	New York	First-year students	600	13

*Our campus contact at University of Connecticut sent the survey link to instructors rather than directly to students and asked instructors to forward to students. Of the 150 instructors who received the e-mail, we were not able to confirm how many forwarded the survey link and how many students responded. None of the 613 participants who identified their institutional affiliation were from the University of Connecticut.

**Community College was not an institutional partner. One participant filled out the survey and likely got the link forwarded from someone else or was co-enrolled at an institution involved in this study.

Table I.2   Number of Responses Analyzed in Each Measure

Measurement	Sample N
Characteristics of Generation Z	759
Styles in working with others	749
Motivations	728
Learning styles and preferences	701
Communication methods and preferences	685
Social media use	673
Friendships and relationships	665
Social concerns/cares	618
Politics	618
Optimism	614
Spirituality	614

Table I.3   Demographic Data of Participants (in percent)

Race/ethnicity	
African American or black	10.11
American Indian or Alaska Native	5.87
Asian	5.87
Hispanic	17.78
Middle Eastern	1.14
Native Hawaiian or Other Pacific Islander	1.96
White	76.18
Gender	
Man	30.83
Woman	69
Transgender	.16
Sexual orientation	
Heterosexual	91.03
Bisexual	5.21
Gay or lesbian	3.26

"select all that apply") as well as open-ended questions to gather qualitative data. The topics included self and peer group characteristic descriptions, learning styles and environment preferences, communication, relationships, social media use, leadership styles, social issues and engagement, and spiritual and political outlook. Some survey measurements were created using models and scales from existing literature.

Learning Styles

The four learning styles from Kolb's Experiential Learning Model were used to develop the descriptions of learning styles (also called learning approaches). Converging was renamed Practical, Diverging was renamed Imaginative, Accommodating was renamed Experiential, and Assimilating was renamed Logical. These changes were done to make the names of these styles easier to understand for the participants. For more information, see:

Kolb, A. Y., & Kolb, D. A. (2005). Learning styles and learning spaces: Enhancing experiential learning in higher education. *Academy of Management Learning and Education, 4*(2), 193–212.

The text for the styles was taken from:

Businessballs.com. (N.d.). *Kolb learning styles.* http://www.businessballs.com/kolblearningstyles.htm

Multiple Intelligences

Gardner's multiple intelligences model was adapted to serve as the list and descriptors of learning methods:

Gardner, H. (1993). *Multiple intelligences: The theory in practice.* New York: Basic Books.

Language descriptors for each intelligence type was taken from:

Bixler, B. A. (N.d.). *A multiple intelligences primer.* http://www.personal.psu.edu/bxb11/MI/MultipleIntelligences_print.html

Optimism

The two measurements of optimism and outlook questions were adapted from the Life Orientation Test. The measurement, "I am optimistic about my future," was adapted from "I'm always optimistic about my future," and "I believe good things will happen for me" was adapted from "Overall, I expect more good things to happen to me than bad." These adaptations were done because the first measurement appeared too extreme with the word *always*, and the second appeared too middle of the road.

Scheier, M. F., Carver, C. S., & Bridges, M. W. (1994). Distinguishing optimism from neuroticism (and trait anxiety, self-mastery, and self-esteem): A re-evaluation of the Life Orientation Test. *Journal of Personality and School Psychology, 67*(7), 1063–1078.

Data Analysis

Quantitative questions were analyzed by looking at response percentages for each measurement. Some findings were reported using only the percentages at either end of the spectrum (e.g., disagree versus agree). In other cases, response categories indicating a favorable or unfavorable response were combined for analysis and reporting (e.g., very concerned and concerned versus not concerned). The margin of error was calculated for each measurement to consider when comparing percentages. In addition, some measurements were analyzed by comparing means. *T*-tests for statistical significance were used for any analysis that involved comparing means. Qualitative responses were analyzed using a content analysis process. Responses were coded into one or more themes and then interpreted for analysis.

Limitations of the Study

As with any other study, this one had its limitations. First, although we attempted to cast the net wide, we could include in our sample only students from institutional partners who were interested in participating in the study. We attempted to reach out across the nation to include a variety of institutional types for partnership, but in the end, we worked only with institutions that were willing to participate. Because of this, the institutions we partnered with are not entirely representative of higher education. We did not have any single-gender institutions, historically black colleges, religiously affiliated institutions, or for-profit colleges. In addition, with only fifteen institutional partners, not all states were represented, although students came from a variety of states regardless of where they went to college. Another limitation is that the number of students in this study is not representative of the Generation Z student population in its entirety, and some institutions are overrepresented and some underrepresented in terms of participants. Because of this, the demographics of the sample may not reflect the exact demographics of Generation Z.

Other Research We Used

To offset these limitations, this book also presents research findings from four additional types of sources: higher education studies, national polling data, market research, and studies about adolescents.

Higher Education Studies

The main source of data for this book was the 2014 Generation Z Goes to College study, but other higher education sources, including Northeastern University's Innovation Imperative study on Generation Z students and the Higher Education Research Institute's Cooperative Institutional Research Program (CIRP) findings, were particularly useful. We worked directly with the Higher Education Research Institute to disaggregate the fall 2014 CIRP findings to only those in the age range of Generation Z providing us with a nationally normed sample of more than 150,000 students.

National Polling Data

Polling data, studies, and reports from entities such as Pew, Gallup, and the US Census also provided valuable insight.

Market Research

The first studies done on Generation Z emerged from market research, which is not surprising since many businesses likely want to understand their consumers and clients in this generation better. Research came from such areas as banking and real estate, but also emerged from market research companies assessing trends of this generation.

Studies about Adolescents

Given that these students were recently adolescents, we chose to look at studies that took place in the last few years focusing on the adolescent population. This was helpful in looking at trends of this group over time. For example, we found that 65 percent of Generation Z college students dislike or only somewhat like engaging in phone calls. This is no surprise given that according to a Pew poll of teenagers in 2010, phone calls were already considered "old school" technology.

Notes

1. IMDB. (1995). *Toy Story plot summary*. Retrieved from http://www.imdb.com/title/tt0114709/plotsummary

2. For more information about George Foreman, go to http://www.biography.com/people/george-foreman-9298881

3. For more information about Michael Jordan, go to http://www.biography.com/people/michael-jordan-9358066

4. World Wide Web Foundation. (2015). *History of the web*. Retrieved from http://webfoundation.org/about/vision/history-of-the-web/

5. Levine, A., & Dean, D. R. (2012). *Generation on a tightrope: A portrait of today's college student*. San Francisco: Wiley.

6. Strauss, W., & Howe, N. (1990). *Generations: The history of America's future*. New York: Morrow.

7. Strauss & Howe. (1990).

1

WHO IS GENERATION Z?

Generations, much like cultures, have their own attitudes, beliefs, social norms, and behaviors that define them. For some, Generation Z students might seem as if they are from a foreign land. Judgmental attitudes, lack of understanding, and stereotyping are barriers that might stand in the way of older generations in understanding this new culture.[1] Natives to the digital and online world, Generation Z will soon fully inhabit higher education and then the workplace, taking on roles that will influence the physical world beyond the screen. Before diving deep into the culture and personality of Generation Z, it is important to take a look at what characterizes and makes this generation unique.

Back in My Day …

"Every generation imagines itself to be more intelligent than the one that went before it, and wiser than the one that comes after it."

George Orwell[2]

Each generation has experienced being "kids these days," but as every new generation emerges, it is subjected to a certain level of disdain from older generations. Could the disdain be coming from the fact the new generations are indeed disrespectful and lazy? Or is it that those in older generations do not fully understand who these young people are and how social rules are changing because of them? In order to embrace and engage Generation Z, it is critical to understand who these students are and what makes them different.

Older generations create the environments that younger ones are raised in, so to fully understand Generation Z, it is important to start by understanding the generations that came before them.

Baby Boomers

The Baby Boomer generation gets its name from the surge of babies born after the end of World War II, between 1946 and 1964.[3] During the war, many men who would otherwise be fathers were busy fighting. As the war ended and troops returned home, there was more stability for the country and certainty for families, and thus began the boom of babies.[4]

Postwar America experienced a healthy economy; consumerism was seen as the cure for the Great Depression and the minor recessions leading up to and through World War II.[5] Baby Boomers grew up with the philosophy that hard work is the path to success[6] and the goal was to achieve the American dream of having their own houses, cars, and material possessions.[7] Driven by ambition to succeed, advance, and earn,[8] Baby Boomers are characterized by a strong traditional 8:00 a.m. to 5:00 p.m. work ethic.

Boomers also saw the civil rights movement and anti-Vietnam war demonstrations unfold before their very eyes, and the oldest participated in the unrest. They have gone on to become parents, some to Generation X, but primarily to Generation Y, also known as the Millennials. At the time of this writing, the 74.9 million people in the United States are Baby Boomers.[9]

Generation X

Those in Generation X, born between 1965 and 1980,[10] grew up during the height of cable television, MTV, leg warmers, and Michael Jackson.[11] They saw the first personal computers from Apple and IBM and likely played Pong on their Ataris. Much smaller in numbers than the Baby Boomers before them and the Millennials after, Generation X has a population of close to 50 million.[12]

With a 25 percent increase in married women in the workforce between 1968 and 1978,[13] Gen Xers were raised during a time in which it was becoming more of the norm for both parents to work. Thus, Gen X children, many of whom let themselves into their homes after school, were deemed "latchkey kids,"[14] leading them to having to be independent at a young age.[15]

Generation X has been viewed as cynical about the world, skeptical, and pragmatic.[16] They are often regarded as the "middle child" between two very large generations that have received a great deal of attention.[17] Where shows like *Leave It to Beaver*[18] idealized the nuclear family for the Baby Boomer generation, Generation X saw increased rates of divorce.[19] As Baby Boomers were excited and hopeful about the country's race to the moon, Generation X witnessed the *Challenger* explosion. Where post-World War II saw an economic boom,[20] the 2008 economic recession began just as many in Generation X arrived at what should have been their peak earning years. But in the end, despite all that defines Generation X, they lack a coherent generational identity of their own.[21]

Despite the rise in divorce rates during their childhood, two-thirds of Generation X are married and 71 percent have children.[22] Generation X plays an important role, if not one of the most important ones for Generation Z: their parents. The level of independence with which Generation X was raised has set an interesting stage for their own parenting. Taking a lesson from their hard-working parents, they strive to balance work and family.[23] They seek to play active and supportive roles in their children's lives and thus place great value on the time spent with family.

Generation Y, aka Millennials

Generation Y, more commonly known as Millennials, falls between Generation X and Generation Z. Although the dates of their birth years range depending on what source is used, one could put it as encompassing the 1980s and early 1990s. And although they are the closest in age to Generation Z, they certainly have their differences. Often referred to as the Me Generation, Millennials are criticized for being entitled and expecting things to be handed to them, leading to the perception of them as self-interested and overconfident.[24] They have used their twenties, a time when previous generations were getting married and starting families, as a time to further their education, launch their careers, and practice introspection to determine what they want in life.[25]

Millennials are used to a strong support system, both financially and emotionally,[26] from their Baby Boomer parents:[27] more than half, even those who are working full time, indicate depending on financial assistance from their family.[28] Millennials are confident, with a can-do attitude, which many attribute to the active parenting style of the Boomers and the "everyone gets a participation trophy" philosophies characteristic of their upbringing.[29]

The healthy economy the Baby Boomers grew accustomed to influenced how they raised their Millennial children, which was to do what it takes to set their children up for future success.[30] Thus, Millennials expect jobs to finance their personal lives, including travel, expensive electronics, and trendy clothes, but they also face large amounts of student loan debt and unemployment.[31] It is no surprise that Millennials have high expectations for their career, including pay, opportunities for advancement, fulfilling work, and work-life balance.[32] Not wanting to fall in line as one of the statistics, 89 percent of Millennials are optimistic about their personal futures.[33] Their confident attitudes, coupled with their lofty work expectations, directly align with how they are perceived as always wanting something bigger, better, and right now when it comes to their professional lives.

Millennials are on track to being the most educated generation to date, with one in three having obtained a bachelor's degree.[34] In the professional world, there can be a clash between them and those from other generations. Growing up in a multimedia and interactive environment, Millennials are used to always being connected. This may create conflict with the traditional workday of 8:00 a.m. to 5:00 p.m.: their employers are likely to be Baby Boomers or even Generation Xers who have developed what they consider healthy boundaries between work and play.[35]

Millennials have been the earliest adopters of social media and Internet technology,[36] likely contributing to their comfort in using the technology available to them. They are known to multitask and use a variety of communication platforms throughout the workday, including instant messaging, e-mail, and social media.[37] Unlike their predecessor generations that did not grow up with such advanced technology, Millennials have had nearly a lifetime of exposure.

Generation Z, Who Are You?

Generation Z refers to those born from 1995 through 2010. Having their world completely shaped by the Internet, they are often also aptly referred to as digital natives, the Net Generation, or iGeneration.[38] They make up a quarter of the US population and will become a third of the population by 2020.[39] They are the most racially diverse generation to date.[40]

Walking through history between 1995 and today paints an informative picture that can help uncover what makes this generation unique. As these students entered kindergarten, they saw the newscasts of September 11, 2001. They witnessed the economy crash and saw the unemployment rate skyrocket. They have known only two US presidents and have lived in a world at war for a majority of their lives. And their schools have always been striving to leave no child behind. Where their predecessors had a special device for video games, another for playing music, another for making phone calls, and a paper calendar, Generation Z can do all of that with one device that fits in their pocket. As they started driving and needed directions, they likely never had to purchase or print a map; instead they plugged an address into their GPS or phone. This highly technological era in which they were born has helped make them smart, efficient, and in tune with the world, both offline and online.[41]

Generation Z has always lived in a virtual and physical reality. With easy access to the world's issues, Generation Z sees problems but wants to find solutions and knows how to wield their tools and knowledge to do so. We predict Generation Z will have a strong work ethic similar to Baby Boomers and the responsibility and resiliency of their Generation X parents, and they may be even technologically savvier than the Millennials. This leads us to the biggest question: Will Generation Z be the group that changes the world?

Personality Characteristics

How Generation Z students describe themselves is influenced not just by the nature of the world they were raised in but the nurture of the families they were raised by: mostly Generation Xers. As parents, they are using an involved parenting style similar to that of the Boomers, but they're also instilling values of individual responsibility and independence.[42] After the Enron scandal, the dot-com bust of 2000, and the 2008 financial crisis, Generation X likely got the message that their company would not always be there to take care of them. To succeed, their children would need to develop entrepreneurial skills and be able to take care of themselves. In our study, Generation Z students described themselves as loyal, thoughtful, compassionate, open-minded, and responsible, suggesting that this could be a mature and focused group of students who have concern for others.

Loyal

Millennials have been branded the Me Generation, as evidence by *Time* magazine's cover story on that generation in 2013.[43] But our study indicates that 85 percent of Generation Z students describe themselves as loyal. They exhibit strong feelings and concern for those around them and align their pledges of support with issues that affect everyone, not just themselves or their small social sphere—quite opposite of a "me" focus.

Consider how loyalty might play out for Generation Z when it comes to the world of work. Having witnessed high levels of unemployment during their youth, this generation is very career minded. One might think they would be always be looking for the next move in their career path and hop from one job to the next. However, given their sense of loyalty, it is likely that they will change jobs less frequently than Millennials do.[44]

Compassionate

Seventy-three percent of Generation Z students in our study described themselves as compassionate, no surprise given the context within which they live. This generation has had access to nearly unlimited information, which has also given them the ability to learn about various topics and current issues. Because of this, they have been able to see the effect of events and experiences on real people. Previous generations heard about the impact of war, tragedies, and disasters in faraway lands, whereas Generation Z students can easily find detailed information, watch videos, and see pictures, making a distant experience close to home.

In addition, their constant connection with others provides a means to be in the know of issues facing their friends and family. They see social media posts and get text messages that describe intimate details of tragedies and misfortune. Being privy to this type of information certainly can make it difficult to be anything less than compassionate.

Thoughtful

Having loyalty and compassion, it is understandable that 80 percent of Generation Z students in our study view themselves as thoughtful, as each of these characteristics is reflective of caring for others. The thoughtfulness of Generation Z is in contrast to Millennials, who have been perceived as selfish and self-absorbed.[45] But are Generation Z students really thoughtful, or do they just say they are? Through our study, Generation Z students described story after story of their concern about issues facing other people. Their concerns appeared genuine, definitely demonstrating a true sense of thoughtfulness.

"To move forward, we all should have well-educated minds so that we will be able to better understand our world, our problems, and each other."

Generation Z student

Open-Minded

Open-mindedness is the ability to consider new perspectives, ideas, and ways of being. And open-minded is exactly how 70 percent of Generation Z students in our study see themselves. This aligns with the findings from another study in which 70 percent described themselves as in the top or above average in understanding others compared to their peers.[46]

This generation is predicted to be the last one in America in which Caucasians are in the majority[47] as only 55 percent of people in Generation Z are Caucasian.[48] This is a considerable difference compared to 72 percent of Baby Boomers who are Caucasian.[49] Instead of shying away or opposing what is different, Generation Z welcomes difference with an open mind and open arms, believing more diversity in America is a good thing.[50] (More information on how Generation Z views diversity, multiculturalism, and social justice is in chapters 2 and 6).

> "This generation is a very open-minded one and accepts uniqueness and the things that make others different."
>
> *Generation Z student*

In addition, just as limitless access to information has helped Generation Z students develop compassion for others and a thoughtful worldview, it has also exposed these students to many different cultures, identities, and ways of living. So if it is not the diversity around them that accounts solely for their open-mindedness, it is the exposure to new ways of thinking and being prevalent in their news and social media that help them see perspectives other than their own.

Responsible

Thank the parents of Generation Z for helping instill a level of responsibility with these students. Ninety percent of parents raising Generation Z students indicated that they assigned chores to their child to help teach responsibility and good habits.[51] This may have led to the foundation these students have for their own sense of responsibility as adults, as 69 percent of students in our study describe themselves as responsible.

> "Independent people who are both excited and fearful for the future."
>
> *Generation Z student*

In addition, the financial and political instability of the post-9/11 world has created a situation in which Generation Z students crave predictability and order.[52] Thus, Generation Z has taken an "if not you, then who?" approach to life. They recognize that they will be responsible for taking the necessary steps to set up a successful life, whether that is getting the most out of college to prepare for a career or saving money to buy a house. They also understand the many issues in the world that are in need of solutions. Coupling responsibility with their compassion, Generation Z could be the generation to address some of the world's most pressing issues.

Determined

This is a generation that will not give up. Given their mentality for taking responsibility, they also bring with them determination. Our study revealed that 74 percent of Generation Z students identify as determined, whereas another study found that 78 percent believe their drive to achieve is higher than that of their peers.[53] This attitude will likely serve them well as they learn that not everyone gets a trophy and that hard work is part of life.

> "Generation Z consists of community-driven individuals who find creative ways to problem-solve. They are extremely driven and intelligent."
>
> *Generation Z student*

Not Like Me at All

There are some characteristics that when asked about, many Generation Z students identified as not describing them or only somewhat describing them. First, 24 percent do not believe they are conservative, and 45 percent more say that conservatism only somewhat describes them. The word, *conservative* in the media reflects the idea of being leaning to the right on issues. Using this definition, not identifying as conservative aligns with our findings of Generation Z as students being moderate to left leaning on political issues.

In addition, we found that 19 percent do not believe they are spontaneous (with another 50 percent only somewhat believing they are) and 18 percent do not believe they are competitive (with another 36 percent only somewhat believing they are). It is clear that they do not see themselves as unplanned, likely because they appear to understand the reality of making sure everything is in order for their college experience so they do not stay longer than they need or pay more than they should. And although they may want to get ahead, their other characteristics of loyalty, compassion, and thoughtfulness likely rein in any desire they might have to be competitive.

Me, But Not You

In our study, we asked Generation Z students to report the personality characteristics that most described themselves and then those of others in Generation Z. We found that this generation of students certainly has a more favorable impression of themselves than they do of their peers. They see others as having high discovery, exploration, and risk-taking characteristics that they themselves do not have. These characteristics include competitive, spontaneous, adventuresome, and curious. They view themselves as responsible and determined individuals with concern for others, but the characteristics they associate with their peers can be interpreted as self-focused and irresponsible. Their perception of peers in Generation Z may fall more in line with traditional teenage stereotypes of being "fast and free." In fact, this perception may not be too far from reality: 40 percent of Generation Z students will take a risk if they feel they have more to gain.[54] In addition, another study found that one in three Generation Z students thinks their peers are lazy and lack focus.[55] So because there is an incongruence between how they see themselves and how they see their generation as a whole, the truth about the personality characteristics they possess may be somewhere in the middle.

"Generally spontaneous and have an open mind because of multiple reasons. They are figuring out what they want to do with their lives, which will induce experimenting. They also want to have fun in their young lives and live carefree."

Generation Z student

Interactivity Trumps Physical Activity

Being constantly connected to a screen contributes to Generation Z's more sedentary lifestyle compared to previous generations.[56] This is one of many factors leading to the quadrupling of adolescent obesity rates over the past thirty years.[57] These students have grown up in an era of the reduction, and sometimes elimination, of physical education and recess in the K-12 school curriculum. And for many, playing video games and surfing the web have replaced playing outside after school.

There has also been a decline in organized team sports for Generation Z.[58] This could be due to the decreased funding for physical activity in their K-12 schools, the potential of injury, or even the fact that some sports, such as baseball or golf, are just too slow paced to keep up with their short attention span.[59] Participation in baseball and soccer, for example, has decreased by 7 percent in youth ages seven to eighteen, even though both sports are considered slower paced and where scoring happens less frequently.[60]

Although these students are entering a world in which they have nearly unlimited access to campus recreation centers and a growing number of fitness centers and personal trainers outside the college setting, Generation Z is still considered to be one of the unhealthiest generations.[61] Will this generation have a greater number of obese individuals than ever before, or will they reclaim fitness in their young adulthood? While they might not be participating in organized sports as often, Generation Z students show increased interest in staying active through working out with weights and machines.[62] Given the changing dynamics of work life, though, we may see a generation of sedentary workers who sit in front of their computers all day eating carrot sticks and hummus, only to interrupt the routine with a one-hour workout at the gym to stay in shape.

Motivation

Equipped with the power of knowledge, concern for the world around them, and technological resources unimaginable to previous generations, Generation Z is speculated to be ambitious and motivated.[63] What motivates them?

Motivators

Our study revealed that more than 70 percent of Generation Z students are motivated by not wanting to let others down, advocating for something they believe in, making a difference for someone else, having the opportunity for advancement, and earning credit toward something. Not wanting to let others down and making a difference for others demonstrate the relational aspect of motivation for this generation, not surprising given their self-identified characteristics of loyalty, compassion, and thoughtfulness. And certainly their sense of responsibility explains why they are motivated by advocating for something they believe in.

Generation Z is also motivated by rewards, such as an opportunity for advancement or earning credit. These are rewards quite different from being motivated by a prize or a tangible gift. They have seen high unemployment rates and are concerned about their financial stability, and so their motivation to advance or earn credit toward a larger goal reflects their commitment to solidifying a stable career path and financial foundation for the future. Consider that they will likely not be motivated by a Starbucks gift card, but by reaching milestones that are steps toward their careers.

We found that gender does play a role in motivation strategies with Generation Z students. Generation Z men are more motivated than women by leaving a legacy, learning something, and competing with others, all of which are more individually focused. Generation Z women are more motivated than men by making a difference and caring about the project, both of which are relationally focused.

Unmotivators

At the other end of the spectrum are motivators that do not work for Generation Z students. We found that more than a quarter of Generation Z students are not motivated by public recognition, acceptance from others, competition with others, or the idea that someone will return a favor. While Generation Z has a high concern for others and issues, they are not driven by the need to be validated by others. It is generally assumed that teens and young adults are highly driven to fit in and find acceptance among their peers, but Generation Z's motivations tell us something different.

Surprisingly, money does not hold weight in motivating Generation Z. Despite being concerned about financial and career stability, only 28 percent of Generation Z students would be motivated to work harder or stay with an employer for financial gains, whereas 42 percent of Millennials would be more motivated to work harder or stay with an employer for financial gains.[64] Even with a concern for financial stability, our study indicates that Generation Z students are more motivated by relationships and the ability to work toward something they care about than financial advancement.

For those who are teaching, managing, parenting, or simply interacting with Generation Z students, understanding what motivates them can be critical in empowering them to act.

Conclusion

Generation Z sees the world through multiple screens, but as evidenced by their we-centric attitudes, they recognize that societal issues are much larger than just themselves. With their loyalty, determination, and responsibility as well as realistic outlook on life inherited from Generation X, this generation is committed to those around them and motivated by making a difference. Add to that their characteristics of care and compassion, and you can expect Generation Z to use both their heads and their hearts to solve the world's problems.

Notes

1. Kiss, G. (2008). Tactics for removing cultural barriers: A practical approach to effective communication. *AARMS*, 7(3), 425–433.
2. For more George Orwell quotes, go to http://www .goodreads.com/author/quotes/3706.George_Orwell

3. United Nations Joint Staff Pension Fund. (2007). *Overcoming generational gap in the workplace.* Retrieved from http://www.un.org/staffdevelopment/pdf/Designing%20Recruitment,%20Selection%20&%20Talent%20Management%20Model%20tailored%20to%20meet%20UNJSPF%27s%20Business%20Development%20Needs.pdf

4. History.com. (2010). *Baby Boomers.* Retrieved from http://www.history.com/topics/baby-boomers

5. United Nations Joint Staff Pension Fund. (2007).

6. Tolbize, A. (2008). *Generational differences in the workplace.* Retrieved from http://rtc3.umn.edu/docs/2_18_Gen_diff_workplace.pdf

7. History.com Staff. (2010).

8. United Nations Joint Staff Pension Fund. (2007).

9. Fry, R. (2015). *This year, Millennials will overtake Baby Boomers.* Retrieved from http://www.pewresearch.org/fact-tank/2015/01/16/this-year-millennials-will-overtake-baby-boomers/

10. United Nations Joint Staff Pension Fund. (2007).

11. For more information about Michael Jackson, go to http://www.biography.com/people/michael-jackson-38211

12. MetLife Mature Market Institute. (2013). *The MetLife study of Gen X: The MTV generation moves into mid-life.* Retrieved from www.metlife.com/assets/cao/mmi/publications/studies/2013/mmi-gen-x.pdf

13. Hayghe, H. (1981). *Husbands and wives as earners: An analysis of family data.* Retrieved from http://www.bls.gov/opub/mlr/1981/02/art5full.pdf

14. Knoll, Inc. (2014). *What comes after Y?* Retrieved from http://www.knoll.com/media/938/1006/What-Comes-After-Y.pdf. See also MetLife Mature Market Institute. (2013). *The MetLife study of Gen X: The MTV generation moves into mid-life.* Retrieved from www.metlife.com/assets/cao/mmi/publications/studies/2013/mmi-gen-x.pdf

15. Buahene, A., & Kovary, G. (2003). The road to performance success: Understanding and managing the generational divide. Toronto, ON: n-gen People Performance Inc.

16. Buahene, A., & Kovary, G. (2003).

17. Taylor, P. & Gao, G. (2014). *Generation X: America's neglected 'middle child.'* Retrieved from www.pewresearch.org/fact-tank/2014/06/05/generation-x-americas-neglected-middle-child/

18. IMDB. (1957). *Leave It to Beaver plot summary.* Retrieved from http://www.imdb.com/title/tt0050032/plotsummary

19. Jones, A.M. *Historical divorce rate statistics.* Retrieved from http://divorce.lovetoknow.com/Historical_Divorce_Rate_Statistics

20. Digital History. (2015). *Overview of the post-war era.* Retrieved from http://www.digitalhistory.uh.edu/era.cfm?eraID=16

21. Henseler, C. (2014). *Generation X: What's in the label?* Retrieved from http://www.huffingtonpost.com/ christine-henseler/generation-x-whats-in-the_b_ 5390568.html

22. MetLife Mature Market Institute. (2013).

23. Regus. (2013). *Boomers struggle to find their balance-Regus work:life balance report 2013.* Retrieved from http://press.regus.com/united-states/boomers- struggle-to-find-their-balance---regus-worklife- balance-report-2013

24. Kingston, A. (2014). *Get ready for Generation Z.* Retrieved from http://www.macleans.ca/society/life/ get-ready-for-generation-z/

25. Raphelson, S. (2014). *Amid the stereotypes, some facts about Millennials.* Retrieved from http://www.npr .org/2014/11/18/354196302/amid-the-stereotypes- some-facts-about-millennials.

26. Elam, C., Statton, T., & Gibson, D. D. (2007). Welcoming a new generation to college: The Millennial students. *Journal of College Admission*, 195, 20–25.

27. Elam, C., Statton, T., & Gibson, D. D. (2007).

28. Arnett, J. J. & Schwab, J. (2013). *The Clark University poll of parents of emerging adults.* Retrieved from http://www.clarku.edu/clark-poll-emerging-adults/ pdfs/clark-university-poll-parents-emerging-adults .pdf

29. Elam, C., Stratton, T., & Gibson, D. D. (2007).

30. Kendzior, S. (2014). *Only Baby Boomers could afford to be helicopter parents.* Retrieved from http://finance .yahoo.com/news/only-baby-boomers-could-afford-161109070.html

31. Raphelson, S. (2014).

32. Ng, E. S. W., Schweitzer, L., & Lyons, S. T. (2010). New generation, great expectations: A field study of the Millennial generation. *Journal of Business and Psychology,* 25(2), 281–292.

33. Levine, A. & Dean, D. R. (2012). *Generation on a tightrope: A portrait of today's college student.* San Francisco, CA: John Wiley & Sons, Inc.

34. Raphelson, S. (2014).

35. United Nations Joint Staff Pension Fund. (2007).

36. New Strategist Publications, Inc. (2010). American generations: Who they are and how they live. Ithaca, NY: New Strategist Publications.

37. Schawbel, D. (2014). *Gen Y and Gen Z workplace expectations study.* Retrieved from http:// millennialbranding.com/2014/geny-genz-global-workplace-expectations-study/

38. Prensky, M. (2001). Digital natives, digital immigrants. *On the Horizon,* 9, 5. Retrieved from http:// www.marcprensky.com/writing/Prensky%20-%20Digital%20Natives,%20Digital%20Immigrants%20-%20Part1.pdf

39. Sparks & Honey. (2014). *Meet Gen Z: Forget everything you learned about Millennials.* Retrieved from www .slideshare.net/sparksandhoney/generation-z-final-june-17

40. Magid Generational Strategies. (2014). *The first generation of the twenty-first century: An introduction to the pluralist generation.* Retrieved from http://magid.com/sites/default/files/pdf/ MagidPluralistGenerationWhitepaper.pdf

41. Sparks & Honey. (2014).

42. Magid Generational Strategies. (2014).

43. Stein, J. (2013, May 20). Millennials: The me me me generation. *Time, 26–34.*

44. Schawbel, D. (2014).

45. Myers, K. K., & Sadaghiani, K. (2010). Millennials in the workplace: A communication perspective on Millennials' organizational relationships and performance. *Journal of Business and Psychology, 25*(2), 225–238.

46. Eagan, K., Stolzenberg, E. B., Ramirez, J. J., Aragon, M. C., Suchard, M. R., & Hurtado, S. (2014). *The American freshman: National norms fall 2014.* Los Angeles: Higher Education Research Institute.

47. Magid Generational Strategies. (2014).

48. Magid Generational Strategies. (2014).

49. Magid Generational Strategies. (2014).

50. Magid Generational Strategies. (2014).

51. JWT Intelligence. (2012). *Gen Z: Digital in their DNA.* Retrieved from http://www.jwtintelligence.com/ wp-content/uploads/2012/04/F_INTERNAL_Gen _Z_0418122.pdf

52. Knoll. (2014). *What comes after Y? Generation Z: Arriving to the office soon.* Retrieved from http://www .knoll.com/knollnewsdetail/what-comes-after-y-generation-z-arriving-to-the-office-soon

53. Eagan et al. (2014).

54. Eagan et al. (2014).

55. Schawbel. (2014).

56. Sparks & Honey. (2014).

57. National Center for Health Statistics. (2011). *Health, United States, 2011: With special features on socioeconomic status and health.* Retrieved from www.cdc.gov/ nchs/data/hus/hus11.pdf

58. Wallerson, R. (2014, January). Youth participation weakens in basketball, football, baseball, soccer: Fewer children play team sports. *Wall Street Journal.* Retrieved from http://www.wsj.com/articles/ SB10001424052702303519404579350892629229918

59. Anderson, W. (2014). Taking their ball and going home. *Wake Up Quarterly: A Strategic Intelligence Report: Generation Z, 25–26.* Retrieved fromhttp://issuu.com/thisisomelet/docs/omelet_ intelligence_report_genz/27

60. Wallerson. (2014).

61. International Health, Racquet, and Sportsclub
    Association. (2011). *U.S. health club mem-
    bership exceeds 50 million.* Retrieved from
    www.ihrsa.org/news/2011/4/5/us-health-club-
    membership-exceeds-50-million-up-108-
    industry.html

62. Physical Activity Council. (2014). *2014 par-
    ticipation report.* Retrieved from http://www
    .physicalactivitycouncil.com/pdfs/current.pdf

63. Schawbel. (2014).

64. Schawbel. (2014).

2

BELIEFS AND PERSPECTIVES

Having interacted with young people in our daily work, we have seen that it is not just adults who hold deeply seated beliefs and perspectives. Youth and young adults can be passionate as well. So what might influence the beliefs and perspectives of Generation Z?

As we will see in upcoming chapters, students in Generation Z are empowered with information and communication tools and have access to thought leaders and power brokers. They possess a mind-set that they can change institutions. Understanding the context that shapes the beliefs and perspectives of Generation Z may shed light on why they communicate, relate, engage, and lead the way they do.

The World around Them

Context shapes the way people see the world. It matters. Consider how growing up after the invention of the automobile opened up geographic boundaries in ways that previous generations would never have been able to conceive. Or imagine how receiving an immunization for polio eliminated the childhood fear of contracting the illness. Although there are factors such as geographic upbringing, education level, family and peer influence, culture, and personal experiences that may have a unique individual impact on a particular Generation Z student, there are common events and contextual factors that cut across the generation as a whole. These include having information at their fingertips, being constantly connected, exposure to creative entrepreneurship, fearing disasters and tragedies, having exposure to issues of diversity and social justice, and experiencing budget cuts. How might each of these affect the beliefs and perspectives of Generation Z?

Information at Their Fingertips

As Generation Z students participate in higher education, many amenities available to them were not to older generations. First, many students come to class with laptops, tablets, and smart phones so they are digitally connected the moment they enter class. Although it might be distracting for instructors to compete with students' technological gadgets, it does create a new type of learning environment, one in which students are connected to more information online than the instructor could ever know and teach in class. This vast amount of online information comes in the form of websites, journal articles, blogs, forums, videos, and sites like Wikipedia, which bring together the old sets of encyclopedias into a digital format.[1] If an answer cannot be found using those resources, Siri, the digital personal assistant built in to the iPhone, can verbally answer nearly any question.[2] Then there are Google Maps[3] and Apple Maps[4] that include far more map and navigation information than any atlas. These map tools use a global positioning system that directly navigates drivers to where they need to be. In addition, e-readers have the capability of storing hundreds of books electronically on one device.[5] Is this too much information? Teachers would say, yes. One study found that 83 percent of Advanced Placement (AP) and National Writing Project (NWP) teachers believe "the amount of information available online today is overwhelming to most students."[6] How might this vast amount of information affect how Generation Z sees the world?

If It's Online, It's True

With so much information available, where does this leave Generation Z students in terms of information literacy? More than three-quarters of the AP and NWP teachers surveyed believe that online search engines have led students to expect to find the information they need quickly and with little effort.[7] This certainly creates a situation in which researching content at the last minute because of the assumption of its availability makes for more reasons to procrastinate, leaving less time to critically examine the information.

> "The ease of access to information has, I've noticed, almost deadened people's curiosity and drive to question the things they hear or see, and they take the first thing they're told."
>
> *Generation Z student*

In addition, information that is found in an online search is not always accurate. AP and NWP teachers agree. Nearly two-thirds believe that the technology available to research information has made it more difficult for students to find legitimate and credible information.[8] And with only 44 percent evaluating the quality or reliability of information they receive,[9] it is no surprise that the mentality of trusting what is on the Internet rings true with them.

Get It When You Want It

In addition to being able to access information all hours of the day, consider the convenience in being able to contact anyone at any time because twenty-four-hour customer service lines are open and online buying sites like Amazon[10] provide a mall-like shopping experience that can happen at 3:00 a.m.[11] Although all generations have this 24/7 access, Generation Z has always known a world with it, making it easy for them to believe that everyone else is and should always be available. This may manifest itself as a middle-of-the-night message to an instructor about an assignment due first thing in the morning or to a supervisor after hours with a question that could have waited.

Adding to the culture of get-it-when-you-want-it, consider the emergence of video streaming services and the many other sites available to watch TV shows and movies. With the advent of Netflix[12] and Hulu,[13] there is no reason to watch a show live on television. Want to see an old episode of a TV show no longer on the air? Stream it. Thinking of a particular movie? Watch it right now. This phenomenon has also created the opportunity to engage in binge watching: staying up all night to watch a season of a TV show or viewing an entire series over a span of a few weeks. Binge watching is not limited to Generation Z students; 50 percent of all adults indicate that they binge-watch TV.[14] But the ability to binge-watch has nearly always been a reality for Generation Z students.

This get-it-when-you-want-it mentality of instant gratification will likely continue to exist and perhaps even grow as technology makes access to information, entertainment, and services even easier.

Constant Connection

> "Teens ... believe they need to be available 24/7 to their friends, because, you know, someone might get dumped or into an argument with their parents. They need instant gratification and solace. Nobody can wait anymore not because they can't—but because they don't need to."
>
> *John M. Grohol, founder and CEO, Psych Central*[17]

The days of coming home to check the answering machine for any missed calls are long gone. Now it is easier than ever to reach someone through text, phone call, e-mail, or instant message right on the cell phone in a person's pocket. Ninety percent of American adults own a cell phone,[15] and 78 percent of Generation Z teenagers had a phone before they arrived at college.[16] How might the ability to be constantly connected shape the perspectives and beliefs of this generation?

Fear of Missing Out

One study found that 100 percent of all Generation Z students indicate being online at least one hour per day with nearly three-quarters of those within one hour of waking up.[18] They do not miss a beat. This ability to connect with others around the clock may be a contributing factor in their suffering from FOMO—the fear of missing out.[19] They want to be in the know and are connected nearly all hours of the day, likely fostering the belief that there is no good time to turn it off.

Time and Space Are More Fluid

Think of the traditional notion of the office job in which there are set hours that employees work. For example, they may arrive at 8:00 a.m. and leave at 5:00 p.m. These are not shift jobs designed to cover the hours an establishment is open, but jobs in which there has previously been an set range of hours allocated for work that in fact could be completed at any time. Generation Z students, by being connected around the clock, are not likely to unplug at 5:00 p.m. As companies move toward more flexible scheduling, project-based work, and the ability to define one's own work time, the benefits associated with these arrangements[20] will certainly be even more pronounced for the constantly connected Generation Z. In addition, this constant connection means that in many cases, Generation Z employees will not be tied to a specific space to get their work done. Only 28 percent of Generation Z have a preference for working in a traditional office setting compared to 45 percent of Millennials.[21] As previous generations may have seen a more structured work situation in time and space, Generation Z is likely to believe that their constant connection and desire to stay plugged in will serve them well in being able to work across time and space norms of the past.

Creative Entrepreneurship

The first year of the birth of Generation Z students, a company called eBay[22] came to be.[23] This online auction site put the power of the retailer in the hands of everyday people, allowing them to post any item they wanted for auction for others to bid on and buy. Since then, companies like Airbnb,[24] Craigslist,[25] and Uber[26] have put people at the helm of their

"Uber, the world's largest taxi company, owns no vehicles. Facebook, the world's most popular media owner, creates no content. Alibaba, the most valuable retailer, has no inventory. And Airbnb, the world's largest accommodation provider, owns no real estate. Something interesting is happening."

Tom Goodwin, senior vice president of strategy and innovation, Havas Media[28]

own entrepreneurial initiatives. They can rent, sell, or serve others without having to own a business and can set the terms in which they offer their products or services. And because these forms of entrepreneurship often provide a secondary source of income for people,[27] individuals can have a great deal of autonomy in their own decision making. What perspectives or beliefs might Generation Z conclude by participating as a producer or consumer through creative entrepreneurship?

Sharing Can Be Revenue Generating

Think of all those tools collecting dust in the garage or closets full of items that have barely been used. These are assets, although many people might not think of them as that. This mind-set may change with the emergence of the sharing economy in which people share their assets with each other in a peer to peer rental market.[29] These assets may be unused or underused, so renting them out can result in unexpected profit.[30] This could include renting a lawnmower to neighbors on the six days a week the owner does not use it or renting a guest room to travelers.

Like many of the other technological and cultural advances of the era, Generation Z will likely never know a time in which the sharing economy did not exist. These students may think, "Why buy a pair of skis when I can rent them from someone online for the weekend?" "Why not rent my textbooks out since I do not need them anymore and I cannot sell them back for an adequate price?" This sharing economy has the potential to transform the way everyone, including Generation Z, does business.

Selling Is Not Just for Businesses

Garage sales have been places that people go to rummage through others' used items to buy things. There is often no rhyme or reason as to how a garage sale might be organized, and there is often a need to sift through boxes and bins to search for a particular item of interest. It can be challenging to find that item at a garage sale, and driving around looking for garage sales can be time consuming. Enter Craigslist, an online bulletin board in which users can post classified ads for items they have for sale.[31] With more than 80 million classified ads posted on Craigslist each month,[32] users can search for exactly what they are looking for without a haphazard search of going to garage sales. Need a white wood table or a pair of hiking boots or even a used car? Search on Craigslist. As 26 percent of Millennials and Generation Zers have sold something on an online site,[33] we can expect that this type of entrepreneurship will continue in the future with both of these generations.

Sometimes people want to sell items other than used manufactured products. Now, anyone can be an artist and sell their handmade, and sometimes customized, items like art, clothing, and jewelry on sites such as Etsy, which hosts

32 million items for sale.[34] No more needing to acquire space in a gallery or shop for selling goods or having to buy from a dealer or store. Generation Z's exposure to buying and selling has always involved online spaces without anyone between the artist and shopper. This phenomenon is fairly popular with both Millennials and Generation Z: 16 percent have indicated selling something handmade on a site like Etsy.[35]

Not only can online bulletin boards such as Craigslist and Etsy streamline the buying and selling process of items, but they provide a means for people to make purchases directly from individuals rather than businesses. As Generation Z has ample access to buy and sell on their own, they may inhabit this space more readily than their generational predecessors.

Be Your Own Boss

Online sites like eBay Classifieds,[36] a web-based bulletin board, provides the opportunity for anyone to post their services on the web and engage in business transactions directly with consumers, removing the intermediary of a business.[37] Posting a service as an individual or finding someone to perform a particular service can be streamlined by using a site like eBay Classifieds. Simply search by category, key word, and location, and it is simple to find a landscaper, mover, or tech repairperson. Individuals can work directly with the person providing the service rather than calling an 800 number or putting in a request on a Contact Us web page for a business. In addition, individuals posting on these sites can have lower overhead, possibly resulting in a lower cost to consumers.

Another realm of services includes the 53 million individuals working for businesses as independent contractors or freelancers[38] providing on-demand work.[39] Examples of businesses that hire independent contract labor include Uber, a ride-share company that touts that drivers can drive their own cars and be their own bosses,[40] and Taskrabbit,[41] a business dedicated to outsourcing peoples' errands with preselected independent taskers. These independent contractors are not technically employees and have the autonomy to define their work hours and projects. This may allow the flexibility and freedom for anyone to be entrepreneurial, but it does muddy job classifications when individuals work for businesses as contractors rather than employees,[42] a situation that may emerge more readily as Generation Z students engage in the workforce. Nevertheless, the sheer number of individuals working for themselves can certainly shape the beliefs about employment that this generation might have. Those in generations before them may have left their career aspirations up to a human resources hiring authority, whereas Generation Z students may see acquiring a career as an opportunity to create the jobs they want.

Disasters and Tragedies

"Just as September 11 changed the way society sees threats from terrorists, [Hurricane] Sandy has changed how we see threats from the ocean and waterways."

Eric Klinenberg, sociologist, New York University[43]

Every generation has its disasters and tragedies, from the stock market crash in the 1920s to the AIDS crisis in the 1980s. Generation Z is no exception. They were likely too young to truly understand the impact of September 11, 2001, but they certainly have witnessed the aftermath by watching US involvement in ongoing wars and conflicts that appear to have no real end in sight. Consider also the widespread loss that many Americans felt during the Great Recession (2007–2009) and the burst of the housing bubble when Generation Z was just reaching adolescence. Whether personally affected by the recession or seeing their peers struggle, lost jobs and lost homes were their reality.

On top of war and recession, these students have seen national and global devastation. The sheer destruction caused by Hurricane Katrina and Superstorm Sandy as well as the tsunami in Japan and earthquake in Haiti have left communities in shambles. Factor in epidemics such as swine flu, bird flu, Severe Acute Respiratory Syndrome (SARS), and ebola, and the world appears to be full of frightening catastrophes. How might these events have shaped the beliefs and perceptions of Generation Z?

The World Is a Scary Place

Generation Z is growing up in a post-9/11 era in which the United States has been at war for years and terrorist acts occur regularly around the world. This has been the reality since these kids were no older than kindergarten age. They have been told that airports are scary places where even a grandma can hide a bomb in her shoe or that more than three ounces of a liquid might do serious damage in flight. Generation Z students have not known otherwise and never recall a time when airports were a place to reunite with others rather than keeping watch to make sure someone does not slip something into their suitcase.

"I believe that America's desire to interfere in many foreign affairs causes the youth to fear another large war or long-lasting consequence that will have to be addressed during our generation's turn at political power."

Generation Z student

Fear of terrorism is not restricted to travel situations. This generation has witnessed many acts of public violence, including school shootings at the elementary, high school, and college levels; incidents such as the 2013 Boston Marathon bombing;[44] and shootings in movie theaters in Aurora, Colorado,[45] and Atlanta, Georgia.[46] Even those who did not personally experience these events may be concerned that they might be a victim in the future.[47] With one click on a website, anyone can delve deeply into an event and watch video footage, read transcripts, or see interviews, making the event feel even closer to home and even more frightening. These events can certainly have an impact on how Generation Z sees their future: we found that 60 percent are optimistic about it, down from 89 percent of Millennials who were surveyed while in college.[48]

Danger Lurks around Every Corner

If it feels unsafe to go out, how about staying in? It has been impressed on Generation Z that the online world can be scary too. With hackers, identity thieves, bullies, and sexual predators out there, it can be easy to be a victim without ever leaving home.

Depending on the issue, scholars debate whether there is an increased risk of personally experiencing dangerous situations today versus in the past. Regardless, the perception of danger has increased over the past twenty years,[49] leaving

Generation Z growing up in what seems to be a dangerous world. It is no surprise that Generation Z students are not risk takers, as we found in our study, and are pragmatic[50] since these characteristics may help these students navigate that dangerous world.

Diversity and Social Justice

Generation Z's beliefs about diversity and social justice are almost certainly influenced by their exposure to a wide range of people different from them. Consider the change in racial composition in the United States. Between 2000 and 2010, the percentage of white people decreased from 75.1 percent to 72.4 percent[51] while the largest racial minority group in the United States, Hispanics,[52] continues to grow.[53] Individuals selecting two or more races during the 2010 Census were 2.9 percent of the total US population, compared to 2.4 percent in 2000.[54] Although racial diversity can certainly be regional and there are pockets of communities that are less diverse, growth in racial minority populations can increase exposure for all Generation Z students to a variety of different people. And it is not just more exposure to diversity in general, but these students see more diversity in higher-profile roles. Consider the growth in the number of female CEOs over the course of their lifetimes. Between 2004 and 2014, the number of female CEOs doubled at the top five thousand fastest-growing privately owned companies.[55] Although there is much more room for more women in the higher ranks, Generation Z students will likely be exposed to more women in leadership roles than previous generations were.

Exposure to diversity is only part of the puzzle that sets the context for Generation Z. It is important to consider issues of social justice in the lives of these students. First, Generation Z students have always lived during a time in which the Civil Rights Act, Voting Right Act, Fair Housing Act, and Americans with Disabilities Act were part of the fabric of society. But issues of equity and equality are still debated today and are often at the center of the national political agenda. In just the two decades following the birth of the first Generation Z students in 1995, laws and policies have been created or upheld around issues of antidiscrimination, women and fair pay, hate crime prevention, marriage equality, work permits for childhood immigrants, and minimum wage increases. Yet, Generation Z students have seen laws limiting women's reproductive rights and enacting stricter voter identification laws. They saw the passage of "Papers, please" laws that require undocumented individuals to provide proof of citizenship or legal residency if stopped for any reason by law enforcement, as well as laws requiring transgender people to use the restroom designated for their biological sex as determined at birth or by chromosomes. In addition, expansion of religious freedom laws has opened up more rights for religious individuals but also has implications allowing discrimination toward other identity groups.[56] Throughout history, there have been battles over laws that directly affect particular groups of people, and this generation will likely continue to see this trend.

So, how might an increase in exposure to diversity affect the perspectives and beliefs of Generation Z? And what beliefs and perspectives can Generation Z draw from debates around issues of social justice?

Diversity Is Good

Generation Z is the most racially diverse generation in recent history, with the most diverse social circles.[57] And more members of this generation than any other generation have a positive opinion about the country's becoming more diverse.[58] Their exposure to diversity through seeing women and people of color in leadership roles and having a diverse social circle of friends has likely contributed to their open-mindedness.[59]

Reach for Your Dreams, But Be Realistic

Barack Obama's election as US president in 2008 challenged historical racial norms of the top elected position. His election inspired youth. During the 2008 election, nearly two-thirds of Generation Z youth who were surveyed indicated that they believed they really could be president if they wanted to. And this number was even higher among African American youth.[60] This perception of being able to achieve what was once reserved for white men can be empowering.

Although it might be empowering for Generation Z students to see historically underrepresented people in critical leadership roles, there is still an element of realism that grounds them in understanding the context within which they exist. They do not live in a world free from oppression, discrimination, and prejudice. For example, Generation Z is least likely of the four most recent generations to believe in the American dream—that is, the notion that initiative and hard work offer an equal opportunity for people to prosper, or at least achieve financial security.[61] This is no surprise given that their parents, mostly Generation Xers, are the second least likely to believe in the American dream.[62] Generation Z students know that it takes more than hard work to achieve their dreams. Their responsible and ambitious[63] nature coupled with their lack of a sense of entitlement[64] may prove to be what challenges notions of access, equity, and equality for everyone.

Equality Matters

Will Generation Z live in or create a postoppressive society, one in which race, class, gender, sexual orientation, and other identities do not play a determining factor in one's life? Probably not. Prejudice, institutional oppression, and discriminatory laws do and will likely continue to exist. Generation Z believes in equality,[65] and these students have a great deal of passion for social justice issues. We found nearly 56 percent of Generation Z students are concerned about racism, another 56 percent about sexism, and 61 percent about poverty. Their interest in and concern for these issues puts them in a situation to be supporters and allies of social justice as college students.

Budget Cuts

Generation Z students have witnessed cutbacks nearly their whole lives. During the Great Recession, 8.7 million jobs were cut,[66] along with funding for education, health care, and social programs.[67] Consider education, for example. Many individuals in older generations can reminisce about their times in art, physical education, and music classes while in school. But when Generation Z students began to take part in K-12 education (the 2000s), cuts in art and physical education programs were beginning to swell. Since the implementation of No Child Left Behind in 2001, nearly 50 percent of school administrators indicate funneling significant amounts of time from physical education into reading and math.[68] In addition, between 1999 and 2009, instruction in visual arts, dance, and theater at the elementary and secondary levels was reduced.[69] Although music programs were offered at elementary and secondary schools at the same or close to the same rate over the ten-year span, music education was less accessible to students in higher-poverty areas.[70] While some individuals in Generation Z may have individually participated in art, physical education, and music classes during their K-12 education, access for the generation as a whole was less than in previous generations.

Generation Z students also fall victim to funding cuts for public higher education. Cuts have been drastic, leading some to predict that it will not be long before states no longer fund public colleges and universities at all.[71] Couple the reduction in funding with the rising cost of doing business, and institutions are left with cutting budgets and increasing tuition rates. These increased tuition rates continue to surpass the rate of inflation,[72] resulting in students bearing higher costs to attend college and higher debt burdens once they graduate.

> "Funding for schools is being cut left and right, and it is time for a change because as cliché as this is, the children are the future and we should care more about the quality of their education."
>
> *Generation Z student*

Be Financially Conservative

This constant exposure to cutbacks has created an environment in which there may appear to be no financial safety net. As we will discuss further in chapter 6, our study found that more than 80 percent of Generation Z students are concerned about the cost of higher education. With the continued rise in tuition, students may be living on the edge just to make ends meet. One missed paycheck from work for being sick or one extra class needed could be just the situation that makes someone in Generation Z go from college student to dropout. With the tendency toward being financially conservative or moderate that we found in our study, it is no surprise that Generation Z students prefer to save money now in case they need it later.[73]

Religion

Critical events and contextual factors can be shapers of beliefs and perspectives. But those are not the only elements of influence. The saying, "stay away from talking religion and politics with those you do not know," is simply a reminder that both of these institutions can also fundamentally affect an individual's beliefs and perspectives.

Religion is such a strong force that wars have been waged over opposing ideologies, and individuals have sought refuge in other nations to avoid religious persecution. The United States embraces the value of freedom of religion through the First Amendment. Consider the diversity of religions in existence today, each having its own unique set of beliefs that shape their followers' perspectives on larger social issues.[74] For example, beliefs on abortion, same-sex marriage, and the death penalty are greatly influenced by one's religious views.[75] Knowing that religion often shapes or defines one's belief system, what are the religious identities and practices of Generation Z students?

Religious Participation

We found that many Generation Z students participate in organized religion—47 percent in fact. And rather than participating only in major holidays and rituals, they are quite involved. Forty-one percent of all Generation Z students say they attend weekly religious services,[76] and given the number who identify as religious, this is a substantial portion. Compared to other generations when they were younger, these rates of attendance are considerably higher than Millennials at 18 percent, Generation X at 21 percent, and Baby Boomers at 26 percent.[77]

Add in those who do not participate in organized religion yet say they believe in God or identify as spiritual, and the number of believers grows. One study found that a whopping 78 percent of Generation Z says they believe in God,[79] whereas our study found that 47 percent of Generation Z students identify as religious and 31 percent as spiritual, also totaling 78 percent. Since these numbers are considerably higher than those associated with religious participation, might there be a cohort of students who believe in a faith but do not want to participate in the organized religion that accompanies it? Organized religion is often aligned with conservative political views, especially around social issues.[80] Given that we found the vast majority of Generation Z students are liberal or moderate in their views on social issues, it would not be unexpected if Generation Z opts out of organized religion to reconcile their faith and social beliefs.

Religious Nonparticipation

If 78 percent of Generation Z students in our study identify as spiritual or religious, what about the rest of Generation Z?

"I think the single most important reason for the rise of the unknowns [no religious affiliation] is that combination of the younger people moving to the left on social issues and the most visible religious leaders moving to the right on that same issue."

Robert Putnam, Harvard University, in identifying a trend that started in the 1990s[78]

We found that 22 percent of Generation Z endorses no religion, lower than the 37 percent of Millennials who were opposed to or indifferent about religion while in college,[81] but slightly higher than the 20 percent of the general American population that does not ascribe to a faith.[82] "No religion" is now the third largest religious group in the world.[83] And if trends continue, the number of those affiliated with an organized religion will likely decrease as Generation Z ages, moving people out of the religious category and into either the spiritual or none categories.[84] Will we see a generation whose faith is not tied to organized religion and where spirituality is more fluid than religious doctrine? What might this mean for organized religion as an institution?

Politics

Politics can be a tangible way to see beliefs and perspectives in action as those at either end of the political spectrum often have a particular ideology in common. For example, as liberals

fight for tighter gun control, conservatives advocate for loosening gun restrictions. And those who identify as moderate, or
politically middle of the road, likely have a viewpoint that falls
somewhere in between.

Political Ideologies

Although there are many political parties in the United States
and certainly many political perspectives, some general beliefs
align with the two major ends of the spectrum: conservatism
and liberalism, with moderates falling in between the two.
Merriam-Webster defines these ideologies as follows:

> *Conservatism*: A political philosophy based on tradition and
> social stability, stressing established institutions, and pre-
> ferring gradual development to abrupt change; *specifically*:
> Such a philosophy calling for lower taxes, limited govern-
> ment regulation of business and investing, a strong national
> defense, and individual financial responsibility for personal
> needs (as retirement income or health-care coverage).[85]

> *Liberalism*: A political philosophy based on belief in progress,
> the essential goodness of the human race, and the autonomy
> of the individual and standing for the protection of political
> and civil liberties; *specifically*: Such a philosophy that consid-
> ers government as a crucial instrument for amelioration of
> social inequities (as those involving race, gender, or class).[86]

> *Moderate*: Professing or characterized by political or social
> beliefs that are not extreme.[87]

Political Leanings of Generation Z

We found that Generation Z students are liberal to moderate
on social issues (see table 2.1), as evidenced by their strong

Table 2.1   Generation Z Political Affiliation

	On Social Issues	On Financial Issues
Identify as liberal	40%	17%
Identify as moderate	38%	51%
Identify as conservative	22%	32%

support of marriage equality at more than 80 percent.[88] But when it comes to financial issues, we found that they are moderate to conservative, as can be clearly seen in their own personal approach to saving and conservative spending.[89]

Generation Z comprises a high number of moderates on both social and financial issues. Ascribing to political parties as they have historically been defined might be challenging for them. This may mean that more Generation Z voters register as independents, or it may simply mean a generation disconnected from the two-party political system, as we explore more in chapter 7.

Conclusion

Although Generation Z students are a diverse group of individuals, many similarities cut across the generation as a whole. Their political ideologies indicate liberal to moderate perspectives for social issues and moderate to conservative for financial issues, whereas their religious participation reflects high levels of spirituality and religious affiliation. Add to that the contextual factors this generation has experienced, such as vast amounts of information available to them, connectivity through technology, opportunities for creative entrepreneurship, dealing with the aftermath of disasters and tragedies, exposure to diversity and social justice issues, and experiencing the effect of budget cuts. Understanding these political, religious, and societal factors can help shed light on how Generation Z sees the world.

Notes

1. Wikipedia. (2015). *Wikipedia: About.* https://en .wikipedia.org/wiki/Wikipedia:About

2. Apple. (2015a). *About SIRI.* Retrieved from https:// support.apple.com/en-us/HT204389

3. Google Maps. (2015). *About.* Retrieved from http:// www.google.com/maps/about/

4. Apple. (2015b). *Maps.* Retrieved from https://www .apple.com/ios/maps/

5. Tecca, C. B. (2012). *Four pros and cons of e-readers vs. textbooks.* Retrieved from http://www.today .com/parents/4-pros-cons-e-readers-vs-textbooks- 2D80556082

6. Purcell, K., Rainie, L., Heaps, A., Buchanan, J., Friedrich, L., Jacklin, A., ... Zickuhr, K. (2012). *How teens do research in the digital world.* Retrieved from http://www.pewinternet.org/2012/11/01/how-teens- do-research-in-the-digital-world/

7. Purcell et al. (2012).

8. Purcell et al. (2012).

9. Eagan, K., Stolzenberg, E. B., Ramirez, J. J., Aragon, M. C., Suchard, M. R., & Hurtado, S. (2014). *The American freshman: National norms fall 2014*. Los Angeles: Higher Education Research Institute.

10. Amazon. (2015). *About Amazon*. Retrieved from http://www.amazonfulfillmentcareers.com/about-amazon/

11. Fitterman, S. (2013). *The ultimate debate: Online shopping vs. brick and mortar shopping*. Retrieved from http://insights.wired.com/profiles/blogs/the-ultimate-debate-online-shopping-vs-brick-and-mortar-shopping#axzz3eSZsFwHC

12. Netflix. (2015). *Company overview*. Retrieved from https://pr.netflix.com/WebClient/loginPageSalesNet WorksAction.do?contentGroupId=10476

13. Hulu. (2015). *About*. Retrieved from http://www.hulu .com/about

14. Beres, D. (2014). *Half of all adult Americans now admit to binge-watching TV*. Retrieved from http://www .huffingtonpost.com/2014/12/11/binge-watching_ n_6310056.html

15. Pew Research Center. (2014). *Mobile technology fact sheet*. Retrieved from http://www.pewinternet.org/ fact-sheets/mobile-technology-fact-sheet/

16. Madden, M., Lenhart, A., Duggan, M., Cortesi, S., & Gasser, U. (2013). *Teens and technology 2013*. Retrieved from http://www.pewinternet .org/files/old-media/Files/Reports/2013/PIP_ TeensandTechnology2013.pdf

17. Grohol, J. M. (2011). *FOMO addiction: The fear of missing out*. Retrieved from http://psychcentral.com/blog/archives/2011/04/14/fomo-addiction-the-fear-of-missing-out/

18. Ipsos MediaCT. (2013). *Generation Z: A look at the technology and media habits of today's teens*. Retrieved from http://www.wikia.com/Generation_Z:_A_Look_at_the_Technology_and_Media_Habits_of_Today%E2%80%99s_Teens

19. Sparks & Honey. (2014). *Meet Gen Z: Forget everything you learned about Millennials*. Retrieved from www.slideshare.net/sparksandhoney/generation-z-final-june-17

20. Elfman, L. (2012). *Flexible workplace is great for employees—and the companies they work for?* Retrieved from http://www.huffingtonpost.com/2012/11/20/flexible-workplace-employees-companies_n_2165727.html

21. Schawbel, D. (2014). *Gen Y and Gen Z Global Workplace Expectations Study*. Retrieved from http://millennialbranding.com/2014/geny-genz-global-workplace-expectations-study/

22. eBay. (2015). *Who we are*. Retrieved from http://www.ebayinc.com/who_we_are/one_company

23. Hsaio, A. (2015). *How did eBay start?* Retrieved from http://ebay.about.com/od/ebaylifestyle/a/el_history.htm

24. Airbnb. (2015). *About us*. Retrieved from https://www.airbnb.com/about/about-us

25. Craigslist. (2015). *Factsheet*. Retrieved from https://www.craigslist.org/about/factsheet

26. Uber. *Uber*. Retrieved from https://www.uber.com/

27. White, G. B. (2015*). In the sharing economy, no one's an employee*. Retrieved from http://www.theatlantic.com/business/archive/2015/06/in-the-sharing-economy-no-ones-an-employee/395027/

28. Goodwin, T. (2015). *The battle is for the customer interface*. Retrieved from http://techcrunch.com/2015/03/03/in-the-age-of-disintermediation-the-battle-is-all-for-the-customer-interface/#.frlq0d:Zl2L

29. Investopedia. (N.d.). *Sharing economy*. Retrieved from http://www.investopedia.com/terms/s/sharing-economy.asp

30. Investopedia. (N.d.).

31. Craigslist. (2015).

32. Craigslist. (2015).

33. eMarketer. (2014). *How elusive is Generation Z after all?* Retrieved from http://www.emarketer.com/Article/How-Elusive-Generation-Z-After-All/1011466#sthash.ex9GqfVz.dpuf

34. Etsy. (2015). *About Etsy*. Retrieved from https://www.etsy.com/about/?ref=ftr

35. eMarketer. (2014).

36. eBay Classifieds. (2015). *About us*. Retrieved from http://www.ebayclassifieds.com/m/About

37. Thompson, C. (2015). *How the "Uber effect" is changing work*. Retrieved from http://www.cnbc.com/id/102503684

38. Freelancers Union and Elance oDesk. (2014). *Freelancing in America: A national survey of the new workforce.* Retrieved from http://fu-web-storage-prod.s3.amazonaws.com/content/filer_public/c2/06/c2065a8a-7f00-46db-915a-2122965df7d9/fu_freelancinginamericareport_v3-rgb.pdf

39. Wald, J. (2014). *What the rise of the freelance economy really means for business.* Retrieved from http://www.forbes.com/sites/waldleventhal/2014/07/01/a-modern-human-capital-talent-strategy-using-freelancers/

40. Uber. (2015b). *Sign up to drive with Uber.* Retrieved from https://get.uber.com/drive/

41. Taskrabbit. (2015). *How Taskrabbit works.* Retrieved from https://www.taskrabbit.com/how-it-works

42. White. (2015).

43. Lewis, T. (2013). *Hurricane Sandy impacts: How the superstorm changed the public's view of weather threats.* Retrieved from http://www.huffingtonpost.com/2013/08/12/hurricane-sandy-impacts_n_3743902.html

44. History.com. (2015). *Boston Marathon bombings.* Retrieved from http://www.history.com/topics/boston-marathon-bombings

45. Frosch, D., & Johnson, K. (2012, July 21). Gunman kills 12 in Colorado, reviving gun debate. *New York Times.* Retrieved from http://www.nytimes.com/2012/07/21/us/shooting-at-colorado-theater-showing-batman-movie.html?_r=0

46. Gargis, J., & Gray, B. (2014). *Two people shot at Midtown movie theater.* Retrieved from http://www.ajc

.com/news/news/local/2-people-shot-at-midtown-movie-theater/njZYQ/

47. Jackson, J., & Gouseti, I. (2014). Fear of crime and the psychology of risk. In G. Bruinsma & D. Weisburd (Eds.), *Encyclopedia of criminology and criminal justice* (pp. 1594–1603). New York: Springer.

48. Levine, A., & Dean, D. R. (2012). *Generation on a tightrope: A portrait of today's college student.* San Francisco: Wiley.

49. Glassner, B. (2010). *The culture of fear.* New York: Basic Books.

50. Anatole, E. (2013). *Generation Z: Rebels with a cause.* Retrieved from http://www.forbes.com/sites/onmarketing/2013/05/28/generation-z-rebels-with-a-cause/

51. Hixon, L., Hepler, B. B., & Kim, M. O. (2011). *The white population: 2010.* Retrieved from http://www.census.gov/prod/cen2010/briefs/c2010br-05.pdf

52. Centers for Disease Control and Prevention. (2013b). *Hispanic or Latino populations.* Retrieved from http://www.cdc.gov/minorityhealth/populations/REMP/hispanic.html

53. Ennis, S. R., Rios-Vargas, M., & Albert, N. G. (2010). *The Hispanic population: 2010.* Retrieved from http://www.census.gov/prod/cen2010/briefs/c2010br-04.pdf

54. Jones, N. A., & Bullock, J. (2012). *The two or more races population: 2010.* Retrieved from https://www.census.gov/prod/cen2010/briefs/c2010br-13.pdf

55. Portillo, C. M. (2014). *Only 14 percent of CEOs on this year's Inc. 5000 list are female-and that's a major improvement.* Retrieved from http://www.bizjournals .com/bizwomen/news/latest-news/2014/08/only-14-percent-of-ceos-on-this-years-inc-5000.html

56. Washington Post Editorial Board. (2015, March 30). Indiana's religious freedom law can have real discriminatory effects. *Washington Post.* Retrieved from http://www.washingtonpost.com/opinions/indianas-religious-freedom-law-can-have-real-discriminatory-effects/2015/03/30/f7470520-d71f-11e4-b3f2-607bd612aeac_story.html

57. Magid Generational Strategies. (2014). *The first generation of the twenty-first century: An introduction to the pluralist generation.* Retrieved from http://magid.com/sites/default/files/pdf/MagidPluralistGenerationWhitepaper.pdf

58. Magid Generation Strategies. (2014).

59. Anatole, E. (2013).

60. Patterson, M. M., Pahlke, E., & Bigler, R. S. (2013). Witnesses to history: Children's views of race and the 2008 United States presidential election. *Analyses of Social Issues and Public Policy, 13*(1), 186-210.

61. Magid Generational Strategies. (2014).

62. Magid Generational Strategies. (2014).

63. Anatole. (2013).

64. Ekins, E. (2014). *65% of Americans say Millennials are "entitled," 58% of Millennials agree.* Retrieved from

http://reason.com/poll/2014/08/19/65-of-americans-say-millennials-are-enti

65. Northeastern University. (2014). *Innovation survey.* Retrieved from www.northeastern.edu/news/2014/11/innovation-imperative-meet-generation-z/

66. Davidson, P. (2014). *U.S. economy regains all jobs lost in recession.* Retrieved from http://www.usatoday.com/story/money/business/2014/06/06/may-jobs-report/10037173/

67. Gordon, T. (2012). *State and local budgets and the Great Recession.* Retrieved from http://www.brookings.edu/research/articles/2012/12/state-local-budgets-gordon

68. Institute of Medicine. (2013). *Educating the student body: Taking physical activity and physical education to school.* Retrieved from http://www.iom.edu/~/media/Files/Report%20Files/2013/Educating-the-Student-Body/EducatingTheStudentBody_rb.pdf

69. Parsad, B., Splegelman, M., & Coopersmith, J. (2012). *Arts education in public elementary and secondary schools 1999-2000 and 2009-2010.* Retrieved from http://nces.ed.gov/pubs2012/2012014.pdf

70. Parsad et al. (2012).

71. Mortensen, T. G. (2012). *State funding: A race to the bottom.* Retrieved from http://www.acenet.edu/the-presidency/columns-and-features/Pages/state-funding-a-race-to-the-bottom.aspx

72. Lorin, J. (2014). *College tuition in the U.S. again rises faster than inflation.* Retrieved from http://www

.bloomberg.com/news/articles/2014-11-13/college-tuition-in-the-u-s-again-rises-faster-than-inflation

73. Intelligence Group. (2013). *Cassandra report.* Retrieved from www.cassandra.co/report/

74. Pew Research Center. (2010). *Religion and the issues.* Retrieved from http://www.pewforum.org/files/2010/09/immigration-environment-views-fullreport.pdf

75. Pew Research Center. (2010).

76. Northeastern University. (2014).

77. Pew Research Center. (2010).

78. Glenn, H. (2013). *Losing our religion: The growth of the "nones."* Retrieved from http://www.npr.org/blogs/thetwo-way/2013/01/14/169164840/losing-our-religion-the-growth-of-the-nones

79. Northeastern University. (2014).

80. Harris, D. (2009). *Young Americans losing their religion.* Retrieved from http://abcnews.go.com/Politics/story?id=7513343

81. Levine, A., & Dean, D. R. (2012).

82. Glenn. (2013).

83. Heneghan, T. (2012). *"No religion" is world's third-largest religious group after Christians, Muslims according to Pew study.* Retrieved from http://www.huffingtonpost.com/2012/12/18/unaffiliated-third-largest-religious-group-after-christians-muslims_n_2323664.html

84. Pew Research Center. (2010).

85. http://www.merriam-webster.com/dictionary/conservatism

86. http://www.merriam-webster.com/dictionary/liberalism

87. http://www.merriam-webster.com/dictionary/moderate

88. Eagan et al. (2014).

89. Intelligence Group. (2013).

3

COMMUNICATION PLATFORMS AND PREFERENCES

Shopping, travel, gathering information, and entertainment: the Internet has changed the way people do everything—most profoundly, the way they connect and communicate with others. With phones seemingly glued to their hands or their heads buried in their laptops, there are concerns that Generation Z will not know how to properly communicate and build relationships.[1] But properly communicating and relating to others can be relative because each generation has its own set of social norms and trends. Some would argue that technology does not just provide a different method of communicating from what was available for previous generations in early adulthood; it forces a rewriting of etiquette rules.[2] What may have been socially inappropriate twenty years ago may now be normal.

The only communication methods that Generation Z students have known include buttons to send messages, mailboxes that cannot be physically touched, and photo albums that are entirely stored in a cloud. Consider that these students have never known a time when plans with others had to be made in person or having a pen-pal meant writing a letter with pen and paper and waiting weeks for a response from across the globe. With text messaging at their fingertips, they have never known the sneakiness of writing and passing notes in class.

So Many Channels, So Little Time

With constant connectivity and real-time access to information, Generation Z has the ability to engage in quick, frequent, and succinct communication. It is no surprise that given their tendency to jump from screen to screen and conversation to conversation, many have short attention spans.[3]

Their smart phones provide text, e-mail, messaging, and social media all from one location, which is likely why the most common connection to the Internet for them is through smart phones.[4] Their phones give Generation Z users not only the ability to communicate more quickly and more often but from anywhere at any time. Although phones are the number one platforms they use to connect with others, 93 percent of Generation Z also has access to a computer, either a personal laptop or shared family computer, making their ability to connect using technology nearly universal for all.[5] As the most mobile device–dependent generation yet, Generation Z may seem distracted by their phones and tablets, yet in their eyes, this is just the way they connect with others. Given all of these communication options, what does Generation Z use most and for what purposes?

Text or iMessage Is Best

Texting has become a prominent mode for communication and widely popular among Generation Z students due to the ability to send and receive messages frequently and from almost any location. One in three Generation Z students report sending over three thousand text messages per month, or roughly one hundred messages a day.[6] In a few seconds, they can send a message to their classmate about homework and let their mom know they will be home after their club meeting.

"It is quick, easy, and allows me to do two or three other things while carrying on a conversation."

Generation Z student

"I like texting because my phone is always in my hand, so why not?"

Generation Z student

The rapid send and response rate that text messaging offers also presents new challenges in the sense that Generation Z has almost created their own language for texting. Shortening words and using abbreviations has been at the core of texting from the beginning due to limits on characters per message and prices set per message. Now, with Wi-Fi accessibility and the commonality of unlimited use plans, Generation Z can use abbreviated language not to save money or characters but to be able to send messages more quickly.

Emojis, or emotion icons, add another layer to the text message language Generation Z is fluent in. Emojis extend beyond just happy or sad faces to include tiny picture icons, such as a piece of pizza or dog, that can accompany a message. Generation Z students can in fact carry on an entire conversation with these tiny pictures alone.[7] How oddly full circle human communication has come in looking back to the days of symbols drawn on cave walls.

Alexander Graham Bell would probably be in awe as to how far his invention, the telephone, has come, especially since Generation Z is not fond of using their mobile phone for its original intent: making phone calls.[8] Sixty-five percent of Generation Z students in our study said they dislike or only somewhat like making voice phone calls. It appears that this old-school technology might be reserved for them to communicate with parents and family members, whereas texting is the communication method they prefer to converse with peers and friends.[9]

Whether You Like It or Not, You've Got Mail

Our study revealed that a quarter of Generation Z students indicate that they do not like e-mail, and almost half indicate that they only somewhat like it. They view e-mails, like phone calls, as a communication method that takes too much time between responses and is more formal. That is why it is no surprise that Generation Z students in our study associated e-mail with adults. E-mail to Generation Z is what hand-written or typed office memos and snail mail were to previous generations.

> "I will only use e-mail messaging if I want to contact a coworker or professor."
>
> *Generation Z student*

Instant Messaging

In the 1990s, AOL Instant Messenger was all the rage.[10] Instant messaging allowed users to connect with each other by sending messages quickly while on their computers. Now, in addition to messaging from computers, there are messaging apps that have instant messaging functions that can be used on smart phones and tablets. Despite its widespread availability, we found that instant messaging is the least preferred communication method for Generation Z. One-third of Generation Z students reported disliking instant messaging, and another third indicated only somewhat liking it.

In fact, instant messaging has many of the same qualities and functions that text messaging does, yet the two have an inverse relationship. The decline in instant message preferences could be due to the similarity in function to text messaging that they like so much. Instant messaging was born as a computer-based method, and in the long run, it might not be able to compete with the mobile friendly perception of texting.

Face-to-Face over Facebook

Despite their widespread use of and potential reliance on technology to communicate, Generation Z students still find in-person communication to be valuable. Our study revealed that 83 percent of Generation Z students prefer face-to-face communication because it allows them to connect better and read the other person. And this is not just communication with family members. More than two-thirds prefer interacting with their friends in person as opposed to online or by social media.[11] They also prefer and expect in-person communication in the workplace with their supervisors and employers.[12]

> "I like to use face-to-face communication because it makes it easier to see emotions and makes it personal."
>
> *Generation Z student*

Although Generation Z students may crave face-to-face communication, consider that much of their communication is instead done through technology. This does not give them as much opportunity to hone their skill sets to communicate effectively in person; the result is that they lack strong interpersonal skills.[13]

Conclusion

Technology has had an enormous affect on the way that Generation Z communicates, which is quickly, efficiently, accessibly, and all the time. Although they can communicate through technology at any time, they still prefer face-to-face communication. They, like other generations before them, crave authentic connection with others. Being able to communicate using multiple methods, however, can certainly augment the face-to-face interactions they enjoy.

Notes

1. Bruzzese, A. (2013). *On the job: New generation is arriving in the workplace.* Retrieved from www.usatoday.com/story/money/columnist/bruzzese/2013/10/20/on-the-job-generation-z/2999689/

2. Selinger, E. (2013). *We're turning digital natives into etiquette sociopaths.* Retrieved from www.wired.com/2013/03/digital-natives-etiquette-be-damned

3. Sparks & Honey. (2014). *Meet Gen Z: Forget everything you learned about Millennials.* Retrieved from www.slideshare.net/sparksandhoney/generation-z-final-june-17

4. Madden, M., Lenhart, A., Duggan, M., Cortesi, S., & Gasser, U. (2013). *Teens and technology.* Retrieved from http://www.pewinternet.org/2013/03/13/teens-and-technology-2013/

5. Madden et al. (2013).

6. Lenhart, A., Ling, R., Campbell, S., & Purcell, K. (2010b). *How phones are used with friends: What they can do and how teens use them.* Retrieved from www.pewinternet.org/2010/04/20/chapter-two-how-phones-are-used-with-friends-what-they-can-do-and-how-teens-use-them/

7. Sparks & Honey. (2014).

8. Mobile Statistics. (2012). *Phone calls are dead says Generation Z.* Retrieved from www.mobilestatistics.com/mobile-news/phone-calls-are-dead-say-generation-z.aspx

9. Lenhart, A., Ling, R., Campbell, S., & Purcell, K. (2010c). *Teens and mobile phones.* Retrieved from www.pewinternet.org/2010/04/20/teens-and-mobile-phones

10. Abbruzzese, J. (2014). *The rise and fall of AIM, the breakthrough AOL never wanted.* Retrieved from http://mashable.com/2014/04/15/aim-history/

11. Northeastern University. (2014). *Innovation survey.* Retrieved from www.northeastern.edu/news/2014/11/innovation-imperative-meet-generation-z/

12. Millennial Branding. (2014). *Gen Y and Gen Z global workplace expectations study.* Retrieved from millennialbranding.com/tag/gen-z/

13. Knoll. (2014). *What comes after Y? Generation Z: Arriving to the office soon.* Retrieved from www.knoll.com/knollnewsdetail/what-comes-after-y-generation-z-arriving-to-the-office-soon

4

SOCIAL MEDIA USE

The past twenty years have seen exponential growth in technological development for the web. Society has come a long way from the dial-up tone of America Online[1] to being able to access the Internet through smart phones. In the early days, the Internet consisted of web pages created by a select few who had the knowledge and capability to build them. Primarily static with read-only functioning, the earliest websites made up what is now referred to as Web 1.0.[2] Increasingly more participatory, Web 2.0[3] was developed to allow users to read and write content, such as posts. Today, sites are based on user-created content and social connectivity. Content can be created in almost real time such as being able to upload a vacation photo just after it is taken.

It is no surprise that Generation Z students, who have grown up in a world shaped by the Internet, are in tune with and connected through social media and online communication technology platforms. Finding out where they hang out in the virtual world can make it easier to connect with them.

Likes, Tweets, Follows, and Pins: The "What" of Social Media

With the versatility and accessibility of today's Internet and devices, Generation Z students are connected online at least one hour every day; some indicate they are connected online nearly 10 hours a day.[4] They spend 41 percent of their time outside the classroom on a computer, phone, or mobile device.[5] Their social media use involves more than just connecting with friends: staying up-to-date on news, researching topics of interest, and general lifestyle improvement such as fitness and nutrition, fashion, or general entertainment. One in four Generation Z students in our study indicated using social media for its speed and ease of use. With a few swipes on their smart phones, they can "like" a picture on Instagram, send a tweet through Twitter, and message a classmate on Facebook. With Generation Z's preference in multitasking and their use of multiple screens to connect and communicate, speed and simplicity are certainly factors for them in using any particular social media tool.

THE Social Network

> "Facebook was not originally created to be a company. It was built to accomplish a social mission—to make the world more open and connected."
>
> *Mark Zuckerberg, CEO, Facebook*[7]

With 1.35 billion monthly active users worldwide, Facebook has been a predominant social media site since its inception in 2004.[6] Facebook allows users to create a personalized profile, upload pictures, share information through what is called a "status," check in at various locations, send messages to friends, invite friends to an event, and even play games in online communities. Facebook has numerous uses and features that have also become intertwined with many other websites and applications. For instance, users can link their Facebook profile to their Spotify account, a music-streaming website, and share with friends what tunes they have been listening to.

Facebook has become far more than just a social networking site to connect with and check in with friends. It permeates multiple sites and platforms. Facebook has become a tool that can be used in many aspects of life: professional networking, business advertising, personal content promotion, advocating for an issue, and entertainment.

A Picture Is Worth a Thousand Likes

Launched in 2010, Instagram makes everyday users photographers. Accessible by smart phone or tablet, the 300 million users of Instagram can upload and edit photos with filters and effects, as well as add 15 second videos to share with friends and followers.[8] Instagram was acquired by Facebook in 2012, which has since allowed users to share content on both platforms and streamline accounts. Like Facebook, Instagram accounts can be set to either public viewing or private sharing, in which users can approve or deny followers.

The Hashtag Generation

Twitter, unlike many other social media platforms, limits user messages to 140 characters per tweet.[9] A tweet can be anything from sharing a personal thought, a live update from an event, a picture, a link to an article, or even just sharing what the user is doing at the moment. The first tweet was posted in 2006, and now 284 million users are on Twitter at least once a month.[10] Usage reports indicate 80 percent of those users are tweeting from a mobile device.[11]

Twitter hosts accounts of celebrities, news sources, and humor sites that allow users to stay up-to-date with what is going on beyond just their friend group. The ability to create lists and categorize Twitter accounts by content provides an avenue to quickly sift through multiple types of information in a few swipes on the smart phone. It provides the ability to keep up with the Kardashians,[12] get the latest score of the big game, and see what a friend from home is up to.

Twitter can be credited with the concept of a hashtag,[13] a pound sign in a tweet that allows that tweet to be discovered in a search. For example, if a user tweets, "Excited to go home for the holidays #familytime," this tweet is then grouped in a stream of other tweets including the hashtag #familytime. Other users who are interested in the topic of family time can search and see any tweet tagged with that hashtag and thus follow users they may not have discovered otherwise.

Tweets have been used as a very quick way to communicate with a large group of people. In their own way of breaking news, Twitter users started "live tweeting" events by sharing their thoughts during events through the use of hashtags. In 2009, news outlets even began using Twitter to break news quickly.[14]

While some still do not understand the point of Twitter, the company summarizes it succinctly: "A tweet is an expression of a moment or idea ... shared in real time, every day."[15] Generation Z is among the millions of users who find this form of expression and sharing to be highly appealing.

Captured on Video

Humor, instructions, music, and personal stories can all be found on YouTube. YouTube allows users to create and upload original content and videos and provides a platform for user comments and conversations. With the first video being an 18 second clip from a zoo,[16] YouTube has come a long way with its more than 300 hours of videos uploaded each minute.[17]

YouTube emerged in 2005 and has not slowed in growth or prominence since its founding.[18] It reports over 1 billion users per month who collectively watch more than 600 billion hours of videos each month.[19] Forty percent of YouTube's global watch time takes place on a mobile device.[20] Thus, it is no surprise that YouTube is hugely popular with young adults. The YouTube analytics report indicates that users from eighteen to twenty-four make up 41 percent of the 25 million total video viewership in the United States.[21] Generation Z is quite fond of YouTube: 93 percent visit the site at least once a week, and slightly more than half visit multiple times per day.[22]

Aside from the video content, YouTube is highly integrated with other social media platforms. As a Google company, a user must have a Google account to upload a video or subscribe to a channel, but anyone can view or share a video. While videos were being circulated by e-mail before YouTube, the platform gave traction to the viral video by allowing users to paste the link to the video on other sites or social media platforms and spread the video out to numerous people.[23] The viral video phenomenon has led to lucrative opportunities for businesses, musicians, advertisers, and everyday individuals.[24] YouTube has grown into more than just a site to stream videos. It has become a marketing tool, an online community, and method for accessing a colossal amount of video content.

Telling Stories

Although the first blog was created in 1994, the term *blog* emerged only in 1997 as a shortened name for *web log*.[25] Blogs were initially created to serve as personal websites and have evolved to include a variety of uses, users, and platforms. With the emergence of sites such as Tumblr, Blogger, and Wordpress, the need for knowledge of HTML and web coding that was present in the early days of blogs no longer existed and opened up access to a larger number of users.

Blog sites provide a template-like approach where users can select a theme and input written content, pictures, or videos. Blogs take on a variety of shapes and cover a range of topics. These platforms can showcase personal portfolios of work, provide a space to share stories of travel or life events, serve as a platform to offer advice, or be an online diary. Users who are interested in similar topics can find community by connecting with others through blogging.

Put It on the Pinboard

Virtual pinboarding allows users to view, save, and organize pictures, websites, and posts to a pinboard. The concept is similar to cutting out a magazine clipping and pinning it to a corkboard to save the idea. Virtual pinboarding grew in popularity with the emergence of Pinterest in 2010.[26] The 50 billion pins on Pinterest are both user created and produced and supported by companies, but they range in topics from recipes, fitness and health, and home decor to fashion and art.[27] Pinterest has seen huge growth in users since its founding, but the main demographic has remained very much the same.[28] Women make up a majority of Pinterest users and are five times more likely to use it than men.[29] The total user numbers sit at 72.8 million and growing.[30]

Sharing Opinions and Getting Advice

Online forums come in all topics, users, and platforms, but their unifying thread is to bring people together in a virtual community. Online forums are usually grouped by topic or interest in which people seek out and give advice or support. Forums can range in levels of privacy from an open discussion board, where anyone can post, to a closed community, which requires users to be granted access.

Reddit, one of the most popular online forums, describes itself as the "front page of the Internet."[31] While Reddit might appear to be news focused, users or "Redditors" can share or create posts about different topics, and other users can view and vote if they like the post. The front page of Reddit has the posts with the most votes. There are various groups of users based on topics and interests. At the start of 2015, over 186 million monthly contributors on Reddit had provided content and post votes.[32]

Avatars and Social Gaming

History shows that humans have been playing games for entertainment dating back to the ancient Egyptians.[33] As technology has evolved, so have games. Instead of having to wait for a friend to come over to play a board game, the Internet has given gamers the ability to play games with others from all over the world at all times of day. Massive multiplayer online role-playing games (MMORPGs)[34] allow users to create an online avatar to represent their presence in the game, which can be entirely made up or accurately align with their offline identities. Based in a fantasy realm, World of Warcraft[35] is one of the most popular MMORPGs, with over 10 million subscribers.[36]

Facebook has also become part of social gaming in which users play with their Facebook friends and their avatar is pulled from their Facebook profile.[37] Through either the web-based platform or mobile application, over 250 million people play games on Facebook.[38] This phenomenon is very popular: 12 percent of the world's population engages in social gaming at least once a month.[39] Social gaming is anticipated to continue to grow to an $87 billion market by 2017 with the continued evolution of mobile and online sources.[40]

Generation Z's "Likes"

With an expansive online breadth, it is not surprising we found that Generation Z students use Facebook the most in comparison to other mass communication methods. These students believe that Facebook incorporates a little bit of everything allowing them to follow, post, keep up, and chat, all in one place. The expansive number of users and various capabilities make Facebook a one-stop-shop for users.

Generation Z students nevertheless are using more than Facebook. One in four in our study report that Twitter is their preferred form of social media. This preference stems from how quick and easy it is to tweet—and tweet often. Some prefer Twitter because they can tweet many times a day and not overwhelm followers as the feed of information refreshes frequently, where an abundance of Facebook posts might be seen as annoying. Twitter's news feed includes all tweets that a user follows, whereas Facebook has an algorithm that determines the posts a user sees on their news feed. On Facebook, you might not see every post from every friend, but the newsfeed algorithm tends to show the same people regularly.

While previous generations take in news from newspapers, radio, TV, or an online news site, Twitter allows students to stay informed of what is going on in the world or worlds of their choosing while easily filtering out the worlds they do not want to learn about. Instead of sitting down to read a news article, they might just take in a tweet at the time the event is happening. Someone who is particularly interested in keeping up with sports, for example, can opt to follow ESPN on Twitter to stay in the know with what is going on with their favorite team. Another user might be very interested in the day-to-day lives of celebrities and pop culture. Twitter gives them the ability to craft their newsfeed by following television channels, magazines, or celebrities. And there is no need to wait: students can stay up-to-date by the second on nearly any topic just by scrolling through their Twitter feed.

Different Keystrokes for Different Folks

People might describe Generation Z students as glued to their phones. And for many, this is true. But why? What is the adhesive that keeps this group glued to their smart phones, tablets, and computers? It is likely that the Internet and social media provide so many different tools that can make communication, connection, sharing, and entertainment easier. But just as a person would not buy a single tool—say, a circular saw—and expect that tool to be effective in completing every household improvement, Generation Z students are using different social media and mass communication platforms to fulfill different needs.

Keeping Up with Others

"I use it most so I can see what's going on in everyone's lives (which is mostly drama, so bust out the popcorn!)."

Generation Z student

Although social media is generally self-focused and usually where personal sharing occurs, Generation Z students use social media more to keep up with others than to share about themselves.[41] For these students, their strong connection to social media is to have a window into the lives of others. In an almost voyeuristic way, Generation Z is very drawn to seeing what is going on with those around them, and social media is a quick and easy way to do just that. Very similar to the appeal of reality television, social media also gives Generation Z users a personal look into the lives of others without having to share their personal information.

We found that more than 80 percent of Generation Z students use Facebook and Instagram as the main platforms to keep up with others. This could likely be linked to the idea that having a large number of Facebook users makes it easy to keep up and connect with others wherever they are, whereas Instagram's growing popularity and focus on pictures and videos appeals to Generation Z. With friends, family, acquaintances, celebrities, and companies having a presence on

Facebook and Instagram, users can check in on a wide array of people in only one or two places.

> "I use Facebook the most because that's where most of my friends are; that's how I keep up with people I care about."
>
> *Generation Z student*

New Knowledge

The Internet can be a powerful tool for learning and gaining knowledge. Being brought up in the midst of a web evolution, the static nature of taking in new information in words alone does not appeal to Generation Z. Watching YouTube videos is the preferred form of social media for learning new information for Generation Z students in our study. The multimedia nature of videos allows students to go beyond just reading about a concept, and instead witness and even virtually experience it.

> "I am exposed to many videos that allow me to learn a variety of things. From strength training to how to make food and so on. It's a great resource."
>
> *Generation Z student*

Some Generation Z students indicated in our study that they use YouTube videos to supplement their academic classes. Video allows students to learn by combining visual, audio, linguistic, spatial, and musical strategies,[42] as well as to select and organize words and images and integrate them with prior knowledge.[43] Many students are also using video as a classroom tool: 33 percent of Generation Z indicate watching lessons online.[44] If students have a preference for taking in knowledge through video, this brings up many important implications for those teaching and educating this generation.

Sharing Personal Information

Although they prefer to access information about others rather than share about themselves, Generation Z students who do share use Facebook and Instagram to do so. Facebook has expansive usership and allows people to post many different types of information: a text-based status, a picture, a short video, or a link to another site. The broad reach of Facebook allows that information to get out to a great number of people. Thus, 54 percent of Generation Z students we studied say they use Facebook for sharing personal information.

> "I mostly use Facebook because it's user friendly. It's an easy place to share ideas, thoughts, and past adventures. It's a fun way to look back and record your past digitally."
>
> *Generation Z student*

However, Instagram inches just ahead of Facebook, with 60 percent of those in our study indicating that they share personal information through this platform. This is probably because Instagram allows users to express themselves in a visual manner through the ability to edit and filter the pictures and videos they post. The simple editing functions add to the appeal of Instagram because users can produce content that was previously exclusive to professional photographers and videographers.[45]

> "I use Instagram the most because it is filled with photographs and it is easiest to control who can view my posts. I can view others' posts and see their experiences."
>
> *Generation Z student*

While understanding how Generation Z shares their information, it is also important to understand with whom they share that information. Facebook and Instagram allow users to pick and choose who can see content, so these students can craft their audience and curate what each audience can view. They capitalize on the ability to tailor posts and followership. For example, 60 percent of Generation Z Facebook users have their profiles set to private so that only approved friends can see information and 26 percent omit or post false information to help protect their privacy.[46] This may include altering personal information or hiding certain elements of personal information from a public profile. Generation Z also cares about their online reputation: 74 percent have deleted, blocked, or "unfriended" someone because of privacy concerns.[47] Generation Z students enjoy sharing about themselves, but they are protective about whom they share with.

Sharing Expertise or Opinion

Generation Z students are comfortable with sharing their opinions or expertise and use multiple platforms, such as Twitter, blogging, personal websites, pinboarding, forums, and social gaming, to do so. All of these platforms give users the option to share using an identity that is built on a spectrum of accuracy with their offline life. While not every Generation Z student may choose to use an alias or craft an avatar identity, doing so provides a safe space for Generation Z students to share without the vulnerability of the information or opinion being linked to their actual identity. Facebook, Instagram, and YouTube, which our study found are the platforms used by the fewest number of Generation Z students in sharing their opinions, entail putting a face to the shared opinion or expertise. Using these sites can create a bit more vulnerability because posts can be easily attached to their offline identities.

> "It's anonymous, I can express myself freely."
>
> *Generation Z student*

> "There is considerable comfort behind a computer screen."
>
> *Generation Z student*

Babble of the Sexes

It is not news that men and women communicate differently, so it should not be news that Generation Z men and women use social media differently as well. When looking at why they use social media, the reasons are starkly different. We found that the main reason women use social media is to keep up with others' lives, while men use social media because it is quick and easy to use.

Although our study found that more than 25 percent of men and women say they use Facebook and Twitter the most for communicating with others, their preference for Instagram varies. Twenty-nine percent of women use Instagram the most (even more than Twitter for them), whereas only 15 percent of men do. Given the widespread use of Facebook and Twitter, it is not surprising that these are preferred platforms. However, the disparity between men's and women's use of Instagram is interesting as this is consistent with the use of Instagram by women in general.[48]

Facebook Is for Family, Twitter Is for Friends

Fostering relationships with family members after going away to college can be difficult, and Generation Z students are using Facebook as a means to stay connected with their families from afar. While it might be a driving factor in why Generation Z students are still using Facebook, the presence of their family members on Facebook is also one of the reasons they are not using Facebook as often.[49]

> "I like voicing my opinion over social media that hasn't been taken over by parents yet."
>
> *Generation Z student*

> "I use Twitter most to communicate with friends in the same age group, with very little parent users."
>
> *Generation Z student*

More than half of adult Internet users older than age sixty-five are using Facebook,[50] meaning Generation Z is likely seeing Grandma posting what she thought about the latest episode of *The Voice* or a picture of her trip to see the grandkids. Generation Z's view of Facebook is changing. While it might not be as hip and cool for Generation Z as it once was for teens, they have not completely abandoned it.[51] They still see it as a necessary utility due to its wide integration with other platforms, websites, and applications. So if Generation Z is still connected multiple hours a day, where are they online? They are where their parents and family members are not.

Facebook allows Generation Z students to stay in touch with Aunt Susan while away at college, but they do not want

Aunt Susan reading their tweets, "liking" their Instagram photos, or reading their blogs. Generation Z students are flocking to platforms like Instagram, Twitter, and various messaging applications such as Snapchat,[52] in which 26 percent of users are Generation Z, and WhatsApp.[53] These sites allow them to connect with users their age and monitor who sees their content.[54] The concept of protecting their privacy from their parents is not new for teenagers. Having a Twitter account free from parents could be the modern equivalent of a teenager having a personal landline phone in his or her bedroom in the 1990s. Social media provides a unique way for Generation Z students to stay connected with family through some platforms, as well as to be candid with their peers through others.

> "Parents don't have Twitters … yet. We can truly be who we want to be, say what we want to say, and post what we want to post."
>
> *Generation Z student*

The role that social media plays with how Generation Z students manage their familial and peer relationships brings up important questions of how best to digitally communicate with this generation. Should higher education administrators, faculty, and staff invade students' "authority-figure-free" zone? If they do crash their online party, will these students keep flocking to newer platforms? Or do those in higher education let Generation Z students have their online freedom in their platforms of choice and capitalize on the platforms in which their presence is welcome?

Conclusion

It is clear that Generation Z students are versatile in their use of social media and use different platforms for different purposes. And although there are trends in social media use, some students might not have familiarity with particular platforms. Parents, family members, and authority figures need to be mindful about what platforms to use, how they use them, and where they enter the virtual space of Generation Z.

Notes

1. America Online. (2015). *About AOL*. Retrieved from http://corp.aol.com/about-aol

2. Aghaei, S., Nematbakhsh, M. A., & Farsani, H. K. (2012). Evolution of the world wide web: From web 1.0 to web 4.0. *International Journal of Web and Semantic Technology*, 3(1), 1–10.

3. Aghaei et al. (2012).

4. Ipsos MediaCT. (2013). *Generation Z: A look at the technology and media habits of today's teens*. Retrieved from http://www.wikia.com/Generation_Z:_A_Look_at_the_Technology_and_Media_Habits_of_Today%E2%80%99s_Teens

5. Sparks & Honey. (2014). *Meet Gen Z: Forget everything you learned about Millennials*. Retrieved from www.slideshare.net/sparksandhoney/generation-z-final-june-17

6. Facebook. (2015b). *Company history*. Retrieved from http://newsroom.fb.com/company-info/

7. Facebook. (2012). *Form S-1 registration statement; Letter from Mark Zuckerberg.* Washington, DC: Facebook.

8. Fiegerman, S. (2014). *Instagram tops 300 million active users, likely bigger than Twitter.* Retrieved from http://mashable.com/2014/12/10/instagram-300-million-users/

9. Twitter. (2015). *About.* Retrieved from https://about.twitter.com/

10. Twitter. (2015).

11. Twitter. (2015).

12. E! (2015). *Keeping up with the Kardashians.* Retrieved from http://www.eonline.com/shows/kardashians

13. Zak, E. (2013). *How Twitter's hashtag came to be.* Retrieved from http://blogs.wsj.com/digits/2013/10/03/how-twitters-hashtag-came-to-be/

14. Twitter. (2015).

15. Twitter. (2015).

16. Giuliano, K. (2015). *YouTube turns 10 today.* Retrieved from http://www.cnbc.com/id/102611949

17. Giuliano, K. (2015).

18. Fitzpatrick, L. (2010, May 31). *Brief history YouTube.* Retrieved from http://content.time.com/time/magazine/article/0,9171,1990787,00.html.

19. YouTube. (2015). *Press room.* Retrieved from https://www.youtube.com/yt/press

20. YouTube. (2015).

21. YouTube. (2015).

22. Ipsos MediaCT. (2013). *GenZ: The limitless genera-tion: A survey of the 13-18 year-old Wikia audience.* Retrieved from http://www.wikia.com/Generation_ Z:_A_Look_at_the_Technology_and_Media_Habits_ of_Today%E2%80%99s_Teens

23. ViralGains. (2014). *The history of viral video.* Retrieved from https://www.youtube.com/watch?v=snHey-snTb8

24. Dickey, M. R. (2013). *The 22 key turning points in the history of YouTube.* Retrieved from http://www .businessinsider.com/key-turning-points-history-of-youtube-2013-2?op=1

25. Thompson, C. (2015). *A timeline of the history of blog-ging: The early years.* Retrieved from www.nymag .com/news/media/15971

26. Jacques, A. (2012). *Parlaying Pinterest: What you need to know about virtual pinboards.* Retrieved from www.prsa.org/Intelligence/Tactics/Articles/view/ 9744/1048/Parlaying_Pinterest_What_you_need_to_ know_about_vi#.VSRyUfnF-4Y

27. Smith, C. (2015c). *By the numbers: 60+ interesting Pin-terest pin and board statistics.* Retrieved from http:// expandedramblings.com/index.php/pinterest-pin-and-board-statistics/

28. Roose, R. (2014). *Pinterest is sneaking up on Twitter, Facebook, and Google.* Retrieved from http://nymag .com/daily/intelligencer/2014/05/pinterest-is-sneaking-up-on-twitter-and-facebook.html

29. Digital Information World. (2014). *#SocialMedia 2014: User demographics for Facebook, Twitter,*

Instagram, and Pinterest -#infographic. Retrieved
from www.digitalinformationworld.com/2014/10/
social-media-user-demographics-linkedin-tumblr-
facebook-and-more-infographic.html

30. Smith, C. (2015a). *90+ amazing Pinterest statistics.*
Retrieved from http://expandedramblings.com/index
.php/pinterest-stats/

31. Smith, C. (2015b) *By the numbers: 40+ amazing Reddit
statistics.* Retrieved from www.expandedramblings
.com/index.php/reddit-stats.

32. Smith, C. (2015b).

33. Orsini, L. (2010). *History of social games.* Retrieved
from http://kotaku.com/5548105/history-of-social-
games#

34. Techopedia. (n.d.). *Massively multiplayer online
role-playing game (MMORPG).* Retrieved from
http://www.techopedia.com/definition/1919/
massively-multiplayer-online-role-playing-game-
mmorpg

35. Blizzard Entertainment. (2015). *What is World of Warcraft?* Retrieved from http://us.battle.net/wow/en/
game/guide/

36. Prescott, S. (2014). *World of Warcraft subscriber count
spikes following release of Draenor release.* Retrieved
from www.pcgamer.com/world-of-warcraft-
subscriber-count-spikes-following-draenor-release/

37. Facebook. (2015c). *Games overview.* Retrieved from
developers.facebook.com/docs/games/overview

38. Facebook. (2015c).

39. Lewis, V., Rollo, J., Devitt, S. Egbert, J., Strawn, M., & Nagasaka, M. (2012). *Social gambling: Click here to play.* http://linkback.morganstanley.com/web/sendlink/webapp/f/u4a8mcp4-3ohe-g001-b7cd-002655210101?store=0&d=UwBSZXNlYXJjaAA0NzE3NTY%3D&user=2t7a7p40q5buy-2365&__gda__=1479106416_6a55cefa848830ece67e9f0e40d5607a

40. Gaudiosi, J. (2012). *New reports forecast global video game industry will reach $82 billion by 2017.* Retrieved from www.forbes.com/sites/johngaudiosi/2012/07/18/new-reports-forecasts-global-video-game-industry-will-reach-82-billion-by-2017/

41. Tamir, D., & Mitchell, J. (2012). Disclosing information about the self is intrinsically rewarding. *Proceedings of the National Academy of Sciences, 109,* 8038–8043. Retrieved from http://www.pnas.org/content/109/21/8038.full

42. Berk, R. A. (2009). Multimedia teaching with video clips: TV, movies, YouTube, and mtvU in the college classroom. *International Journal of Technology in Teaching and Learning, 5*(1), 1–21.

43. Berk. (2009).

44. Sparks & Honey. (2014).

45. Hill, K. (2013). *Vine, Instagram and the appeal of apps that turn us into artists.* Retrieved from www.forbes.com/sites/kashmirhill/2013/01/25/vine-instagram-and-the-appeal-of-apps-that-turn-us-into-artists

46. Pew Research Center. (2013). *Teens, social media, and privacy.* Retrieved from http://www.pewinternet.org/2013/05/21/teens-social-media-and-privacy-3/

47. Pew Research Center. (2013).

48. Duggan, M. & Smith, A. (2013). *Social media update 2013.* Retrieved from http://www.pewinternet.org/2013/12/30/social-media-update-2013/

49. Hempel, J. (2013). *Are teens fleeing Facebook or not?* Retrieved from http://fortune.com/2013/07/31/are-teens-fleeing-facebook-or-not/

50. Duggan, M., Ellison, N. B., Lampfe, C., Lenhart, A., & Madden, M. (2015). *Social media update 2014.* Retrieved from http://www.pewinternet.org/2015/01/09/social-media-update-2014/

51. Hempel. (2013).

52. Snapchat. (2015). *3V Advertising.* Retrieved from https://www.snapchat.com/ads

53. WhatsApp. (2015). *About WhatsApp.* Retrieved from https://www.whatsapp.com/about/

54. Neal, R. (2013). *WhatsApp, SnapChat, and LINE: Why mobile messaging apps are taking teens away from Facebook.* www.ibtimes.com/whatsapp-snapchat-line-why-mobile-messaging-apps-are-taking-teens-away-facebook-1464804.

5

FRIENDS, FAMILY, AND ROMANCE

As the Internet has changed the way we communicate, it has also affected the way Generation Z creates and maintains relationships with the people in their lives. Technology presents new opportunities, but also new challenges and boundaries in managing relationships. Whether their best friend, significant other, or family members, relationships look different for Generation Z than for generations before them. Where previous generations managed relationships solely in person or through written communication, Generation Z has a multitude of ways for building and managing relationships.

Friends and Followers: Creating and Sustaining Peer Relationships

In the 2013 comedy film based on the 1980s TV series by the same name, *21 Jump Street*,[1] police go undercover to bust a drug problem at a local high school and find that the cool kids have changed drastically since their glory days. Instead of the attractive athletes being the in clique, the cool kids are the ones who recycle, participate in theater, are in tune with what is going on in the world, and want to be a part of finding a solution to today's issues. It is in fact a profile of today's Generation Z students.

What Matters in Friendships

Our study found that Generations Z students prefer friends they can relate to: shared values and shared hobbies are the most important factors for them in making friends and sustaining friendships. Unlike the teen movies from the 1980s and 1990s where the plot involved a makeover of the ugly duckling to the unknowingly attractive heartthrob, Generation Z students in our study indicated that physical appearance is least important to them when creating and sustaining friendships. To Generation Z, the cool kids are not necessarily only the attractive jocks and pretty cheerleaders.

Generation Z students are not just the most diverse generation yet;[2] they are also open-minded and embrace diversity.[3] Fewer than 20 percent believe that a shared culture or background is important when creating or sustaining friendships. Differences in culture and background play only a minimal role in whom they choose to be friends with, which is why it is no surprise that they have the most diverse social circles of any other generation.[4]

Following, Friending, Linking, and Liking Friends

Technology and Internet access have been important in the way that Generation Z creates and sustains friendships. Where proximity may have played a more prominent role with older generations in their friendships, fewer than half of Generation Z students in our study find it important to live near friends, and that is likely because technology has provided ways to fill that gap. Haven't seen their best friend from high school who now goes to college on the opposite coast? Video chatting allows them to have face-to-face communication. Need to wish someone happy birthday and forgot to send a card? Generation Z can post on their Facebook wall or share a picture on Instagram.

Networks on social media also allow Generation Z students to "follow" and "friend" people they have never met in person, thus creating online relationships that are socially acceptable for this generation. Depending on the platform, they might follow someone whom they have similar interests with or become friends on Facebook with someone who is second- or third-degree connection based on a mutual friend. Regardless of whether the intent is to create or sustain friendships, technology provides more opportunity for users to create connections and keep in touch than ever before.

Family Matters

With increased rates of home schooling, Generation X has taken an involved approach to parenting, instilling the value of close family relationships with their Generation Z children.[5] Eighty-eight percent of those in Generation Z feel they are extremely close to their parents, whom they see as playing roles more like friends and advisers,[6] except perhaps on Facebook as discussed earlier. They see their parents and family as sources of emotional and financial support.[7] As described further in chapter 8, Generation Z's parents are their role models. It is no wonder, then, that our study revealed that Generation Z students have high regard for their parents, and more than half take the opinions and perspectives of their family into consideration in their decision making.

Similar to Millennials, those in Generation Z value their close family relationships and call, text, and connect often with their parents.[8] Phones and social media can be comforting as they provide a way for all of them to stay in contact no matter where they are.[9]

Romance in a Digital World

Chivalry as it was once conceived may be drawing its last breaths, but the desire to form romantic relationships is alive and well among Generation Z students. Technology also plays a role in their romantic relationships and helps to shape dating norms.

Dating Sites and Meeting "The One"

Dating has certainly taken on a new form due to how integrated technology and social media have become in the lives of Generation Z. Online dating has rapidly grown in popularity and accessibility, with over 65 percent of Americans being comfortable with it.[10] Online dating allows users to meet more and a wider diversity of people than they would in the usual course of life, but it can also encourage moving on to another prospect quickly because there is always another option available.[11] Generation Z is likely engaging in their first adult romantic relationships, and for them, the pursuit of finding a match will be very different than it was for previous generations. When they were in early adulthood, Baby Boomers and Generation Xers would have to be in the right place at the right time to meet "the one." For Generation Z, they can be sitting in their

apartment with access to profiles of hundreds of potential partners in their area simply by swiping a screen to decide whom
they would be interested in chatting with. The days of romantic
comedy-like love stories and serendipitous meetings could
be all but gone.

Consider how the online dating world has opened up opportunities to find specific groups of people to date. Sites aimed
at connecting individuals from particular religious groups and
ethnic communities, as well as gays and lesbians, have made dating more accessible.

Connecting, Communicating, and Canoodling

Social media and technology present opportunities for Generation Z couples to connect, communicate, and canoodle in new
ways. First, social media can reduce the stigma of blind dating.
Connecting on social media with someone through a shared
connection can certainly reduce the anxiety of showing up at
a restaurant looking for the person wearing a red shirt. Both
knowing that the date is vetted through a mutual friend and having the ability to connect virtually before meeting might make
the situation feel less intimidating.

Social media and texting can also be a platform for flirting.
Quickly sending words through cyberspace might embolden
people to be more candid. And once they have started dating,
social media sites can become places to express affection for
one another or display exciting endeavors as a couple, such as
trips and date nights. This may be out of the norm for how
other generations grew up dating, but not so for Generation
Z. One in three members of Generation Z uses social media
as a way to post details or pictures from a date.[12] Although

these sites have added a new dimension of public display of affection, Generation Z's desire for privacy might prevail as they choose to keep their posts private and their intimate details to themselves.

> "It's a territorial thing. It's like an online hickey."
>
> *Generation Z student*

> "Sometimes it [technology] can get in the way of the actual relationship. Someone may be posting something about the relationship that doesn't need to be shared to the public."
>
> *Generation Z student*

Technology has also revolutionized long-distance relationships with no more long-distance phone bills or mailed love letters. Texting allows more frequent connection, and video chatting provides a space to see each other in real time.

> "We FaceTime [Apple's online video chat][13] several times a week and it's like our own form of dates. We text all day so it doesn't feel like he's that far."
>
> *Generation Z student*

Drama and Trust Issues

Some find technology to be extremely helpful in their romantic relationships, but technology can also create drama. Working through trust and jealousy is a reality of many relationships regardless of generation. As social media and technology have developed, they have given users more access to view the lives of their friends and followers. This access can allow someone to uncover unfavorable information about their partner's past that can trigger trust issues about behavior and experiences.

In addition, social media gives users the ability to see where others are, whom they are with, and what they are doing, creating opportunities for individuals to monitor the social media behavior of their partners by seeing whom they are looking up as well as potentially wander off themselves and look up old flames. The ability of social media to offer such great transparency creates new issues for Generation Z's romantic relationships. Whether they see too much or too little, technology and social media will certainly have an impact on romantic relationships for Generation Z.

> "It [social media] is more of a burden than anything else. I am able to see anything, even things I don't want to see regarding my significant other."
>
> *Generation Z student*

Starting Up and Breaking Up

While technology and social media can play a role in Generation Z's romantic relationships, that role does not include creating or ending relationships formally. In starting a relationship, fewer than 20 percent of those in Generation Z prefer to ask someone out online as opposed to in person.[14] And, at the other end of the spectrum, only 22 percent have broken up with someone online.[15] Technology may be an easy solution to many other issues in the world of Generation Z, but they still believe that the somewhat daunting moment of asking someone out or the sticky situation of ending a relationship should be handled in person. This certainly furthers the idea that technology and social media can be useful in sustaining relationships but not for starting or ending them. This may change as Generation Z ages. As their access to viable romantic relationships may decrease not having access to a wide dating pool in the college environment, they may be left to turn to technology and social media to find "the one."

Conclusion

Today's technology and access to the Internet have had an impact on Generation Z's relationships, as it has on other aspects of their lives. The social aspect of technology allows Generation Z to build and maintain relationships with friends, family, and romantic interests in new ways. Being able to access each other more often and across distance, Generation Z can hurdle obstacles in managing relationships with others. Where some generations might view technology as a barrier to relationships, Generation Z views it as a bridge to the people in their lives. It is important to recognize, though, that Generation Z believes technology is useful in developing existing relationships but not as a replacement to forging authentic relationships with friends, family, and romantic partners built on shared values and interests.

Notes

1. IMDB. (2012). *21 Jump Street plot summary*. Retrieved from http://www.imdb.com/title/tt1232829/ plotsummary

2. Magid Generational Strategies. (2014). *The first generation of the twenty-first century: An introduction to the pluralist generation*. Retrieved from http://magid.com/sites/default/files/pdf/ MagidPluralistGenerationWhitepaper.pdf

3. Magid Generational Strategies. (2014).

4. Magid Generational Strategies. (2014).

5. Knoll. (2014). *What comes after Y? Generation Z: Arriving to the office soon.* Retrieved from www .knoll.com/knollnewsdetail/what-comes-after-y-generation-z-arriving-to-the-office-soon

6. Intelligence Group. (2013). *Cassandra report.* Retrieved from www.cassandra.co/report/

7. Marchetti, T. J. (2014). *Three fundamental ways Generation Z differs from Millennials.* Retrieved from www .imediaconnection.com/content/37005.asp

8. Levine, A., & Dean, D. R. (2012). *Generation on a tightrope: A portrait of today's college student.* San Francisco: Wiley.

9. Lenhart, A., Ling, R., Campbell, S., & Purcell, K. (2010a). *Attitudes towards cell phones.* Retrieved from www.pewinternet.org/2010/04/20/chapter-three-attitudes-towards-cell-phones

10. Smith, A., & Duggan, M. (2013). *Online dating and relationships.* Retrieved from www.pewinternet.org/ 2013/10/21/online-dating-relationships/

11. Smith & Duggan. (2013).

12. Smith & Duggan. (2013).

13. Apple. (2015b). *FaceTime.* Retrieved from https:// www.apple.com/ios/facetime/

14. Northeastern University. (2014). *Innovation survey.* www.northeastern.edu/news/2014/11/innovation-imperative-meet-generation-z/

15. Northeastern University. (2014).

6

CARES AND CONCERNS

E very generation faces social issues paramount to the times. The Baby Boomer era was marked by the Vietnam War, Generation X era with the fall of communism, and the Millennial era with September 11, 2001. The era that Generation Z is coming of age in is no different in that the current state of the world shapes their cares and concerns.

Issues of Greatest Importance

This generation cares about a lot of issues, and we found that education, employment, and racial equality are of most importance to them. Our findings indicate, that they care about these issues because they have an impact on others as well as themselves personally. In addition, some issues elicit more than care on their part; they are of grave concern.

Education

Almost everyone can reflect back on their K-12 school days full of drama, excitement, friends, romances, and new experiences. Photos and yearbooks can capture the essence of the glory days, but nothing can take the place of the actual memories. Generation Z college students just left the K-12 education system, and so their memories are fresh and their experiences salient. Thus, the importance they place on education is no real surprise.

Generation Z students believe that education is the foundation for individual success and societal prosperity. We found that these new college students' global view of education aligns with five themes (see table 6.1, which also has quotations from our study):

1. Education leads to future personal success.

2. Education is an investment in America's future.

3. An educated society is a better society.

4. America's education system is declining.

5. There is limited access to quality education.

The Reality of Higher (Cost) Education

The high cost of health care in the United States has spawned major debate over the Affordable Care Act, federal legislation aimed to provide more people with quality, affordable health care. Consider, though, that in just the past ten years while the focus was on the rising cost of health care and the Affordable Care Act, college tuition rose more than 80 percent, almost twice as much as the cost of medical care.[1] Tuition that could once be paid for with a summer job, part-time work, and maybe a small loan has now skyrocketed to nearly a universally unaffordable experience for students. Even attending a public in-state institution can lead to insurmountable debt. The rising cost of community college tuition,[2] which has been a viable financial alternative for many, can also create financial barriers.

Anxiety over being able to afford a college education is forefront on the minds of these students;[3] we found that more than 80 percent report being concerned about higher education

Table 6.1 What Generation Z Believes about Education

Education leads to future personal success.	Education is an investment in America's future.	An educated society is a better society.	America's education system is declining.	There is limited access to quality education.
"I need it to be able to survive in today's world." It is the "path to a successful life."	Education is the "building block," "foundation," and "best investment" in America's future. "Our children are our future."	"Education leads to a better society with better jobs, and thus [a] better economy." "Providing children with an education can prevent so many problems."	"If America continues to fall behind in educating its children to the same extent that other developed nations do, then America cannot hope to maintain its position as a world superpower."	"Education should be accessible for everyone and it's sad that [it] is not possible." "EVERYONE should have the opportunity to become someone great."

costs, and 17 percent indicate it as their number one social concern. It is no real surprise: going to college today will likely result in accumulating a debt these students cannot pay off. They worry they will not find adequate employment after college to support themselves and their families as well as pay off their student loans. These students might end up accruing debt to earn a degree that prepares them for a job that has a salary too low to pay off their loans. This is a trend; 72 percent of Millennials surveyed while in college who had student loans were concerned about their ability to pay them back.[4]

> "I'm most concerned about the cost of higher education because it is necessary now, but is priced so far above even a well-off family's budget that it will end up destroying the economy by saddling the new working age group with huge amounts of debt that will take decades to pay off."
>
> *Generation Z student*

Generation Z students have an idea for how to address the rising cost of college. They do not propose increasing state subsidies for public institutions, reducing institutional expenses through budget cuts, or raising more private money to offset costs. And they certainly do not want to raise tuition. Generation Z seems to prefer an option of having a limited college experience. This includes access to courses and faculty but leaves all the extras, like residence halls and athletics, out of the experience and out of the price tag.[5] Consider it college à la carte. Why pay to have access to a computer lab if a student has a computer? Or membership to the recreation center if a student does not use it?

Despite the growing cost of college, two-thirds of Generation Z students believe that the benefits of a college degree outweigh the costs, and more than three-quarters believe that having a degree is essential to having a career.[6] The question is, What kind of higher education might this be? Alternatives to the traditional four-year degree-granting institution, such as technical and vocational colleges, online programs, and bachelor's-granting community colleges, are continuing to play a role in the higher education system. As we see more technical occupations arise, the training for those will likely not be in the form of a traditional four-year degree. This may drive students aspiring to these fields to reimagine what type of higher education they need, if any. The continued debate about the value of a college education certainly highlights for these students that there may be other alternatives to gaining meaningful employment outside a four-year degree that do not bury them in a lifetime of debt.

> "I would like to be able to attend college in order to better contribute to this society without financially ruining myself with a mountain of debt. This doesn't seem likely."
>
> *Generation Z student*

Employment

Remember being asked as a child, "What do you want to be when you grow up?" as if any job is for the taking and it just takes dedication and heart to land it. While it certainly does take hard work to get that dream job, there is more at play, and Generation Z students know that. Having recently come out of a recession and many having witnessed people lose their jobs, they know that even loyal, smart people who work very hard might not get or keep a good job. We found that their noble, yet realistic outlook, reflects four themes as illustrated in table 6.2, which also has quotations from our study:

1. Job = survival.
2. Jobs are hard to find.
3. Why attend college?
4. Everyone should have the ability to be employed.

Table 6.2   What Generation Z Believes about Employment

Job = survival.	Jobs are hard to find.	Why attend college?	Everyone should have the ability to be employed.
"[Employment is important] so that I can survive" and "so I don't starve to death." "Without it, there is no way to make a living and fulfill needs." "Without a job, I can't do anything in this world."	"With the economy today, it is hard to find a job."	"What is the point of going to school for years and getting a high degree but no job to apply it toward?" "I'm not attending college and paying all this money for nothing."	"Everyone deserves an equal chance to work and make currency." "A lot of people are unemployed, and it's affecting households and families."

No Guarantees

Generation Z students worry about getting a job, and they know there is no guarantee that a college education leads to employment. After the recession, unemployment rates were high compared to recent years,[7] especially for Millennial graduates, who were unemployed at the rate of 9.1 percent.[8] Although that rate has decreased,[9] Generation Z students understand that simply having a job does not ensure indefinite employment, as situations such as downsizing, mergers, and the fear of receiving a pink slip can create uncertainty.

> "I want to be financially secure and not have to worry about finding a new job every month or if I will be able to make the upcoming rent."
>
> *Generation Z student*

It's Not a Job; It's a Passion

Members of Generation Z may skip working for an employer altogether. Nearly half expect to become their own bosses during their careers.[10] With self-employment predicted to grow at a rate of 6 percent for the next five years,[11] entrepreneurship is an even more viable option for this generation to make a living. Work must be meaningful for Generation Z. Although they recognize that getting any job can be challenging, they also do not want to settle for a job that is not fulfilling. Two-thirds want their careers to have a positive impact on the world,[12] and nearly 40% plan to invent something that will "change the world."[13] This perspective diverges from that of Millennials who, when in college, were willing to major in a program that they were not really interested in if it meant getting a job, especially in industries with potential growth.[14] Obtaining employment from a traditional employer may be more of a concern in theory, but in practice, expect to see many in Generation Z graduates create their own employment opportunities that suit their styles and passions.

> "When I graduate college, I want a good job in something I love."
>
> *Generation Z student*

Racial Equality

Incidents such as the shooting deaths of unarmed Black teens by police officers or by everyday Americans under the auspice of Stand Your Ground laws have drawn attention of the media. These incidents have resulted in community uprising, bringing issues of racial equality to the front and center of the ongoing debate about race. This continued debate is getting old for Generation Z students. They are frustrated that there is not racial equality and that people are still arguing about it at this time in history. Our study found that 68 percent of Generation Z students care about racial equality. Considering that 40 percent of Generation Z students who participated in our study indicate caring about racial equality identify as white, it appears to be an issue of concern not just of racially oppressed groups. Three beliefs about racial equality are particularly prevalent among Generation Z (see table 6.3, which also has quotations from our study):

1. Equality is the right thing to do.

2. Racism is terrible.

3. Why is racism still around?

Table 6.3   What Generation Z Believes about Racial Equality

Equality is the right thing to do.	Racism is terrible.	Why is racism still around?
"I cannot even fathom why in this day and age, people don't recognize that everyone should be treated equally from a racial standpoint." "I think that if there was more equality, there would be more opportunities, less crime, less poverty, and more peace."	"[Racism] affects everyone around me." "[Racism] can ruin people's lives forever." ∗ "Racism—it shouldn't be like that."	"It's incredibly barbaric that there isn't a basic human line drawn yet that states we all have equal worth." "I believe that rights for all people should be completely established and respected by this point in time." "This stuff should have been over with 70 years ago." "It shouldn't even be an issue anymore."

Financial Security

Readers from older generations may reminisce about graduating from high school and looking forward to the "I can make my own decisions" time of their lives. One might think that Generation Z students are entering their post–high school world making the same youthful and potentially shortsighted decisions that previous generations made, like racking up the credit card bill or spending the last bit of the week's paycheck on an unnecessary purchase. But the Great Recession has made Generation Z, as they are growing up in a time of great fiscal crisis, very attuned to money. We found that more than three-quarters of these young people, even as new, traditional-aged college students, are already concerned about their financial security. Many have a fear that they will not be able to afford college now, and they also fear they will not have enough money to take care of their families in the future. Because of this, more than half would rather save money than spend it now.[15] Aside from saving to pay off student loan debt, they are saving to buy their own homes. Our study indicates that nearly two-thirds are concerned about having affordable and accessible housing available to them.

> "Considering I'm eighteen and in my first year of college, my biggest concern is the fact that I could potentially be paying for the classes I am enrolled in right now, for the rest of my life."
>
> *Generation Z student*

> "I hardly have any savings. I have to make it through college and make my car payments and such, and soon have to gather up some money for affording my own home."
>
> *Generation Z student*

With easy-to-use tools for budgeting and tracking money through mobile banking and financial management apps that help them set financial goals and send high spending alerts, this is a generation, well equipped, not to mention motivated, to be financially savvy.

Limitations on Personal Freedom

Generation Z students have seen both the tightening and loosening of government regulations over their lifetimes.

For example, nearly all Generation Z students have lived in a world of the Patriot Act, which enhanced the ability of law enforcement to access personal information though surveillance, search, and record retrieval. In New York City, legislation was passed to regulate the size limit on the sale of sugary beverages but was eventually overturned by the courts.[16] These are examples of what some might consider attempts at government overreach. Some limitations have been lifted during the lifetimes of these students. Lawmakers did not renew the assault weapons ban from the 1990s, and some weapons that were formerly illegal to purchase are now available.[17]

Generation Z students have lived in an era of balancing personal freedom and government regulation. Our findings indicate that nearly three-quarters of them are very concerned about limitations on personal freedom and do not want the government to control gun ownership, access to abortion, euthanasia, and marriage, reflecting more of a libertarian viewpoint. Be prepared for this generation to decide how much soda they want to consume without having to answer to the government.

"When people try to limit my personal freedoms, it makes me feel like less of a human being."

Generation Z student

Other Issues of Importance

In addition to the issues of greatest importance to Generation Z, they care about and have concern for a number of others surrounding violence, human rights, and political dysfunction.

Violence Everywhere

Generation Z has watched footage of wars streamed on the Internet and read stories and seen pictures of roadside explosives and suicide bombers. Mass shootings have become a widespread phenomenon in their childhood experience. Everywhere they turn, there is real or depicted violence, whether on TV, in the movies, or in video games. And these depictions of violence include graphic killings, torture, mutilation, and rape.[18]

Even ten years ago, it seemed rare to see child characters as victims of violence on television and in the movies. Now, shows like *Law and Order: Special Victims Unit*[19] focus on heinous crimes toward children, and movies like *The Hunger Games*[20] depict children killing other children. Just because incidents of violence might be all around them, Generation Z students are not numb to it, as one might expect. In fact they are acutely aware of its prevalence: our study finds that violence is the biggest social concern for nearly 25 percent of Generation Z students.

> "Any time of any day, I know that anyone could commit any act of violence toward me or others around me, and that I am never safe."
>
> *Generation Z student*

Endless Wars

For Generation Z, most of their lives have been spent in a post-9/11 wartime setting. They have always known the United States to be in conflict in the Middle East and have been exposed to terrorist organizations that not only battle against military forces, but engage in unthinkable violence toward their own people. War to Generation Z involves fighting organizations instead of nations; it means air strikes and drones instead of boots on the ground, as in previous generations' wars. Although war may look different today than it did forty years ago, we found that more than half of Generation Z students are concerned about war, especially its financial impact and human cost. They believe that too many innocent people are affected, that war today has the potential to wipe out humanity, and that there are more peaceful ways to deal with conflict.

"The worst wars are yet to come."

Generation Z student

School Is Not a Safe Haven

Although they have witnessed violence through the media, it might be easy to think that Generation Z students do not relate to incidents of actual violence or that they believe violence takes place somewhere else with other people. But fear of violence is very real to Generation Z students, especially when it occurs in a place that is supposed to be safe: their schools. Consider the number of school shootings that have taken place in the lifetime of Generation Z, which is why it is not surprising that we found more than half of Generation Z students have great concern about school shootings. And with shootings also occurring at the college level, Generation Z students do not leave these fears behind after high school graduation. Nearly half believe that school shootings will have a bigger impact on their generation than having the first African American president or the advent of social networking.[21]

"No one should be afraid of going to school because of violence, shootings, or bullying."

Generation Z student

Bullying is another concern for a majority of Generation Z
students. In an era of technology, bullying permeates students'
social media, e-mail, text, phone, and messaging. There is no
safe haven free from bullies. Prior to the Internet, bullies were
the big mean kids at school whose identities were not a mystery.
Today's technology allows bullies to hide behind a screen and
be armed with the power of a keyboard and social media.[22] In
some instances, such as platforms that allow users to engage
under aliases, the bully is actually unidentifiable. More than 60
percent in Generation Z know someone who has been cyber-
bullied or stalked online,[23] and nearly one-third have been
bullied themselves.[24] Our study revealed that Generation Z
students are aware of the impact of bullying on a student's
self-esteem and know that it can even lead to suicide. They
believe that it is preventable, but that school administrators
and peers are not doing enough to stop it.

Internet Security

In an era of widespread technology use, the Internet can be
used for more types of violence than mere bullying. Identity
theft and unauthorized access to personal information can
make the Internet a scary place to be. And Generation Z knows
that identity theft can happen easily and can have devastating
implications: more than half indicated through our study that
they are concerned about it. The news is filled with stories of
mass hacker jobs, security breaches at major trusted companies

and the military, and individuals having their lives ruined by identity theft. As a generation that appears more private than the previous generation, it is no surprise that they are concerned about who has access to their information.

"It could change your life completely if someone got a hold of your personal information."

Generation Z student

Human Rights

"With Gen Z, because the world is so much more blended— we're this mélange of cultures, with DIY religions and blended families, both generationally and ethnically, that's created what we think is a concept of not tolerance but one step even better, which is togetherness. It's not just that I tolerate you but it's that I am you."

Sarah DaVanzo, chief strategist, Sparks & Honey[25]

Generation Z students are acutely aware of discrimination and the oppression of particular groups of people and are growing up in an era of great attention to equity and equality (see chapter 2). Many cannot fathom why there are still people who are disrespectful to others and that there are policies that prevent people from achieving their dreams. With Generation Z's liberal to moderate views on social issues and concern for government regulation, it is no wonder that they are concerned about restricting rights of individuals based on identity. This commitment to human rights is so critical for them that they deem fairness and the absence of discrimination in the workplace as more important than money or status.[26] And although previous generations may have attempted to address oppression with the notion of tolerance (putting up with differences), this generation does not buy that.[27] Generation Z is about togetherness.[28] They believe that diversity is not only an asset, but an essential factor in solving the world's problems and that as collaborators, their bringing together different perspectives, experiences, and cultures makes a stronger society.

"It's time to start treating each other like human beings."

Generation Z student

The Gender-Bending Generation

In 2014, Lego released its wildly popular female scientist collection aimed to showcase women in male-dominated professional settings.[29] It sold out. Prior to that, other toy companies had created construction sets and foam dart guns for girls.[30] And My Little Pony has certainly created inroads with boys, especially as reflected by Bronies, the name that male My Little Pony fans have given themselves.[31] Although these toys are a noble attempt to challenge gender stereotypes, we found that more than half of Generation Z students are concerned about sexism, and 16 percent believe gender equality is the biggest issue facing society.[32] Add to that the notion that gender today is perceived as more fluid, with roles challenged and stereotypes unraveled. Gender-neutral bathrooms and inclusive language have become more commonplace during the lifetimes of Generation Z students, and transgender celebrities such as Laverne Cox[33] and Caitlyn Jenner[34] have appeared on the cover of mainstream magazines. Has this exposure opened the hearts and minds of Generation Z to transgender equality? Probably: nearly three-quarters of Generation Z students believe that transgender people should have equal rights.[35] Generation Z's open views on gender will likely propel them front and center in discussions around policies and practices related to gender identity, especially as they move into decision-making roles in adulthood.

> "I would like to see the stereotyped female roles broken; times have changed and so have we."
>
> *Generation Z student*

Economic Inequality

Housing bubble, financial crisis, unemployment, bank bailouts: these are all descriptions of phenomena related to the Great Recession, which had a direct impact on nearly three-quarters of Americans.[36] While families were scrambling to make ends meet and not lose their homes, it became apparent that a high concentration of wealth in society was disproportionately in the hands of large corporations, banks, and a few individuals. When the Occupy Movement was born in 2011, it appeared in nearly every major city, calling attention to the 99 percent of the population that does not control the world's wealth.[37]

> "I am very concerned about big businesses and corporations controlling almost every network, business, etc. in the US."
>
> *Generation Z student*

It is not too far removed to recall the financial devastation the Great Recession had. Many older Generation Z students witnessed it for themselves. And if not, they likely have felt the aftermath as unemployment and foreclosures dragged on for years. That is why it is no surprise that we found that 39 percent of Generation Z students indicate their biggest social concern is the economy. They also believe banks and corporations have too much control over money in the United States.[38] Nearly two-thirds are concerned with the rising wage gap between the rich and the poor, as well as poverty.[39] As Generation Z students struggle with issues of their own financial security, they know that their challenges exist in a larger economic context.

Interestingly, Generation Z students differ vastly from their Millennial counterparts on issues of economic inequality. Where Generation Z students are concerned about the rising wage gap, high concentrations of wealth, and poverty, 67 percent of Millennials, while in college, believed that most people who were living in poverty could get out of it.[40]

> "It's way too difficult to live without a good amount of money, and a good amount of money is hard to come by."
>
> *Generation Z student*

Political Dysfunction

Growing up with government shutdowns, political scandals, and establishment politicians who "got primaried," or beaten by a challenger within their own party, it is no wonder that our findings indicate more than half of Generation Z students are concerned about political dysfunction. This is on par with the 55 percent of Millennials who, while in college, believed the country was going in the wrong direction.[41] Students from both generations have been witness to leaders not compromising and important legislation not getting passed. In addition, Generation Z's political experience will be wholly shaped by Citizens United and the emergence of super-PACS, which have created an unprecedented means to funnel money into the political process. The way that campaign financing is conducted and the record amounts of money entering politics by big businesses will be the norm for Generation Z. Will they join in and participate, check out of the process altogether, or try to reshape it? (Chapter 7 explores how Generation Z sees their involvement in the political process.)

> "It worries me that our political institutions are unable to find any passable options or even compromises. All the infighting is preventing us from moving forward and truly prospering as a nation."
>
> *Generation Z student*

At the Forefront of the News, But …

Issues related to gay rights and immigration seem to take up much of the airwaves on the news as political maneuvering for these hotly debated issues continues to deepen cultural divides. The same might be said for climate change, food production practices, and the legalization of marijuana. Despite the prominence of these issues in the media, fewer Generation Z students care deeply about these compared to other issues. But, for those who do, they have varied, and sometimes opposing, opinions.

Gay Rights

Generation Z students likely have no idea who Matthew Shepard was, the gay college student who in 1998 died of brutal injuries after being a victim of a hate crime.[42] They have always known Ellen DeGeneres as an "out" lesbian on national television. In short, most have not known how unsafe the world can be for gay, lesbian, or bisexual people. These students have grown up in an era in which being gay, lesbian, or bisexual is more normalized than in the past. Consider that Generation Z students have witnessed same-sex marriage since they were in elementary school, never will serve in the military under Don't Ask, Don't Tell, likely had a Gay/Straight Alliance at their high school, and many likely had a childhood friend who is gay, lesbian, or bisexual.

Ask a Baby Boomer, Gen Xer, or even a Millennial, and they will be hard-pressed to think of the gay, lesbian, or bisexual people they knew as a child (although one could argue that they were present, just not out of the closet). Times are different and Generation Z is living in the middle of a major social movement. Consider the momentum of the legalization of same-sex marriage as it has become legal in state after state and finally upheld by the Supreme Court. This hotly contested debate on marriage equality is not a debate for most Generation Z students, although they are witnessing it from other generations. Nearly three-quarters of Generation Z believe that everyone, regardless of sexual orientation, should have the right to marry.[43]

> "I realized I have been exposed to a lot of things relating to this topic [gay rights] lately through social interaction and personal experiences."
>
> *Generation Z student*

Our study revealed that more than half of Generation Z students care about issues related to gay rights, but that does not equate to a blanket support of expanding rights. Some believe too many rights are extended to gay, lesbian, and bisexual individuals, others believe marriage should be between a man and a woman, and 16 percent do not care about gay rights one way or another.

Being gay, lesbian, or bisexual today is vastly different than it was twenty or even ten years ago. Today gay rights are often associated with the larger LGBTQIA[44] rights movement, which includes issues related to sexual orientation as well as gender identity. And as the LGBTQIA community continues to strive for rights around issues of adoption, workplace protection, and antidiscrimination, it will likely be Generation Z that shapes these policies in years to come.

LGBTQIA is one of many different acronyms used to encompass sexual orientation and gender identities. L for lesbian, G for gay, B for bisexual, T for transgender, Q for queer and/or questioning, I for intersex, and A for Asexual and/or Ally.

Immigration and the Border Debate

Much of the news that Generation Z has been exposed to in their lifetimes has been around the immigration debate—build a wall to fortify the border with Mexico, take down the wall; criminalize undocumented presence in the United States, pave a way to citizenship; "show me your papers," and extend temporary rights to those who immigrated as children. Some Generation Z students are DREAMers, and those who are not likely know a DREAMER because 1 million US children under age eighteen are undocumented.[45]

"DREAMers" refers to undocumented immigrants who came to the United States as youth. Having grown up and attended school in the United States, they seek the educational and occupational opportunities of their peers who are citizens. The name *DREAMers* comes from the DREAM Act designed to grant legal status to immigrants who were brought to the United States as children.[48]

Like other issues that are hotly debated politically, Generation Z students have many opinions about immigration. More than half believe that everyone should have the right to U.S. citizenship regardless of which country in which they were born and how they arrived to the United States.[46] This differs considerably from the 60 percent of Millennials who, while in college, believed that undocumented immigrants should be deported.[47]

Some Generation Z students in our study believe that the government is not addressing the immigration issue adequately and needs to do more, whether that means granting more rights or fewer rights to immigrants. We found that only 21 percent of Generation Z students care a great deal about the issue of immigration and 11 percent do not care at all. Could the issue be so complex that Generation Z students have not formed an opinion on it? Or maybe they philosophically have an opinion about the issue but do not care enough about the particulars to even say they care at all. Or it could be that the political debate around immigration is just too exhausting and Generation Z has checked out.

Climate Change

In 2006, when the oldest of Generation Z students were eleven years old, Al Gore shocked the world with his documentary on global warming and climate change, *An Inconvenient Truth*.[49] The film brought conversations on large-scale environmental issues to the forefront. Although the environmental movement began long before this film, it certainly brought the scientists to the people to attempt to explain the complexities of climate change. Between greater exposure to knowledge on environmental issues through movies like Gore's, along with discussions and videos on social media, as well as the prevalence of environmentally friendly practices (e.g., residential recycling, removal of plastic shopping bags, the availability of compostable materials, and the use of limited and recycled packaging), the idea of saving the planet is embedded into the day-to-day consciousness of Generation Z students.

But different studies point to different findings in regard to Generation Z's concern for the environment. In one study, three-quarters believe global warming and climate change are a greater threat to society than war, violence, or drugs,[50] and in another study, more than two-thirds believe that addressing global climate change should be a priority for the federal government.[51] In our study, however, 23 percent of Generation Z students indicate not caring about climate change, and in another study, more than half indicate not being concerned about it at all.[52]

Do findings related to the lack of concern about environmental issues reflect the idea that climate change is already being addressed? After all, many people are driving energy-efficient vehicles and bringing reusable grocery bags to

> "The challenge of the next generation is to use human ingenuity to set things up so that the planet can accomplish its 21st-century task."
>
> *William G. Ross, Jr., visiting professor of environmental science and policy, Duke University*[53]

the store. Or perhaps environmentalism is already a culturally established norm, having been embedded in the fabric of higher education by the time even Millennials were in college.[54]

This generation will feel the impact of environmental decisions made by previous generations and their own. With their hopeful attitudes and desire to change the world, perhaps the keys needed to ensure the planet's longevity will come from Generation Z.

Unhealthy Food Production and Factory Farming

In 2008, when the movie, *Food, Inc.*,[55] was released, Baby Boomers, Generation Xers, and Millennials were exposed to an industry hidden from the average consumer. The movie may have frightened older generations as they learned about what they might be consuming, but by the time Generation Z came of age, cage-free eggs, antibiotic-free meat, and organic produce and dairy had become commonplace. With the availability of many of these products at the grocery store and an increase in the number of farmers' markets over the years,[56] Generation Z students can opt in to eating foods produced in healthy, sustainable, and ethical ways. And they are the most willing among the generations to pay for it.[57] Perhaps that is why we found that fewer than 50 percent are concerned about the mass production of unhealthy foods and factory farming, whereas 15 percent are not concerned at all.

Legalization of Marijuana

Like the other issues described in this chapter, the news is full of stories about the legalization of marijuana, and policies continue to be debated and enacted at the state and federal levels. This issue is not one that Generation Z students as a whole care a great deal about, however.

Every living generation has known marijuana, whether from Woodstock in the 1960s, raves in the 1980s, or simply at a party today. Marijuana has become a hot issue as states have debated legalizing the cultivation and use of it for medicinal or recreational purposes (or both). Some Generation Z students live in a state with policies legalizing marijuana, whereas others know of these policies only from hearing about them. Do Generation Z students care? Not really. We found that only 17 percent indicate caring a great deal about the legalization of marijuana and 38 percent not caring at all. This may be because their rates of drug use are lower than those of previous generations,[58] leading to fewer who might be directly affected by marijuana laws. Or perhaps, as with under-age, alcohol consumption, they may partake anyway regardless of the law.

Conclusion

After experiencing a childhood cloaked with social concerns that may have directly affected them, it is surprising to note that

Generation Z students are generally concerned about the welfare of everyone and not just themselves. We found that nearly half of all the social issues that Generation Z students identify as caring about are we-centric, meaning that whatever the issue is "affects all of us." Less than one-third of all the concerns put forth by Generation Z students are other-centric in that they are about issues that do not directly affect them, such as others' well-being and rights. Only one-quarter of the issues they identify as caring about are me-centric, or focus entirely on the impact the issue has on oneself.

In addition, we must wonder why the issues front and center in politics today are not necessarily the issues that Generation Z students care most about. In an era of sweeping legislation for same-sex marriage, executive orders affecting rights for immigrants, alternatives to fossil fuels, sustainable farming practices, and the legalization of marijuana, these issues may pose little to care about in that they appear to be progressing through the legislative process and gaining more cultural acceptance.

Notes

1. Kurtzleben, D. (2013, October 23). CHARTS: Just how fast has college tuition grown? *U.S. News & World Report*. Retrieved from http://www.usnews.com/news/articles/2013/10/23/charts-just-how-fast-has-college-tuition-grown

2. College Board. (2014). *Trends in college pricing 2014*. Retrieved from http://trends.collegeboard.org/sites/default/files/2014-trends-college-pricing-final-web.pdf

3. Northeastern University. (2014). *Innovation survey.* Retrieved from www.northeastern.edu/news/2014/11/innovation-imperative-meet-generation-z/

4. Levine, A., & Dean, D. R. (2012). *Generation on a tightrope: A portrait of today's college student.* San Francisco: Wiley.

5. Northeastern University. (2014).

6. Northeastern University. (2014).

7. US Bureau of Labor Statistics. (2015). *Labor force statistics from the current population survey.* Retrieved from http://data.bls.gov/timeseries/LNS14000000

8. Levine & Dean. (2012)

9. US Bureau of Labor Statistics. (2015).

10. Northeastern University. (2014).

11. Pofeldt, E. (2014). *Obama: Is the job of the future a freelance one?* CNBC. Retrieved from www.cnbc.com/id/101371164#

12. Sparks & Honey. (2014). *Meet Gen Z: Forget everything you learned about Millennials.* Retrieved from www.slideshare.net/sparksandhoney/generation-z-final-june-17

13. Gallup & Operation Hope. (2013). *The 2013 Gallup-Hope Index.* Retrieved from www.operationhope.org/images/uploads/Files/2013galluphopereport.pdf

14. Lewin, T. (2012, November 4). Digital natives and their customs. *New York Times.* Retrieved from http://www.nytimes.com/2012/11/04/education/edlife/arthur-levine-discusses-the-new-generation-of-college-students.html?_r=0

15. Intelligence Group. (2013). *Cassandra report* Retrieved from www.cassandra.co/report/

16. NYC Health. (2015). *Sugary drinks*. Retrieved from http://www.nyc.gov/html/doh/html/living/cdp_pan_pop.shtml

17. Plumer, B. (2012, December 17). Everything you need to know about the assault weapons ban, in one post. *Washington Post*. Retrieved from http://www.washingtonpost.com/blogs/wonkblog/wp/2012/12/17/everything-you-need-to-know-about-banning-assault-weapons-in-one-post/

18. Parents Television Council. (2013). *An examination of violence, graphic violence, and gun violence in the media*. Retrieved from http://w2.parentstv.org/main/Research/Studies/CableViolence/vstudy_dec2013.pdf

19. IMDB. (2012). *The Hunger Games plot summary*. Retrieved from http://www.imdb.com/title/tt1392170/plotsummary

20. IMDB. (1999). *Law & Order: Special Victims Unit plot summary*. Retrieved from http://www.imdb.com/title/tt0203259/plotsummary

21. Intelligence Group. (2013).

22. Galley, L. (2014). *Generation Z: A world gone cyber*. Retrieved from www.huffingtonpost.com/lauren-galley/generation-z-a-world-gone_b_6349074.html

23. Northeastern University. (2014)

24. Intelligence Group. (2013).

25. Dawson, A. (2014). *Generation Z (or is that Edge?) shows a fluid sense of style*. Retrieved from http://www.latimes.com/fashion/la-ig-edge-generation-20141102-story.html#page=1

26. Euromonitor International. (2011). *Make way for generation Z: Marketing for today's teens and tweens.* Retrieved from http://oaltabo2012.files.wordpress .com/2012/03/make-way-for-generation-z1.pdf

27. Sparks & Honey. (2014).

28. Sparks & Honey. (2014).

29. Abrams, R. (2014, August 22). Short-lived science line from Lego for girls. *New York Times.* Retrieved from http://www.nytimes.com/2014/08/22/business/short-lived-science-line-from-lego-for-girls.html?_r=0

30. Abrams. (2014).

31. Abrams. (2014).

32. Salt Communications. (2014). *Generation Z.* Retrieved from www.salt-communications.com/generation-z/

33. For more information about Laverne Cox, go to http://www.lavernecox.com/bio-2/

34. For more information about Caitlyn Jenner, go to http://www.biography.com/people/bruce-jenner-307180

35. Northeastern University. (2014).

36. Sparks & Honey. (2014).

37. Glass, A. (2013). *Occupy Wall Street began, Sept. 17, 2011.* Retrieved from http://www.politico.com/story/2013/09/this-day-in-politics-96859.html

38. Northeastern University. (2014).

39. Board of Governors of the Federal Reserve System (2013). *Survey of consumer finances.* Retrieved from http://www.federalreserve.gov/econresdata/scf/scfindex.htm

40. Levine & Dean. (2012).

41. Levine & Dean. (2012).

42. Matthew's Place. (2015). Matthew's story. Retrieved from http://www.matthewsplace.com/matthews-story/

43. Northeastern University. (2014).

44. Schulman, M. (2013, January 9). Generation LGBTQIA. *New York Times.* Retrieved from http://www.nytimes.com/2013/01/10/fashion/generation-lgbtqia.html?_r=0

45. Passel, J. S., & Cohn, D., (2011). *Unauthorized immigrant population: National and state trends, 2010.* Pew-Research Hispanic Trends Project. Retrieved from www.pewhispanic.org/2011/02/01/unauthorized-immigrant-population-brnational-and-state-trends-2010/

46. Northeastern University. (2014).

47. Levine & Dean. (2012).

48. Anti-Defamation League. (2014). *What is the DREAM Act and who are the DREAMers?* Retrieved from http://www.adl.org/assets/pdf/education-outreach/what-is-the-dream-act-and-who-are-the-dreamers.pdf

49. IMDB. (2006). *An Inconvenient Truth plot summary.* http://www.imdb.com/title/tt0497116/plotsummary; Gore, A. (2006). *An inconvenient truth.* New York: Rodale Books.

50. Grail Research (2011). *Consumers of tomorrow.* www.grailresearch.com/pdf/ContenPodsPdf/Consumers_of_Tomorrow_Insights_and_Observations_About_Generation_Z.pdf

51. Eagan, K., Stolzenberg, E. B., Ramirez, J. J., Aragon, M. C., Suchard, M. R., & Hurtado, S. (2014). *The American freshman: National norms fall 2014.* LosAngeles: Higher Education Research Institute.

52. Northeastern University. (2014).

53. Ross, W. G. (2013). *Environmental challenges facing Generation Z.* Retrieved from http://iei.ncsu.edu/wp-content/uploads/2013/01/Environmental-Response.pdf

54. Levine & Dean. (2012).

55. IMDB. (2008). *Food, Inc. plot summary.* Retrieved from http://www.imdb.com/title/tt1286537/plotsummary

56. US Department of Agriculture. (2014). Number of U.S. *farmers' markets continue to rise.* Retrieved from http://ers.usda.gov/data-products/chart-gallery/detail.aspx?chartId=48561&ref=collection&embed=True&widgetId=37373

57. Nielsen Company. (2015). *We are what we eat.* Retrieved from http://www.nielsen.com/content/dam/nielsenglobal/eu/nielseninsights/pdfs/Nielsen%20Global%20Health%20and%20Wellness%20Report%20-%20January%202015.pdf

58. Centers for Disease Control and Prevention. (2013a). *Cigarette smoking among U.S. high school students at lowest level in 22 years.* Retrieved from www.cdc.gov/media/releases/2014/p0612-YRBS.html

7

ENGAGEMENT AND SOCIAL CHANGE

Generation Z comprises inventors, researchers, philanthropists, and activists. Some have changed the world before their eighteenth birthday. But saving the planet, curing cancer, and developing life-saving technology is a tall order for Generation Z, and most will never be on the cover of a magazine for their contributions. Nevertheless, Generation Z's change agent mentality reflects their desire to make the world a better place even if it does not result in widespread public recognition for them. With far more Generation Z students envisioning changing the world than do Millennials,[1] knowing how they plan to do so can help in providing them the guidance and means necessary.

E-Drink is a coffee mug that can charge a cell phone using the clean energy heat of the coffee. It was created by seventeen-year-old Ann Makosinski who was also the winner of the Google Science Fair at age fifteen for her invention of a flashlight powered by the heat of the hand.[2]

Community Engagement Practices across the Spectrum

Community engagement is not a new phenomenon specific to Generation Z. Each generation has made its mark on society

> "In previous generations, there was a feeling that when you were young, you were a passive bystander, an adult-in waiting, but today because of technology, young people have this sense of self-confidence and a belief that they can change the world."
>
> *Craig Kielburger, cofounder of youth development charity, Free the Children*[3]

through community engagement efforts, whether through volunteering with the PTA, running for public office, participating in the Rotary Club, or belonging to the Masons or Elks. But what might have been engaging for members of other generations may not necessarily be engaging for those in Generation Z. Technology has created new forms of community engagement, and changing social dynamics and pressing societal needs have created opportunities for Generation Z to engage in ways that might be different from those of other generations. So how does Generation Z engage in their communities?

Spreading News and Views

There's no question that the way Generation Z gets its news is distinct from prior generations. The witty, satirical lists of news once limited to David Letterman's Top Ten[4] are now pervasive on the web. And there are potentially thousands of these lists with pictures, videos, animations, and clever banter. For example, topics like Top 10 Cartoon Characters That Look

Like a Political Figure and 14 Reasons Why People Still Have Landlines are commonplace on sites like Buzzfeed and Reddit, drawing people in to get the news in a unique way.

Consuming the News

Consider, though, that sites like Buzzfeed and Reddit that offer both serious and pop culture news stories, mainstream news sites like CNN, platforms like Flipboard that aggregate news from many sites, blogs like Tumblr, and social media platforms are not just static places to go for information. Many of these sites have the ability to push out notifications through their apps, sending news stories specific to each person's interests right to their phones, allowing them to stay up-to-date without having to seek out the news themselves. Although everyone today has access to endless, customized news feeds, Generation Z has always lived with this phenomenon.

> "I share the same sense of humor with the users [on Tumblr]; the content is so diverse (funny cat videos, to news overseas, to recipes, and fun facts)."
>
> *Generation Z student*

> "Twitter for me is like the news on TV for the older generations."
>
> *Generation Z student*

Just because those in Generation Z have access to nearly infinite amounts of information does not mean that they stay informed about all news, however. Our study found that Generation Z students have specific issues they like to follow, particularly those around civil rights, especially gay rights, women's rights, and racial equality. It is particularly interesting that they like to follow stories about gay rights, but as discussed in chapter 6, few are concerned about issues facing the gay community. They also have issues they do not keep up with, specifically around health care and healthy and safe food.

If they want more information about a specific major current event, like finding out the winner of a sporting event, following an election, or learning more about a natural disaster, rather than just waiting for news updates that might be of interest, they use filters such as Twitter hashtags to parse available information from a variety of channels. They do, not only use news aggregators and push notifications to get the news; they also seek out news on mainstream websites, through word-of-mouth, and on television to get information that is timely like who won the World Series.[5]

Regardless, if the news comes to them or they seek it out, Generation Z students like to stay informed about what they are interested in. That is why it is no surprise we found that keeping up on news is by far the number one way Generation Z students engage with the world around them.

Sharing and Forwarding

With nearly every online news story having "share this story" or "forward to a friend" buttons and the ability to use various social media platforms to get the word out, it seems easier than ever before for Generation Z to educate others on social issues. Nearly half report having communicated their opinion about a cause in a public manner using social media, a blog, or an online petition.[6] That does not even take into account sharing views through word-of-mouth, remembering that face-to-face communication is the main communication preference for Generation Z students.

> "I mostly use Reddit to learn about various things and Tumblr to share things that I want others to know."
>
> *Generation Z student*

Still, for as much information as they are consuming and the ease in being able to share it, far fewer Generation Z students are passing that information along to others. Why might that be? Our findings indicate that for the most part, Generation Z students educate others on what they know about and care about. They like sharing their views on gay rights, education, and women's rights, but not on the economy, military intervention, employment, or health care. In a world of viral videos, flash mobs, online petitions, and "likes" for social causes, there are many ways that Generation Z students can educate others, but they need to feel connected to and educated about the issue to share their views.

> "[We] are just trying to figure out what [we] believe to be [our] true opinions and values."
>
> *Generation Z student*

Inventing the Next Big Thing

You do not have to be a reality television contestant pitching your invention to a panel of funders to have access to start-up funding. Crowdfunding sites like Kickstarter "help bring creative projects to life"[7] by serving as online platforms to raise money for ideas, inventions, and causes. The concept of inventing is no longer left solely to scientists in labs or researchers behind closed doors. Inventing is something that anyone can engage in, regardless of background or age. Inventors include the mom who creates a new ergonomic backpack for her son, the kid who writes a book to help younger kids save the planet, and the fourteen-year-old app developer creating new ways of learning and entertaining. Whether it is due to their motivation and drive or the opportunities available to them, nearly 40 percent of Generation Z intend to change the world by developing an invention.[8]

> · Described as a do-it-yourself fundraising site, GoFundMe offers users the opportunity to raise money for personal campaigns.[9]

> · Hackathons are competitions for inventors to bring a great idea to life. Individuals and teams compete to share their innovation, for a chance to win start-up money, and as a way to showcase their products and ideas to investors.[10]

Creating a Business with a Social Mission

With information on entrepreneurship readily available through MOOCs (massive open online courses offered for unlimited participants),[11] online videos, websites, and youth training programs, Generation Z students have the resources they need to be entrepreneurial. Add in opportunities to connect virtually with mentors and access to start-up money through crowdsourcing, and students have ample opportunity to engage in entrepreneurship. With nearly half wanting to start their own businesses,[12] it is no surprise that almost two-thirds of Generation Z think colleges should teach students the entrepreneurial skills important to starting and running a business.[13] The reality, however, is that 30 percent of Generation Z students believe their institution has not taught them applicable business skills.[14]

These students are not just interested in making money; actually, it is quite the contrary. They want to change the world. With the emergence of B corporations, for-profit businesses dedicated to a social mission, expect to see Generation Z participating in social entrepreneurship by developing revenue-generating opportunities that pay the bills and fill a social need.

ASHOKA is a worldwide network of social entrepreneurs that provides "start-up financing, professional support services, and connections to a global network across the business and social sectors, and a platform for people dedicated to changing the world."[15]

Engagement Practices That Work for Some, But Not for All

Once people are informed about particular social issues, they have choices to make. Some people do not wear leather to show their support for animal rights; others bike to work to do their part to save the environment; others choose not to patronize a business because their values do not align. But, does the same mentality hold true for Generation Z? Our research returned mixed results when it came to Generation Z's willingness to make lifestyle changes to support a cause. Similarly, we found no strong trends either way when it came to voting, participating in campaigns, taking leadership roles, and fundraising.

Making a Lifestyle Change

Chick-fil-A,[16] famous for its chicken strips and waffle fries, was in the middle of the cultural divide on the issue of same-sex marriage. After making an offensive remark, the founder propelled the popular restaurant chain into a political frenzy. Supporters of same-sex marriage were boycotting the restaurant, whereas those in support of the founder's views flocked to support Chick-fil-A through their buying power.[17] Other issues are similarly positioned but might not garner support on both sides. Consider companies that have been found to use sweatshop labor, jewelry stores that stock blood diamonds, or toy companies that knowingly produce toys that contain lead. Once it is discovered that the values or practices of a business do not align with one's personal values, individuals have the option to not buy certain products or use particular services as a way of taking a stand on an issue. On the contrary, they can also choose to engage in lifestyle practices that align with their beliefs. These can include purchasing from stores with fair employee wages or patronizing businesses in which the company donates money to social issues or candidates they support.

> "It seems like the most easily changeable thing and yet people continue to destroy the environment. Even just having every person recycle would help, let alone if we could get large companies on board to go much greener."
>
> *Generation Z student*

Whether making a lifestyle change around a social issue is common only to older generations depends on the issue. Consider the environment. We found that nearly one-third of Generation Z students have already made lifestyle changes to support the environment, and more than 40 percent plan to "go green."[18] This likely aligns with the findings in chapter 6 that Generation Z has varying levels of concern for the environment because many already engage in or plan to engage in environmentally conscious practices. We also found that many Generation Z students have made lifestyle changes around consuming healthy and safe food, but that few have made any lifestyle changes in relation to human rights issues despite their concerns. Be prepared, though, as they become more educated on human rights issues, Generation Z students will find ways to stop supporting businesses that are not socially just and engage in more inclusive behavior to work toward enhancing human rights.

Voting

"I care about voting and politics because I want to have my say in various issues."

Generation Z student

"I find it important that we have the right leader to oversee our country."

Generation Z student

The 2008 election demonstrated the power of the youth vote, as 49 percent of eighteen- to twenty-four-year-olds turned out to vote, a 2 percent uptick from 2004.[19] Young adults were excited and energized and they wanted to vote.

Generation Z has a different take on political participation. Some are not engaged or knowledgeable enough to care, and many are exasperated with what they see as corruption and dysfunction in the political system as we noted in chapter 6. For some, this feeling could lead to motivation to participate, while for others it might do nothing but engender apathy and disconnection. Even if they are knowledgeable, motivated, and do care, will they show up to vote? Fifty-six percent of those in Generation Z are registered to vote,[20] but being registered to vote and actually voting are two different things. Consider that only half indicate there is a good chance that they will vote in a local, state, or national election.[21] Since that is only intention to vote, that number will likely decrease when it comes to actual voting behavior, especially given their previous voting patterns—one-third never even voted in a student election.[22] Will Generation Z students continue the trend of being an energized youth vote, or will they be disengaged from the political process?

Only 21 percent of Generation Z students believe that influencing the political structure is essential,[23] a continuation of the lack of faith in politics felt by 61 percent of Millennials, despite their presence in past elections, who believed that meaningful social change could not be made through the traditional political process.[24] Generation Z's distaste for politics in America, coupled with their desire to create social change outside the political process, may lead them to skip the ballot box altogether. This begs the question of who will serve as elected politicians from this generation if they are disengaged with politics in its entirety.

"I don't feel informed enough to vote, so I am not registered."

Generation Z student

"Many of the young people in the country today feel they don't care enough about politics to vote now when, later in their lives they'll see the repercussions and consequences of their choice not to act."

Generation Z student

Campaigning for Candidates

College students were out in full force during the Obama election bid in 2008, campaigning in person or virtually through their social media networks. They were sending viral videos and forwarding campaign e-mails and posts to their friends to encourage them to vote.[25] Many did this informally simply because of their support for a candidate, and some served in more official roles as staffers. Will Generation Z students do the same for candidates they believe in? Fewer than 10 percent worked on a political campaign prior to entering college,[26] but more than half have helped raise money for a campaign or cause.[27] Because they were not of voting age, working on a political candidate's campaign might be distant from their day-to-day reality. Yet they were engaged enough to help raise money for candidates. Perhaps this is more of a reflection of an interest in philanthropy than politics.

Leading 5Ks and PTAs

The United States has a strong history of involved citizenry in community associations,[28] and this generation will likely continue the trend. Americans serve on boards of directors for nonprofit organizations, are active in PTAs, lead scout troops, take on roles in their homeowners' associations, and plan and coordinate community events. More than one-third of Generation Z students have the goal of taking on some type of leadership role in the community.[29] Like generations before them, they hope to actively participate in community associations and organizations.

Raising Money

With the Internet and social media at their fingertips, Generation Z has access to far more knowledge at a younger age than previous generations did. But social media is more than just a news platform or a place to connect with friends; it can also be fundraising space in which these students can engage in philanthropy to collect money from friends and family to support social causes. If a twelve-year-old wants to send money to Africa to build a school, he or she can use social media to raise the money needed. Because of this, today's youth have been dubbed "philanthro-teens."[31] They use the money they raise to donate directly to organizations that support causes they believe in, start their own nonprofit organizations, or engage in microlending to grant small loans to people in need through programs like Kiva[32] or Accion.[33] As financially conservative as Generation Z students are and given the concern for their own financial security after college, Generation Z may not donate their own money to causes but could very well serve as the coordinators or conduits to raise money from others.

Alex's Lemonade Stand was started in 2000 by four-year-old Alexandra Scott to raise money for cancer research to help other kids diagnosed with cancer. Now a foundation, Alex's Lemonade Stand has raised over $4 million for cancer research.[30]

Community Engagement Practices That Just Do Not Fit

Although community service has been around for centuries, the Millennial generation has taken it to new heights. Their high rates of volunteerism[34] have been a call to colleges and workplaces to integrate service into the culture. Whether that is tutoring youth in math, serving soup at a food kitchen, or fixing up a playground, the possibilities for volunteering are limitless given the number of unmet societal needs. Now it seems as if every K-12 school, college, and company or other organization has service projects and volunteer days.

Volunteering or Being Voluntold?

The prevalence of service opportunities likely explains why nearly 90 percent of Generation Z students indicate having frequently engaged in community service as high school seniors.[35] More than half of these students, however, indicate that their community service work was required as part of a class.[36] Since they have arrived in college, either their mentality for volunteerism has changed or their opportunity to engage in it has. One study notes that a third believe there is a very good chance they will participate in community service in college,[37] and another puts that number just over half.[38] But when it comes to actually volunteering versus planning to volunteer, that number drops to 6 percent for participants in our study. We found that their lack of volunteering holds true across race and gender lines. Volunteering is the least used engagement strategy for all races and for men; for women, volunteering is tied with advocacy for the least used strategy.

Generation Z students' participation in volunteerism differs vastly from that of Millennial students. Where we found that Generation Z students engage in volunteering at lower rates compared to other engagement activities, the primary form of activism for Millennials has been focused primarily on service.[39] One study found that sixty-five percent of Millennials had engaged in service sometime during the twelve months prior to the study and said they engage in service because it makes them feel like they are helping people.[40]

Is the lack of interest and participation in volunteering for Generation Z students an issue of time? Opportunity? Interest? It may be that a social change–oriented generation sees their contribution to the world as being more about addressing the root cause of problems than addressing the symptoms.

Advocating and Protesting

The days of campus protests and student sit-ins seem to be subsiding even more with this generation. Stories of college as a place to challenge authority and stand up for personal values are passed from parents to their children but are rarely realized on campuses today. Generation Z has the mentality of wanting to change the world, make a difference, and stand up for rights, but is advocacy and activism the way of the future with these Generation Z students? Slightly more than 20 percent indicated that they have participated in a boycott, rally, or protest to demonstrate for a cause.[41] This is higher than the 11 percent of Millennials who participated in a demonstration, protest, sit-in, or other advocacy experience before or during college.[42]

Generation Z students who do engage in advocacy or activism do not fight for all causes. Our study revealed that more Generation Z students advocate for education (15 percent) and youth development (12 percent) than for immigration (2 percent) and health care (3 percent).

Since the advocacy behaviors studied are likely associated with their high school experience, the question is whether Generation Z students will engage in advocacy in college. Although Generation Z students may be more active than their Millennial predecessors, based on our study, we do not anticipate that they will be much more active. Only slightly more than 5 percent said they plan to participate in future demonstrations on campus.[43] Such numbers lead us to wonder: What, if anything, will be the cause that does bring this generation out in mass to boycott or rally? Or are those forms of participation destined to die away?

New Solutions for New Needs

Pollution does not stop at a nation's boundaries, and addressing war and conflict has become a multinational priority. The global problems facing this generation are immense. Generation Z's great concern for many social issues as described in chapter 6 and the desire to understand and confront these issues[44] makes

"Young people must be able to envision pathways forward, be positively engaged in the process, and see themselves as important voices for systemic change. Historically, protests have played a vital role in social change. What makes today's youth motivated to speak up for change as we did in my generation?"

Marilyn Price-Mitchell, Ph.D., developmental psychologist, Roots of Action[46]

"[Our generation] sees a problem and they want to fix it; they aren't leaving it for someone else to fix."

Linda Manziaris, fourteen-year-old founder of Body Bijou and 2014 Young Entrepreneur of the Year at the Startup Canada Awards[47]

them uniquely situated to create massive social change.

One way they plan to do this is by engaging in work that is meaningful to them and will change the world.[45] Instead of working in a job that they see as just a means to make a living and then volunteering on the weekends to give back to their communities, Generation Z students will turn their community engagement experiences into paid work. This blending of work and passion will likely provide them with enriching and fulfilling career experiences and redefine the concept of work for them. They do not plan to change the world on weekends. Rather, they plan to make that their life's mission.

Conclusion

Like the generations that came before them, community engagement is paramount to Generation Z. But what is different is the form that their community engagement will take. Helping Generation Z students engage civically in ways that fit their needs can be useful in capitalizing on their passions resulting in both learning and career preparation.

Notes

1. Sparks & Honey. (2014). *Meet Gen Z: Forget everything you learned about Millennials.* Retrieved from www .slideshare.net/sparksandhoney/generation-z-final-june-17

2. McElroy, J. (2015). *Saanich teen's newest invention can use hot coffee to power devices.* Retrieved from http:// globalnews.ca/news/1933356/saanich-teens-newest-invention-uses-hot-coffee-to-power-devices/? hootPostID=3a43918d6c03e0dab48395972ac64f32

3. White, S. (2014, September 25). Generation Z: The kids who'll save the world. *Globe and Mail.* http:// www.theglobeandmail.com/life/giving/generation-z-the-kids-wholl-save-the-world/article20790237/

4. Murray, N. (2015). *"From the home office … ": 10 David Letterman top 10 lists.* Retrieved from http:// www.avclub.com/article/home-office-10-david-letterman-top-ten-lists-219375

5. Northeastern University. (2014). *Innovation survey.* Retrieved from www.northeastern.edu/news/2014/ 11/innovation-imperative-meet-generation-z/

6. Eagan, K., Stolzenberg, E. B., Ramirez, J. J., Aragon, M. C., Suchard, M. R., & Hurtado, S. (2014). *The American freshman: National norms fall 2014*. Los Angeles: Higher Education Research Institute.

7. Kickstarter. (2015). *Seven things to know about Kickstarter*. Retrieved from www.kickstarter.com

8. Gallup & Operation Hope. (2013). *The 2013 Gallup-Hope Index*. Retrieved from www .operationhope.org/images/uploads/Files/ 2013galluphopereport.pdf

9. GoFundMe. (2015). *How it works*. Retrieved from http://www.gofundme.com/tour/

10. Leckart, S. (2012). *The hackathon is on: Pitching and programming the next killer app*. Retrieved from http:// www.wired.com/2012/02/ff_hackathons/

11. Educause. (2015). *What is a MOOC?* Retrieved from http://www.educause.edu/library/massive-open-online-course-mooc

12. Sparks & Honey. (2014).

13. Northeastern University. (2014).

14. Adecco Staffing USA. (2015). *Generation Z vs. Millennials*. Retrieved from http://pages.adeccousa.com/rs/ 107-IXF-539/images/generation-z-vs-millennials.pdf

15. ASHOKA. (2015). *About us*. Retrieved from https:// www.ashoka.org/about

16. Chick-fil-A. (2015). *Company fact sheet*. Retrieved from http://www.chick-fil-a.com/Company/ Highlights-Fact-Sheets

17. Barbash, F. (2014, August 9). Chick-fil-A founder dies. Built chain from one small restaurant. Provoked controversy on gay-marriage. *Washington Post*. http://www.washingtonpost.com/news/morning-mix/wp/2014/09/08/chick-fil-a-founder-dies-built-chain-from-one-small-restaurant-provoked-controversy-on-gay-marriage/

18. Eagan et al. (2014).

19. US Census Bureau. (2009). *Voter turnout increases by 5 million in 2008 presidential election, U.S. Census Bureau reports*. Retrieved from https://www.census.gov/newsroom/releases/archives/voting/cb09-110.html

20. Northeastern University. (2014).

21. Eagan et al. (2014).

22. Eagan et al. (2014).

23. Eagan et al. (2014).

24. Levine, A., & Dean, D. R. (2012). *Generation on a tightrope: A portrait of today's college student*. San Francisco: Wiley.

25. Dutta, S., & Fraser, M. (2008). *Barack Obama and the Facebook election*. Retrieved from http://www.usnews.com/opinion/articles/2008/11/19/barack-obama-and-the-facebook-election

26. Eagan et al. (2014).

27. Eagan et al. (2014).

28. Skocpol, T. (1997). The Tocqueville problem: Civic engagement in American democracy. *Social Science History, 21*(4), 455–479.

29. Eagan et al. (2014).

30. Alex's Lemonade Stand Foundation. (2015). *Alex's lemonade stand.* Retrieved from http://www .alexslemonade.org/

31. Tiller, C. (2011). Philanthro-teens: The next generation changing the world. *Media Planet, 2 (USA Today).* Retrieved from http://doc.mediaplanet.com/ all_projects/6574.pdf

32. Kiva. (2015). *About us.* Retrieved from http://www .kiva.org/about

33. Accion. (2015). *What we do.* Retrieved from https:// www.accion.org/what-we-do

34. Achieve. (2013). *The 2013 Millennial impact report.* Retrieved from http://casefoundation.org/wp-content/ uploads/2014/11/MillennialImpactReport-2013.pdf

35. Eagan et al. (2014).

36. Eagan et al. (2014).

37. Eagan et al. (2014).

38. Northeastern University. (2014).

39. Levine & Dean. (2012).

40. Lewin, T. (2012, November 4). Digital natives and their customs. *New York Times.* Retrieved from http:// www.nytimes.com/2012/11/04/education/edlife/ arthur-levine-discusses-the-new-generation-of- college-students.html?_r=0

41. Eagan et al. (2014).

42. Levine & Dean. (2012).

43. Eagan et al. (2014).

44. Anatole, E. (2013). *Generation Z: Rebels with a cause.* Retrieved from http://www.forbes.com/sites/onmarketing/2013/05/28/generation-z-rebels-with-a-cause/

45. Sparks & Honey. (2014).

46. Price-Mitchell, M. (2015). *Youth protests: A positive sign of the times?* Retrieved from https://www.psychologytoday.com/blog/the-moment-youth/201501/youth-protests-positive-sign-the-times

47. White. (2014).

8

LEADERSHIP STYLES AND CAPACITIES

The quest for effective leadership is not limited to any single generation, as each has had its call to lead. What does the future hold for Generation Z students as leaders? Are they the leaders of the future, or are they already leading? What they believe is effective leadership and who their leader role models are will surely shape their leadership styles and behaviors.

Shaping Generation Z's Ideas about Leadership

The notion of leadership has changed over the past century, with each generation having a definition shaped by their societal context:[1]

1920s	"[Leadership is] the ability to impress the will of the leader on those led and induce obedience, respect, loyalty, and cooperation."
1940s	"Leadership is the result of an ability to persuade or direct men, apart from the prestige or power that comes from office or external circumstance."
1960s	"[Leadership is] acts by a person, which influence other persons in a shared direction."

1980s   "Regardless of the complexities involved in the study of leadership, its meaning is relatively simple. Leadership means to inspire others to undertake some form of purposeful action as determined by the leader."

2000s   "Leadership is the process of influencing others to understand and agree about what needs to be done and how to do it, and the process of facilitating individual and collective efforts to accomplish shared objectives."

These definitions showcase just how leadership has changed through time. For example, motivating others changes from inducing obedience to persuading, then influencing, then inspiring, and ultimately facilitating individual and collective efforts. Definitions go from leader dominated to leader-centric to leadership as a process of collectivity. How might Generation Z define leadership in their era? What factors might shape that definition and how they practice leadership?

Skills Employers Want

According to the National Association of Colleges and Employers, nearly 80 percent of employers seek graduates with leadership skills and the ability to work on a team, and more than 70 percent expect these new employees to have written communication skills and the ability to solve problems.[2] Being able to develop the skills necessary for postcollege employment is essential for Generation Z students, especially given their concern about getting a job after graduation. Thus, it would be no surprise that the skills employers want become essential components of the leadership definition of Generation Z.

Strengths-Based Leadership

"From this point of view, to avoid your strengths and to focus on your weaknesses isn't a sign of diligent humility. It is almost irresponsible. By contrast the most responsible, the most challenging, and, in the sense of being true to yourself, the most honorable thing to do is face up to the strength potential inherent in your talents and then find ways to realize it."

Don Clifton, author, Now, Discover Your Strengths[6]

Strengths-based leadership can be traced back to the late 1960s, but it is Don Clifton's work with Gallup that put the approach on the map.[3] By the mid-2000s, strengths had become mainstream with the release of books including *Now, Discover Your Strengths* and *StrengthsFinder 2.0.*[4] The strengths-based approach focuses on polishing talents into strengths rather than trying to fix deficits or improve weaknesses, providing a new way of developing the capacities of people. Programs like Gallup's StrengthsFinder, StrengthsQuest, and StrengthsExplorer for youth are designed to help individuals identify their top strength areas. Nearly 12 million people have discovered their strengths with Gallup's StrengthsFinder program alone, indicating its widespread use in such a short time.[5] Certainly Generation Z students are not the only ones exposed to this philosophy; people across various generations have taken to strengths and use it in their organizations and workplaces.

But unlike other generations, Generation Z is growing up in an era in which the strengths-based approach has nearly always existed. Some may have learned of their personal strengths while in middle and high school, bringing with them to college a philosophy of strengths. More than six hundred schools and higher education institutions use StrengthsQuest.[7] Many Generation Z students have or will become exposed to a strengths-based approach during high school or college, which will certainly affect the way they view and practice leadership. And because older generations also use the strengths-based approach, it would not be surprising to find parents of Generation Z students who have assessed their personal and professional strengths as well. Gallup has found that the strengths-based approach is even being used to better understand and develop parenting skills.[8] Because nearly all children under age eighteen belong to Generation Z, it is safe to say that their parents who have discovered their strengths are likely applying their findings to their households. Given that strengths-based leadership is all around them, it would make sense that Generation Z students define leadership from a lens of strengths rather than one of deficits.

A Complex World Needs a Complex Definition of Leadership

Leadership today involves complex thinking,[9] adaptability,[10] and interdependence.[11] Problems no longer require one answer; innovation does not stop with the latest and greatest invention. Diversity of experiences, perspectives, and cultures highlights the importance of connection and collaboration. Consider the problem of reducing carbon emissions, a highly complex issue that calls for multiple approaches and involves nearly infinite numbers of stakeholders. There have been both policy and innovation advancements in some nations, but a lack of an all-encompassing global approach is evidenced by the Kyoto Protocol. The protocol aimed to have every nation agree to policies and practices that would reduce their carbon emissions. Nearly every country in the world signed and ratified the Kyoto Protocol between 1997 and 2013.[12] The United States is one of only a handful of nations that has never ratified it. Regardless of people's opinions of the protocol, it was a global attempt to address carbon emissions. The leadership required to pull together nearly the entire world to agree on how to proceed with environmental standards must have been monumental.

"Most of our problems could be solved with … leaders who are capable of enacting change."

Generation Z student

Like the effort behind the Kyoto Protocol, the charge for Generation Z will be to focus on a variety of global issues such as international business, trade, crime, disasters and epidemics, money and currency, and military intervention. These complex issues will require a coordinated, adaptive, and interdependent approach, calling Generation Z to action in political, entrepreneurial, and technological leadership roles. And given their determination, open-mindedness, and sense of responsibility, those in Generation Z will surely be able to step up to the challenge.

> "We are a generation that will have to be creative to solve the problems of the past generation."
>
> *Generation Z student*

As Generation Z students define and develop the leadership capacities of themselves and others, they will be influenced by what is around them. The skills employers want, the strengths-based approach, and the complexity of leadership issues today will likely be driving forces in the way Generation Z defines leadership.

Who Are Leader Role Models for Generation Z?

Role models can be fundamental role in shaping the ideals and perceptions of youth. Consider the parent who offered support and guidance during the tumultuous middle school years, the teacher who provided mentorship to a struggling high school student, or the best friend who influenced a peer to make positive choices. These individuals embody the persona of someone to look up to. Who does Generation Z look to as their leader role models?

> "I believe we need more mentors."
>
> *Generation Z student*

Parents

Parental relationships in each generation have defining characteristics. For example, Generation X is often referred to as the latchkey generation due to the transition to a dual-income household, leaving many children to care for themselves until their parents came home from work. The Millennials, on the other hand, are associated with *helicopter parents* who flew so closely overhead that the decisions of the kids were shaped by their parents' opinions.[13] Generation Z, however, is marked by a different parental relationship, one of a trusted mentor. This stems from the idea that Generation Z students like their parents,[14] and 88 percent say they are extremely close to them.[15] For teens, this is fairly remarkable. This close relationship certainly influences how these students tend to see their parents, which is as guides rather than enforcers or influencers. That is why it is not surprising that we found that more than half of Generation Z students consult their parents on important matters.

In considering what has fostered this type of relationship, it is likely the honesty, trust, and openness that their parents have displayed early in their lives.[16] Nearly all Generation Z students report that their parents have talked with them about avoiding drug and alcohol use, and most have talked with them about practicing safe sex.[17] And more than 90 percent of Generation Z parents trust their children when using social media.[18] This demonstration of openness and trust certainly reflects a mentoring relationship, and explains why nearly half say they are most influenced by their parents.[19] It is no wonder that 69 percent indicate that parents are their number one role models, over teachers, political leaders, celebrities, and athletes,[20] a number considerably higher than the 54 percent of Millennials in 2012 who named their parents as their heroes and drastically higher from the 29 percent of Generation Xers in 1993.[21]

Teachers

Many individuals can reflect back to their K-12 education experiences and recall a teacher who made a difference in their lives. Those memories do not typically involve a lesson plan or class assignment, but rather the guidance and mentorship from the teacher to achieve what might have felt like an unattainable goal. That is why it is no surprise that more than half of Generation Z students identify their teachers as role models.[22]

Coaches

Many movies portray the extraordinary coach who led a ragtag team of misfits to victory and, more important, led the players to greatness. Many children who played a sport as a child would be able to identify a coach who served as a role model or mentor. This coach did not shout at their players, argue with referees, or push their players to the brink. And, coaches who engage in these behaviors do not sit well with Generation Z. Rather, this generation's role models are the coaches who do not yell, but remain calm, care and encourage their players, and involve the team in decision making.[23]

Peers

Generation Z students can easily seek out information and advice from their friends, not unlike other generations. But with their abundant access to technology, they can reach each other any time of day for guidance or support. Since they value the opinions of their peers[24] and respond well to strong peer leaders,[25] it makes sense that peers can be influential role models for Generation Z.

Fictional Characters

Fictional characters can also be role models for Generation Z. Although they have no ability to interact with fictional characters, making guidance and mentorship impossible, fictional characters can be role models in the sense that how their characters behave in the story can be inspirational and motivating, showcasing to their fans leadership characteristics to emulate. Consider that the favorite books of Generation Z include *Harry Potter*, *Hunger Games*, *Diary of a Wimpy Kid*, *Twilight*, and *The Hobbit*, all which have been made into blockbuster movies.[26] Each of these stories

—⟞———————

"Pity does not get you aid. Admiration at your refusal to give in does."

Katniss Everdeen, character from Hunger Games, *by Suzanne Collins*[27]

—⟞———————

—⟞———————

"It is a curious thing, Harry, but perhaps those who are best suited to power are those who have never sought it. Those who, like you, have leadership thrust upon them, and take up the mantle because they must, and find to their own surprise that they wear it well."

Albus Dumbledore, character from Harry Potter and the Deathly Hallows, *by J. K. Rowling*[28]

—⟞———————

showcases a teens overcoming obstacles and persevering as unassuming leaders.

Collaboration and optimism help each of these leaders achieve the impossible. Like their on-screen heroes, Generation Z students are confident in their ability to succeed, are collaborative team players, are optimistic about their place in the world,[29] and believe they have great determination, factors that make them like their on screen heroes, Katniss Everdeen and Harry Potter.

Can fictional characters actually influence behaviors? One study found that teenagers who were exposed to prosocial media role models had an increase in altruistic inclinations when asked to personally reflect on the significance of the character. In other words, exposure to media role models may result in changing behavior.[30]

The Harry Potter Alliance is a nonprofit organization inspired by characters from the Harry Potter books with a mission to "turn fans into heroes." It offers high school, university, and community chapters for members to engage in international projects that support equality, human rights, and literacy.[31]

Who Are Not Leader Role Models for Generation Z?

All of the real people who serve as Generation Z role models appear to be in their inner circle. Those outside that tight circle such as bosses, religious leaders, professional athletes, celebrities, and political leaders might seem obvious choices for role models, but not so much for Generation Z.

Bosses

Although many Generation Z students plan to work for themselves, many others will end up having jobs with supervisors. Because these students tend to follow authority[32] and prefer a well-defined chain of command in the workplace,[33] it is not surprising that they view relationships with a boss as highly transactional.[34] Although they need to be engaged in intensive working relationships to perform,[35] very few are motivated by their bosses, even good ones.[36] This type of relationship does not lend itself to one of mentoring and leadership as Generation Z defines it. The question is, What will be the role of the supervisor as a leader as these students move into postcollege employment? Will those in Generation Z follow only because they are expected to, or will the most-admired bosses lead Generation Z individuals to achieve greatness?

Religious Leaders

As we noted in chapter 2, 41 percent of Generation Z students indicate attending religious services regularly,[37] and our study found that nearly half participate in organized religion. Local, national, and international religious leaders can be prominent figures in these students' lives. Consider the individual leading religious services at a person's place of worship, the youth group leader who serves as a formal mentor, the teacher educating individuals on the religion itself, or even prominent religious leaders like the Pope who appeal to audiences beyond a particular religion. Does Generation Z see religious leaders as their role models? Not really: only 8 percent identified them as their first choice of all role models.[38]

Professional Athletes and Celebrities

With celebrities and professional athletes in high-profile roles, there is abundant news of their views and behaviors. Examples are athletes such as Michael Sam, the first openly gay NFL player,[39] and Tim Tebow, who is known more for his public displays of his Christian faith than his football talent.[40] But the limelight is bright, and these high-profile individuals do not always stay in the public's good graces for very long. Michael Phelps[41] and Lance Armstrong,[42] who have tarnished their legacies with drug use and doping, are testimony to this. Add to that celebrities who have pushed the envelope with their eccentric behavior. That is why it is no surprise that only 5 percent of Generation Z rate celebrities and 4 percent rate professional athletes as their number one role models.[43] Furthermore, 30 percent rated celebrities as their last choice of role model.[44] This is likely because Generation Z students tend to see through the superficial, looking to people close to them as role models.[45] As great as these contributions might be, will Generation Z students care that Angelina and Brad are doing philanthropy in Africa or that Leonardo DiCaprio has been an active global environmentalist?[46] Probably not.

Political Leaders

There are a handful of politicians who, despite the fact that their legacies are rooted in a particular time, are still deemed great leaders today: Abraham Lincoln, for example, and John F. Kennedy. They are revered by individuals across party lines for their leadership. Generation Z, however, has witnessed political leadership filled with contention, scandal, and defiance rather than collaboration and integrity. As noted in chapter 6, we found that more than 50 percent of Generation Z students are concerned about political dysfunction, and youth in general think there is little to admire in politicians because they see them as argumentative, dishonest, and selfish.[47] That is likely why only 3 percent of Generation Z students identify political leaders as their number one role models, and 27 percent would choose political leaders last out of every other type of role model.[48] Do not plan on these students to emulate the politicians they see today. Perhaps their values will shape the politicians of tomorrow.

Based on their experiences and perceptions, Generation Z will likely view effective leadership as

- Leveraging the capacities of others
- Engaging in complex thinking and innovative problem solving
- Utilizing a collaborative and interdependent approach
- Communicating effectively
- Being adaptable
- Guiding others to greatness
- Being optimistic
- Persevering through adversity
- Employing honesty and altruism

Generation Z as Leaders and Followers

Given the factors influencing their leadership perception and values, how do Generation Z students lead? Generation Z students are style shifters, which means they consciously employ a specific style appropriate for the situation at hand.[49]

The Act of Leading

In using style shifting, Generation Z students fluctuate from the Doing style (executing a task) to Thinking (strategizing a plan) to Relating (building the team) to Leading (taking initiative) depending on the context. Our findings revealed that more than 60 percent of Generation Z students use each of the four styles always or often, and no students use only one style.

They do, however, have preferred styles. Generation Z students see themselves as workhorses of projects and tasks: most favor the Doing style over other styles. This may come as no surprise since these students describe themselves as determined and responsible, characteristics that contribute to getting things done. After the Doing style, Generation Z students use the Thinking and then Relating styles most frequently, leaving the Leading style as the least frequently used. Interestingly, Generation Z men and women use the styles in that same order.

If the Leading style is used least of the four styles, does this mean that Generation Z students are not leaders themselves? Probably not. All four styles can contribute to effective leadership because different situations may call for the use of different styles. And, being able to employ style shifting by going back and forth between styles based on what is needed makes Generation Z students versatile leaders. For example, using the Thinking style, they could develop a shared vision for an organization and then engage in the Relating style to leverage the strengths of others by matching individuals with roles that fit them to work toward the vision.

Even for those who envision leadership as using only the Leading style, we found that more than 60 percent employ that style always or often. That seems to align well with the notion that 63 percent of Generation Z students identify as having higher leadership ability than their peers.[50] Whether they are simply confident engaging in leadership or actually truly effective leaders, we can expect Generation Z students to take the lead.

The Act of Following

Generation Z students see being followers as keeping up with another person's Twitter feed or regularly reading someone's blog. But what about being a follower in a leadership situation? Generation Z respects authority[51] and adheres to hierarchies in place,[52] so they have the capacity to effectively follow when engaged in formal, positional, leader-follower relationships. Nevertheless, they want their leaders to listen to them, consider their ideas, value their perspectives,[53] and involve them in decision-making.[54] The expectation for this level of engagement may not be readily embedded into more defined leader-follower relations. Thus, they will likely excel most in a structured, hierarchical, environment that has the fluidity and flexibility for active participation and engagement at all levels. In such an environment, anyone can share ideas, and consensus decision-making is the goal. There is an understanding, however, that the leader will have the final say in important matters.

Conclusion

The days of shielding others from bad news in order to protect them may be challenged by this generation. They are problem solvers who believe the only way they can help is if they know what the problem is. Their parents likely did not protect them from any financial woes they faced during the Great Recession, and their own openness with their parents in general likely created a transparent family unit. Thus, it is no surprise that Generation Z values honesty and wants leaders to be open with them rather than hide information just because of their age or title in the organization.[55] This transparency and openness is also reflected in their desire for their leaders to have effective communication skills, especially face-to-face communication as that is their preferred method. And nearly two-thirds want their leaders to listen to their ideas and value their opinions,[56] a practice that more than 70 percent of Generation Z youth experienced with their parents.[57] Their desire to be innovative[58] and engage in problem solving[59] will likely affect both what they value in leaders and how they themselves lead others, resulting in seeing leadership as dreaming big and making things happen.

Notes

1. The quotations for the 1920s through 1980s are from Ciulla, J. B. (2004). Ethics and leadership effectiveness. In J. Antonakis, A. T. Cianciolo, & R. J. Sternberg (Eds.), *The Nature of Leadership*. Thousand Oaks, CA: Sage, pp. 302–312. The quote from the 2000s is from

Yukl, G. (2006). *Leadership in organizations* (6th ed.). Upper Saddle River, NJ: Pearson-Prentice Hall.

2. National Association of Colleges and Employers. (2014). *The skills/qualities employers want in new college graduate hires.* Retrieved from http://www .naceweb.org/about-us/press/class-2015-skills-qualities-employers-want.aspx

3. Burkus, D. (2011). Building the strong organization: Exploring the role of organizational design in strengths-based leadership. *Journal of Strategic Leadership, 3*(1), 54–66.

4. Buckingham, M., & Clifton, D. O. (2001). *Now, discover your strengths.* New York: Free Press. Rath, T. (2007). *StrengthsFinder 2.0.* New York: Gallup Press.

5. Gallup. (2015). *Gallup strengths center.* Retrieved from https://www.gallupstrengthscenter.com/

6. Buckingham & Clifton. (2001).

7. Gallup. (2015).

8. Reckmeyer, M. (2015). *Strengths based parenting: Making the most of your children's innate talents.* New York: Gallup Press.

9. Uhl-Bien, M., Marion, R., & McKelvey, B. (2007). Complexity leadership theory: Shifting leadership from the industrial age to the knowledge era. *Leadership Quarterly, 18*(4), 298–318.

10. Heifetz, R., Linsky, M., & Grashow, A. (2009). *The practice of adaptive leadership: Tools and tactics for changing your organization and the world.* Boston: Harvard Business Press.

11. Lipman-Blumen, J. (1996). *Connective leadership*. New York: Oxford University Press.

12. United Nations. (2015). *Status of ratification of the Kyoto Protocol*. Retrieved from http://unfccc.int/ kyoto_protocol/status_of_ratification/items/2613.php

13. The definition of *latchkey kid* can be found at http://dictionary.reference.com/browse/latchkey per-cent20kid?s=t. The definition of *helicopter parent* can be found at http://dictionary.reference.com/browse/H +parent

14. Euromonitor International. (2011). *Make way for Generation Z: Marketing for today's teens and tweens*. Retrieved from http://oaltabo2012.files.wordpress .com/2012/03/make-way-for-generation-z1.pdf

15. Intelligence Group. (2013). *Cassandra report*. Retrieved from www.cassandra.co/report/

16. Schawbel, D. (2014). *Gen Y and Gen Z global workplace expectations study*. Retrieved from http:// millennialbranding.com/2014/geny-genz-global-workplace-expectations-study/

17. Northeastern University. (2014). *Innovation survey*. Retrieved from www.northeastern.edu/news/2014/ 11/innovation-imperative-meet-generation-z/

18. JWT Intelligence. (2012). *Gen Z: Digital in their DNA*. Retrieved from http://www.jwtintelligence.com/wp-content/uploads/2012/04/F_INTERNAL_Gen_Z_ 0418122.pdf

19. Schawbel. (2014).

20. Northeastern University. (2014).

21. Levine, A., & Dean, D. R. (2012). *Generation on a tightrope: A portrait of today's college student.* San Francisco: Wiley.

22. Northeastern University. (2014).

23. Parker, K., Czech, D. R., Burdette, T., Stewart, J., Biber, D., Easton, L. E., … McDaniel, T. (2012). The preferred coaching styles of Generation Z athletes: A qualitative study. *International Sport Coaching Journal,* 5(2), 5–23.

24. O'Leary, H. (2014). *Recruiting Gen Z: No more business as usual.* Retrieved from http://www.eduventures .com/2014/09/recruiting-gen-z/

25. Tulgan, B. (2013). *Meet Generation Z: The second generation within the giant "Millennial" cohort.* Retrieved from http://rainmakerthinking.com/assets/uploads/ 2013/10/Gen-Z-Whitepaper.pdf

26. Intelligence Group. (2013).

27. Collins, S. (2008). *The hunger games.* New York: Scholastic Press.

28. Rowling, J. K. (2009). *Harry Potter and the deathly hallows.* New York: Scholastic.

29. Euromonitor International (2011).

30. Farsides, T., & Pettman, D. (2013). Inspiring altruism: Reflecting on the personal relevance of emotionally

evocative prosocial media characters. *Journal of Applied Social Psychology, 43*(11), 2251–2258.

31. Harry Potter Alliance. (2015a). *Home.* thehpalliance .org. Harry Potter Alliance. (2015b). *Chapters.* Retrieved from thehpalliance.org

32. Euromonitor International. (2011).

33. Tulgan. (2013).

34. Tulgan. (2013).

35. Tulgan. (2013).

36. Schawbel. (2014).

37. Northeastern University. (2014).

38. Northeastern University. (2014).

39. Goodbread, C. (2014). *Michael Sam, NFL draft prospect, announces he's gay.* http://www.nfl.com/ news/story/0ap2000000324603/article/michael-sam-nfl-draft-prospect-announces-hes-gay

40. Van Riper, T. (2013). *Tim Tebow tops Forbes' 2013 list of America's most influential athletes.* Retrieved from http://www.forbes.com/sites/tomvanriper/2013/05/ 06/americas-most-influential-athletes-2/

41. Almasy, S. (2014). *Michael Phelps suspended by USA Swimming for six months.* http://edition.cnn.com/ 2014/10/06/sport/michael-phelps-suspended/

42. Shin, P. H. B. (2015). *Lance Armstrong on doping: "I would probably do it again."* Retrieved from http://abcnews.go.com/Sports/lance-armstrong-doping/story?id=28491316

43. Northeastern University. (2014).

44. Northeastern University. (2014).

45. Euromonitor International. (2011).

46. Martinez, O., & Pentchoukova, K. (2014). *Sixteen admirable celebrities who are actively changing the world for the better*. Retrieved from http://www .epochinspired.com/inspired/1117982-16-admirable-celebrities-who-are-actively-changing-the-world-for-the-better/

47. Lawless, J. L., & Fox, R. L. (2015). *Running from office*. New York: Oxford University Press.

48. Northeastern University. (2014).

49. Hersey, P., Blanchard, K. H., & Johnson, D. E. (2012). *Management of organizational behavior: Leading human resources*. Upper Saddle River, NJ: Prentice Hall.

50. Eagan, K., Stolzenberg, E. B., Ramirez, J. J., Aragon, M. C., Suchard, M. R., & Hurtado, S. (2014). *The American freshman: National norms fall 2014*. Los Angeles: Higher Education Research Institute.

51. Euromonitor International. (2011).

52. Tulgan. (2013).

53. Schawbel. (2014).

54. Parker et al. (2012).

55. Schawbel. (2014).

56. Schawbel. (2014).

57. Viacom. (2012). *Consumer insights: Nickelodeon's "International GPS: Kids' influence."* http:// blog.viacom.com/2012/08/consumer-insights-nickelodeons-international-gps-kids-influence/

58. Gallup & Operation Hope. (2013). *The 2013 Gallup-Hope Index.* Retrieved from www .operationhope.org/images/uploads/Files/ 2013galluphopereport.pdf

59. Anatole, E. (2013). *Generation Z: Rebels with a cause.* Retrieved from http://www.forbes.com/sites/ onmarketing/2013/05/28/generation-z-rebels-with-a-cause/

9

MAXIMIZING LEARNING

As Generation Z goes to college, it is necessary to understand how to create learning environments that maximize these students' capacity to learn. Advancing technology certainly does play a role in learning, but technology and learning are not necessarily synonymous for this generation. Learning in college takes place in a variety of settings, and the lessons range from content in books to interactions and experiences with peers, faculty, and staff.[1] What contributes to learning for Generation Z students?

Learning Resources

Baby Boomers relied on the Dewey Decimal System to locate books and articles. Generation X transitioned from typewriters to computers. Millennials had the technology to keep up with their grades through online platforms and saw blogging incorporated as part of their course work. The technology available for Generation Z, however, might do more than make learning easier; it might help students learn more simply by having access to more information.

Instantaneous, Accessible, Abundant Information

The convenience and instant access the Internet and technology provide have made a difference in learning and education in general. For example, where previous generations attended history class to learn about a historical event, Generation Z can quickly look up any event and find something about it online; they do not need to wait to learn. Powerful online search engines help Generation Z find a multitude of answers in just a few seconds. These search engines, as we noted in chapter 2, might not always produce sources that are academically sound. Educators are now spending time teaching students how to determine what is credible for academia as research shifts from peer-reviewed journals and books in a library to blogs and op-eds.[2]

With search engines, Wikipedia, YouTube, and other social media sites as places where Generation Z gets information, research has become less about the process of knowledge acquisition and more about quickly finding the answer needed for an assignment.[3] While the accessibility of the Internet presents new challenges in sifting through sources for credibility, it also allows students to access educational resources on demand. Gone are the days of physically going to the library to find various books and articles to complete an assignment. Now there is access to many books and articles without ever having to leave home to get them.

Virtual Student Support

The resources available online to help students complete assignments are abundant. Online tutoring sites, practice tests, how-to videos, and reference materials are just a click away and can certainly support students in being academically successful. For example, the Khan Academy allows users to engage in practice activities and watch instructional videos to learn at their own pace in a variety of subjects, including math, science, history, and even computer programming.[4] Khan Academy lessons are free of charge to users and geared to all ages. Just as they would stream an episode of their favorite TV show, Generation Z students can quickly find an informational video to help with their math homework or even learn an entirely new subject.

Generation Z as Learners

Ninety percent of online content that exists today has been created in just the past two years.[5] With so much that can be accessed online, learning for Generation Z is likely going to be more than just about the content they access, but also about the process in which they learn and comprehend it.

Practical Makes Perfect

It is not surprising that logic-based approaches and experiential learning are the forms of learning that Generation Z students in our study said they use most frequently. First, logic- and mathematical-based approaches focus on organizing information into solutions and applications.[6] Add to that experiential learning, which allows students to learn hands-on and experimentally by applying previously learned content to a real-life setting.[7] Logic-based and experiential learning together allow students to make sense of information through trial and error and then apply this information to a real problem.

Based in Sacramento, California, HackerLab aims to spark innovation through technology at the intersection of education and business. Providing collaborative space, classes, and start-up support, HackerLab works to educate and inspire the next generation of entrepreneurs. It is just one of many collaborative work spaces providing Generation Z opportunities to use their intelligence and technological aptitude to gain practical experience to address issues hands on.[8]

Because they have grown up in a financial recession and have seen employment rates on a roller-coaster, Generation Z students demand an education that will be useful and relevant in getting a job after graduation. These students are drawn to learning that will help fill their toolbox with applicable knowledge and skills for the workforce.[9] They view education as a utility toward their eventual career, which could blur the lines between the classroom and that postgraduation place they keep hearing about called the "real world." Their preference for experiential learning highlights their forward-looking nature to prepare for life beyond graduation. In addition to gaining real-world experience, Generation Z students may seek out courses that hone the critical skills employers want.[10] Their desire for practical and useful learning does not stop at the lecture hall. Seventy-nine percent of those in Generation Z think it is important that educational programs integrate practical experiences such as internships.[11] Concerned about their future, they look at experiences for their usefulness and the long-term benefit for getting a job after graduation.

Imagination Is Imaginary

Creativity requires generating multiple unique ideas and combining those ideas into the best result,[12] which is why it is no surprise that it is one of the most sought after attributes by employers in recent college graduates.[13] Whereas IQ has steadily increased with each generation, the creativity quotient of America's youth has decreased since 1990.[14] Are Generation Z students being exposed to learning approaches and methods that help develop creativity? Consider that imaginative learning—looking at problems from multiple perspectives and imagining a solution—is related to the concept of creativity, but for Generation Z students in our study, imagination is the least preferred approach.[15]

Why might this be? Are students not engaging in creative methods of learning? As we discussed in chapter 2, with the No Child Left Behind Act, less time has been allocated in K-12 for visual arts, dance, theater, and music classes.[16] These types of classes are typically associated with creativity, and less time in them might have meant less opportunity to engage in creative thinking and expression.

Artistic courses are not the only place students can learn creativity. Teachers of more traditional academic subjects might employ innovative pedagogies like project-based learning, which can boost creativity by challenging students to solve a complex problem.[17] But 84 percent of parents and 79 percent of teachers believe that not enough time is allocated in school to help students develop their creativity.[18] Time spent in standardized testing rather than other courses could certainly have limited their exposure. Since 2002, schools have implemented federally mandated standardized tests, sending a wave of testing through the states.[19] Between federal assessments, state assessments, and end-of-course and graduation assessments, students spent a significant amount of time just taking tests.[20] Both teachers and parents have found this problematic and cite "an education system that is too reliant on testing and assessment" as the number one barrier to teaching creativity."[21]

It is difficult to expect that Generation Z students would prefer imaginative learning methods that foster creative thinking if they seldom engaged in this type of learning before college.[22] This highlights a disconnect between the type of learning Generation Z students prefer to engage in and the creative thinking that employers seek. It is not to say this group is not creative, but that the schools many have grown up attending gave them limited exposure to learning associated with creativity.

Learning Alone

Of all the learning methods, intrapersonal learning is the one most preferred by Generation Z students in our study. They are comfortable with and like being able to learn independently and at their own pace. It is understandable that Generation Z students, self-described as responsible, determined, and thoughtful, prefer to use learning methods that require self-reliance. Armed with these attributes, they have what it takes to stay on track to monitor their own progress.

> "My ideal learning environment is one where I can participate with the group only if I choose. I like to be mentally engaged, but learn best by myself, and would prefer that collaboration were an option."
>
> *Generation Z student*

Technology has always had a presence in educational environments for students in Generation Z and likely contributes to their preference for working alone. With 85 percent of these students reporting engaging in online research for assignments, using technology allows individuals to access an immense amount of information with little to no need for interaction with others.[23] Instead of going to class to gain baseline knowledge, they can access foundational information from a few websites and videos, allowing them to learn on their own before coming to the group.

Facilitated Learning

Our study uncovered a great deal about how Generation Z students view their instructors, peers, and learning environments. While these students prefer an intrapersonal learning method, they also enjoy working in group settings, a sign of their desire for social learning. They want to have some role in setting the tone and pace for their own learning but also see the value and benefit of working with others or at least near them.

Educators play a large role in learning for Generation Z. They call for engaging and passionate instructors. It should not be surprising that this hands-on and participatory group of learners do not like to be lectured at. They view their instructors as facilitators of learning as opposed to talking heads. Instructors who solely lecture for the class period will likely become the dull and unintelligible teacher from Charles Schulz's *Peanuts* cartoons.[24] Generation Z wants to play an active role in creating their learning, not listen silently to their instructors' pontification.

"[My ideal learning environment is] a place where I can work on my own until I need help from another peer or teacher."

Generation Z student

"[My ideal learning environment is] with an instructor who is both highly knowledgeable of the subject and deeply passionate for teaching students."

Generation Z student

The Myth of Multitasking

"If our attention span constricts to the point where we can only take information in 140-character sentences, then that doesn't bode too well for our future. The more we become used to just sound bites and tweets, the less patient we will become with more complex, more meaningful information."

Dr. Elias Aboujaoude, director, Stanford University's Impulse Control Disorders Clinic[29]

Generation Z students are comfortable with multitasking and splitting their time and focus among multiple screens.[25] Consider that they might search through nearly endless information on the Internet while posting messages to their social media sites, watching a video and trying to write a paper all at the same time. Research has found, however, that as Internet accessibility has increased over the past ten years with smart phones and Wi-Fi, the average attention span has decreased by half.[26] Some suggest that technology is leading to the rewiring of human brains.[27] Because the Internet can satisfy the need for instant gratification, some health experts believe it may contribute to the development of attention difficulties.[28] What Generation Z students might refer to as multitasking is likely an inability to focus. With the many benefits technology presents in student learning, it is important to be wary of the myth of being able to multitask effectively. Helping students focus their attention so they are not distracted from their learning will serve them well in creating healthy habits and being academically successful.

Group Work

Consider Generation X students doing a group project, where they might all have attended regularly scheduled group meetings to collaborate as well as report on their individual progress. Then Millennials came along and could divide up tasks using social media and text messaging without feeling the need to meet in person to work on the project. Generation Z's approach is different. In capitalizing on their need for both intrapersonal and social learning, group projects might entail having the group meet. But instead of collaborating on the project verbally, they work independently next to each other on the same Google Doc.[30] Because students spend a great deal of time doing group projects in college, it is critical for instructors to understand how Generation Z students might work together. This knowledge can aid instructors in creating a learning environment or structuring an assignment conducive to their approach.

Gender Preferences in Learning

It is not surprising that men and women have very different preferences in learning methods.[31] We found that women prefer intrapersonal learning and find linguistic learning methods most effective. Combined, this may include journaling, reflection, and reading.[32] While overall, the interpersonal method is one of Generation Z students' least preferred ways to learn, women like being able to relate to and connect with others, as evidenced by their higher rates than men in using the Relating style. Women might not want a full-blown group project, but incorporating opportunities for them to share their thoughts and opinions with others might work well.

> "I love learning with people who fuel the conversation and ask questions."
>
> *A Generation Z woman*

We found that men prefer logical learning and find the spatial method most effective. Together, this may include using visuals to find patterns, classify information, and solve problems and then showcasing findings through design.[33] Couple the logical and spatial learning methods with their use of the Thinking style, and these men will likely prefer to learn with others through finding solutions to problems. While there may be some across-the-board commonalities in terms of learning preferences, gender can make a difference.

Learning Environments

While there will never be an exact prescription for the ideal learning environment, Generation Z has pointed educators in a direction a bit closer to that ideal. The students in our study described their ideal learning environment as one that incorporates independent and hands-on work with engaging instructors and supportive peers.

Learning Spaces

The physicality of the learning space is critically important to Generation Z students, as we learned in our study. These students want a designated zone for learning so they can focus and be free from distractions. The space needs to contain the tools necessary for learning, like access to the Internet and being well lit and open, with adequate table space.

> "My ideal learning environment has calming music, as well as tools or resources to aid me."
>
> *Generation Z student*

Interestingly, we found that Generation Z students enjoy having music as part of the learning environment despite not having a preference for using music as a learning method. In this case, music serves as a background for the learning environment. This might explain why libraries appear to be filled with students furiously typing papers with ear buds or headphones.

Modern Libraries

Libraries serve as the academic central hub on college campuses. While Generation Z might not be diving into books as frequently as previous generations have, the library as a study facility still serves an important role in the learning process. Libraries have the opportunity to not only provide the necessary

research resources, but to offer a physical atmosphere conducive to Generation Z's learning styles and preferences.
Opening its doors in 2013, the Hunt Library at North Carolina
State University is a five-story facility dedicated to providing
everything students might need.[34] The types of meeting spaces
ranges from rooms for small groups, fishbowl setups for
innovative projects, presentation practice rooms, a game lab,
indoor and outdoor reading lounges, and the NextGen Learning Commons with multiple interactive learning options.
Libraries today might look different than fifty or even twenty
years ago, but they certainly can play an important role in
fostering student learning.

Tools for School

Generation Z excels at wielding the Internet and technology to
accomplish things, learning included. Having been exposed
to technology their whole lives, Generation Z students are
likely comfortable using technology in an educational setting.
Their instructors, who are older and perhaps still adjusting
to the online and technologically infused culture of learning,
may find integrating technology challenging. Traditional
school work using paper and books is rapidly being replaced
by online work modules, instructional videos, and handheld
learning devices such as smart phones and tablets.[35] Although
Generation Z students may be able to seamlessly navigate
this technology, their instructors also need to be able to use
it effectively.

Making Major Decisions

Generation Z views their choice of educational institution as a major investment, but a worthwhile investment that will help them achieve their goals.[36] They are looking for an institution where the price is right and the path to a job looks bright. But that is not all. More than half say that location and campus facilities are important in their college choice.[37] Institutions should therefore think about how buildings can be brought up to today's technology standards for creating innovative learning spaces.

Generation Z students seek flexibility in their programs of study as well. More than 70 percent think it is important to be able to design and build their own course of study or major.[38] They prefer to learn on their own time and in their own way, and that will be evident in how they want to earn a degree.

Two-thirds of Generation Z students believe that preparation for life in the working world is a joint responsibility between the institution and the student.[39] This expectation is something to make note of to ensure that Generation Z students are making wise college choices for what they need but also that institutions can meet the expectations they have.

Conclusion

Preparing for their future is paramount for Generation Z, so providing transferable and translatable learning experiences is imperative. They do not plan on taking a back seat in addressing the world's issues or in their education. They want the resources to access and learn information independently, but also the option to engage with peers socially and to reinforce what they have learned. They want instructors who are knowledgeable and passionate, as well as empowering and inclusive, and environments that are conducive to practical learning. Generation Z is the new wave of engaged learners who want to drive their college education.

Notes

1. Kolb, A. Y., & Kolb, D. A. (2005) Learning styles and learning spaces: Enhancing experiential learning in higher education. *Academy of Management Learning and Education, 4,* 193–212.

2. Purcell, K., Rainie, L., Heaps, A., Buchanan, J., Friedrich, L., Jacklin, A., ... Zickuhr, K. (2012). *How teens do research in the digital world.* Retrieved from http://www.pewinternet.org/2012/11/01/how-teens-do-research-in-the-digital-world/

3. Purcell et al. (2012).

4. Khan Academy. (2015). *A personalized learning service for all ages.* Retrieved from https://www.khanacademy .org/about

5. IBM. (2015). *What is big data?* Retrieved from http:// www-01.ibm.com/software/data/bigdata/what-is-big-data.html

6. Bixler, B. A. (N.d.). *A multiple intelligences primer.* Retrieved from http://www.personal.psu.edu/bxb11/ MI/MultipleIntelligences_print.html

7. Businessballs.com. (N.d.). *Kolb learning styles*.
    Retrieved from http://www.businessballs.com/
    kolblearningstyles.htm

8. HackerLab. (2015). *About*. Retrieved from http://
    hackerlab.org/about/

9. Northeastern University. (2014). *Innovation survey*.
    Retrieved from www.northeastern.edu/news/2014/
    11/innovation-imperative-meet-generation

10. National Association of Colleges and Employers.
    (2014). *The skills/qualities employers want in new
    college graduate hires*. Retrieved from http://www
    .naceweb.org/about-us/press/class-2015-skills-
    qualities-employers-want.aspx

11. Northeastern University. (2014).

12. Bronson, P., & Merryman, A. (2010). *The creativity
    crisis*. http://www.newsweek.com/creativity-crisis-
    74665

13. National Association of Colleges and Employers.
    (2014).

14. Bronson, P., & Merryman, A. (2010).

15. Businessballs.com. (N.d.).

16. Parsad, B., Splegelman, M., & Coopersmith, J. (2012).
    *Arts education in public elementary and secondary
    schools 1999-2000 and 2009-2010*. Retrieved from
    http://nces.ed.gov/pubs2012/2012014.pdf

17. Bell, S. (2010). Project-based learning for the 21st cen-
    tury: Skills for the future. *Clearing House, 83*, 39–43.

18. Berland, E. (2013). *Barriers to creativity in education:
    Educators and parents grade the system*. Retrieved

from http://www.adobe.com/content/dam/Adobe/en/
education/pdfs/barriers-to-creativity-in-education-
study.pdf

19. Kamenetz, A. (2014). *School testing: How much is
    too much?* Retrieved from http://www.cgcs.org/cms/
    lib/DC00001581/Centricity/Domain/31/National
    %20Public%20Radio.pdf

20. Kamenetz. (2014).

21. Berland. (2013).

22. President's Committee on the Arts and the Human-
    ities. (2011). *Re-investing in arts education: Winning
    America's future through creative schools.* Retrieved
    from http://www.pcah.gov/sites/default/files/photos/
    PCAH_Reinvesting_4web.pdf

23. Sparks & Honey. (2014). *Meet Gen Z: Forget everything
    you learned about Millennials.* Retrieved from www
    .slideshare.net/sparksandhoney/generation-z-final-
    june-17

24. For more information about *Peanuts*, go to http://
    www.peanuts.com/

25. Sparks & Honey. (2014). Furham, A., & Bradley, A.
    (1997). Music while you work: The differential dis-
    traction of background music on the cognitive test
    performance of introverts and extroverts. *Applied
    Cognitive Psychology, 11*(5), 445–455.

26. Vidyarthyi, N. (2011). *Attention spans have dropped
    from 12 to 5 minutes: How social media is ruining
    our minds.* Retrieved from http://www.adweek.com/

socialtimes/attention-spans-have-dropped-from-12-
minutes-to-5-seconds-how-social-media-is-ruining-
our-minds-infographic/87484

27. Prelude Consulting Limited. (2014). *Generation Z and
    learning.* Retrieved from http://www.prelude-team
    .com/articles/generation-z-and-learning.

28. Evangelista, B. (2009). *Attention loss feared as
    high-tech rewires brains.* Retrieved from http://www
    .sfgate.com/business/article/Attention-loss-feared-as-
    high-tech-rewires-brain-3281030.php

29. Prelude Consulting Limited. (2014).

30. Google. (2015b). *Docs.* Retrieved from https://www
    .google.com/docs/about/

31. Gross, G. (2014). *How boys and girls learn differently.*
    Retrieved from http://www.huffingtonpost.com/dr-
    gail-gross/how-boys-and-girls-learn-differently_b_
    5339567.html

32. Bixler, B. A. (N.d.).

33. Bixler, B. A. (N.d.).

34. North Carolina State University. (2015). *About Hunt
    Library.* Retrieved from http://www.lib.ncsu.edu/
    huntlibrary/about

35. Kiefer, A. (2013). *The learning environment sweet spot:
    Elevating the educational paradigm.* Retrieved from
    https://www.ki.com/uploadedFiles/Docs/literature-
    samples/white-papers/Learning-Sweet-Spot-White-
    Paper.pdf

36. Northeastern University. (2014).

37. Northeastern University. (2014).

38. Northeastern University. (2014).

39. Schawbel, D. (2013). *Millennial Branding and Intern-ships.com release study on the future of education.* Retrieved from http://millennialbranding.com/2013/the-future-of-education/

10

WORKING WITH GENERATION Z

G eneration Z is a dynamic and complex generation, making it challenging to capture all aspects of the perceptions, experiences, beliefs, characteristics, and styles of those in the generation. In deciding what to highlight in this book, the topics selected are those that have emerged across the research as being particularly salient to Generation Z students as well as informative for those who want to be able to understand and effectively work with them. As this generation is just coming into adulthood, it is anticipated that there will be much more to learn about them over time.

It is important to understand that although several trends have been identified about Generation Z, not every student is the same. Looking at trends by demographics such as race, class, and gender can provide more nuanced insight about particular student populations. In addition, each individual has values, concerns, characteristics, styles, and behaviors unique to them. Because this book aims to highlight themes and trends that cut across the generation as a whole, disaggregation at the demographic or individual levels was outside its scope.

Looking at general trends about this population offers insight and a baseline of understanding in order to create and adjust policies, practices, curriculum, programs, environments, and cultures to best educate, relate to, and work with Generation Z.

This chapter provides an overview of strategies to assist college administrators, faculty, and staff in the higher education setting. These strategies may also be helpful to high school teachers, administrators, and parents as they prepare their students for college, policymakers as they consider funding allocations and new programs, and employers as they gear up for the transition of these students from college to career. We examine six strategies in this chapter:

- Relational strategies: Connecting with Generation Z
- Operational strategies: Designing a campus that fits
- Instructional strategies: Designing learning environments
- Programmatic strategies: Creating real-world learning experiences
- Developmental strategies: Building student capacity
- Technological strategies: Using the right social media

Relational Strategies: Connecting with Generation Z

Generation Z students are different from the generations of students that have come before them, and what worked for these previous generations might not work for them. Although it might be tempting to immediately reassess and redesign programs, processes, and institutional priorities to better fit with what Generation Z needs, it might be best to start with how to relate to them as people.

Make Time for Face Time

Not to be confused with Apple's video chatting function,[1] face time with another person is something that Generation Z students crave and value. This is important to keep in mind as technology continues to shape higher education environments, creating more options that replace face-to-face connections with virtual ones. While it is convenient to send out an e-mail or even social media message or text message, there is still value in the personal experience of meeting face-to-face. Students in Generation Z know this too. These in-person interactions are helpful in understanding emotions and reading expressions, something that a written message does not allow, even with emoticons. Rather than move all communication to the virtual world, we must put down the smart phone and focus on engaging in real life.

Be Transparent

Generation Z students are realistic problem solvers who appreciate honesty and authenticity from those who lead them. They do not like to be protected from problems or to have them sugar-coated. They would rather face an issue head-on and be part of the solution. With their problem-solving nature and desire to be consulted in decision making, it is a win-win scenario for those working with Generation Z students to be transparent and involve them in addressing issues. Not only can this be empowering for the students, it might result in a great solution.

Understand Family Roles

Although the term *helicopter parent* has been around for decades, it was not until Millennials came to college that the term became so mainstream.[2] These parents were often highly involved in decision making for their students, even sometimes in lieu of the students themselves, and have been known to sign their students up for clubs and even pick out their classes. Institutions have had to find ways to creatively integrate these parents into the fabric of the institution by offering parent newsletters, parent services, and even parent programs to satisfy their need to be engaged. Being a parent of a college student has become an identity all to itself.

Generation Z brings with it a different role for parents: co-pilot. Generation Z students value family input in their decisions and see their parents as their primary role models, which creates a situation in which students make the decisions but seek their parents' thoughts and advice. It is important to understand that parents will be highly influential in the college experience of many Generation Z students. In fact, Generation Z students will likely ask their parents for advice on just about everything. Like helicopter parents, Generation Z parents are important institutional stakeholders. Building strong relationships with Generation Z will also include building strong relationships with their parents and families.

Operational Strategies: Designing a Campus That Fits

Students select which college they attend by looking at far more than the academic offerings.[3] Everything from the records of the sports teams to the size of the institution can be important factors for students in their decision making. Will they commute or live on campus? Where will they exercise? What will social life be like? Generation Z also wants to know, Is the environment welcoming and safe? And what services are offered? Are they services they could access elsewhere without paying a huge fee, for example? These may be more important factors for Generation Z than academic rankings or student-to-faculty ratio. What might administrators need to consider in campus culture, services, and policies that align with this generation?

Enhance Safety

Generation Z students are highly concerned about violence, especially school shootings. They are aware that school violence is not limited to their K-12 experience and can be a reality in the college setting as well. Creating more robust and transparent policies and practices around campus safety, safety presentations for students, and having students participate in an active shooter training may not just put their minds at ease, but also prepare them in the case a violent incident does occur.

Their concern for school violence also brings up issues about acquaintance and date rape on campus. Educational campaigns and training sessions are standard at many institutions, but grassroots movements like #YesAllWomen have empowered women to use Twitter to share information about incidents of violence and harassment.[4] Consider creating a campus wide hashtag that empowers everyone to report incidents of violence and harassment.

Ensure an Inclusive and Affirming Environment

Generation Z students are concerned about equity, access, inclusion, and oppression. Take a hard look at policies, practices, and environments at the institutional, departmental, and program levels. How can they be more inclusive? Does the campus have safe spaces for students of color? Women? LGBTQIA students? Veterans? Students with disabilities? Other identity groups salient to the campus? Do programs and events reflect the diversity of the campus? Are support services available to first-generation and low-income students? In addition, it is critical that Generation Z students feel that their institutions support their desire to expand inclusion. Generation Z students may be the ones to champion issues such as creating gender-neutral housing and public restrooms as well as expanding nondiscrimination policies on campus so that all students feel safe, supported, and welcome.

Support Mental Health

Generation Z students have had exposure to many large-scale, high-stress events during their lifetimes that have had the potential to contribute to personal fear and anxiety and the construction of unhealthy beliefs about themselves. It is no wonder that increasing numbers of students are coming to college with mental health issues.[5] In fall 2014, 12 percent of all first-year Generation Z students indicated that they intended to seek personal counseling.[6]

Students may not receive the counseling they need for any number of reasons: limited accessibility for counseling due to high fees, limited hours, or even the lack of a counseling center on campus,[7] as well as the stigma associated with receiving counseling.[8] Consider offering free or low-cost long-term personal counseling on campus during a wide spectrum of times, including evenings and weekends, to help increase access. Regarding what can be done about the stigma of seeing a counselor, perhaps if campus administrators and faculty members talk openly and frequently about the benefits of counseling and encouraged students to take advantage of on-campus counseling services, Generation Z students may be more comfortable in using them.

Help Students Access Funding

With the cost of higher education skyrocketing, Generation Z students will need to be able to access funding or not go to college at all. But with student debt being a great concern for them, simply extending the loan amounts is not the answer for this generation. If the price of higher education is not coming down, how can Generation Z students access more funding for college? First, consider centralizing all external scholarships in a database so that students can easily find funding opportunities they are eligible for and apply online for multiple scholarships simultaneously. Scholarships in the database should include those posted by donors and foundations or by staff in financial aid. Students can then search through thousands of scholarships by entering the criteria they meet to see what scholarships they are eligible for. This can increase access to funding opportunities as well as streamline the process of applying.

Reconsider Housing Requirements

When considering the whole package of higher education costs (tuition, fees, books, and living expenses), Generation Z students might opt out of some of the nonessentials of the college experience like living on campus instead of choosing not to attend college. Some institutions have an on-campus residency requirement, which may ultimately be the deciding factor for some students in attending a particular institution or attending college at all. Forty-five percent of first-year students in 2014 picked their college due to the cost; 14.1 percent were unable to afford their first choice.[9]

With private apartments often near campus boundaries and some students choosing to go to college near home, Generation Z students recognize that they can save money by not living in an on-campus residence hall. It is imperative to consider the viability of the on-campus residency requirement and the high price tag of residence hall living. This may be challenging for the institution because many campuses rely on housing revenue to pay for other campus services. Regardless of the need for campuses to continue mandatory housing requirements for revenue and the benefits that on-campus students might receive from that experience, the financial reality is that some Generation Z students may opt out of college altogether or go somewhere else to avoid the costly fees associated with on-campus living. This may leave not just empty residence halls but empty lecture halls.

Make Healthy Food Options the Norm

Many members of Generation Z care about what they eat. They are aware of the impact of processed food, and they have a desire to eat a more organic and fresh diet. In addition, vegan, vegetarian, gluten-free, and lactose-free diets have been accessible in their upbringing in ways in which they were not for previous generations. The days of traditional fast food are numbered. Generation Z will likely want food cooked to order and meals with a great deal of vegetables and other healthy ingredients. Consider wraps, salads, freshly cooked pastas, stir fry, sandwiches, and options that include fresh vegetables and fruits.

This desire to eat healthy may also be important in their choice to live on or off campus. If the on-campus residences do not have kitchens and students are left to eat at campus dining halls that do not offer what they want to eat, it might not matter how great on-campus living can be. Living off campus in an apartment ensures students a full kitchen in their private residence to cook their own food rather than eating in a dining hall or food court, buying food from a vending machine, or using a microwave in their room. Cooking at home may be both healthier and cheaper, alleviating concerns of both finances and health. It is time to take a good look at swapping out some of the pizza, burgers, and greasy food for healthier options for these students.

Offer Expanded Services

Generation Z students (and those in other generations too) are used to having 24/7 access to resources. Unlike other generations, though, Generation Z has grown up in this culture and knows only a world in which immediate access to a human being who can help is always available. But other than a resident assistant and maybe campus police, students do not have much access to campus services at night or on the weekends. It is not essential to make every service available twenty-four hours a day, yet there are some critical services that might be helpful for students to have greater access to. Think of expanding hours so students can access academic advisors, financial aid specialists, and even librarians when they need help.

Generation Z is in a culture of just-in-time learning, and although it is not a good idea to encourage last-minute inquiries, having more expanded hours might fit better with their work schedules and even how they learn. Some older people might think that this generation can just wait until Monday morning the way everyone else had to when they were in college. But the reality is that everyone, Generation Z included, has access to nearly everything all the time. Higher education is simply behind the times.

Cultivate Generation Z Donors

Securing donors to the institution is often a high priority. Donated funds can pay for new buildings, new initiatives, enhancements to existing programs, and scholarships. To acquire this funding, many campuses launch large-scale campaigns, with the goal of raising millions of dollars by asking local entrepreneurs, past donors, alumni, and friends of the institution to give money. Institutions have come to rely on this funding to pay for endeavors not allocated in the institutional budget.

Understanding Generation Z can shed light on how they will be as donors and how to best engage them in the fundraising process. The mantra is often to engage students while they are in college so they will give back when they graduate. But this donor cultivation may need to start early with Generation Z students, because they might not wait until they are alumni before they give money to the institution. This is a passionate, philanthropic group who may find ways to contribute while they are students. Keep in mind that as savers who are worried about the cost of higher education and thus are financially conservative, they may not give their own money. They may, however, be great at helping to shake the money tree with their crowdsourcing mentality during and after college. They are well versed at setting up online campaigns through fundraising platforms like Kickstarter as well as connecting with their networks through social media. This will serve them well as they can readily generate money from others for campus initiatives.

Also, do not discount them if they do not donate money; they may have other assets they are more willing to give. An architect might offer to design plans for a new campus building at a discounted rate or a car dealer might donate five vans for the motor pool. Generation Z students want to contribute, and institutions could greatly benefit in finding ways to get them connected.

Instructional Strategies: Designing Learning Environments

Learning environments that capitalize on Generation Z's interests and strengths are and should be vastly different from those of other generations. Education is less about the transfer of knowledge from teacher to student and more about helping students make sense of the overabundance of information available to them. How can educators design curriculum and learning environments that capitalize on Generation Z's strengths, styles, and preferences for learning?

Align Learning Outcomes with Industry Standards

Higher education continues to experience budget cuts and scrutiny for its questionable ability to effectively prepare students for the workforce. Some institutions are responding by creating majors that tie to emerging occupations, and higher education as a whole is being held to accountability standards related to career placement. Those in Generation Z might still feel there is a value in a college degree. At some point, though, if they are being priced out or take on soaring student loan debt, not being adequately prepared for their careers, and gaining postcollege employment with low salaries, this generation may stop enrolling.

It is critical to ensure that the learning outcomes of degree programs include both technical and leadership competencies that prepare students to move to a viable career on graduation.[10] This may be easier to do in accredited academic programs because of the need to prove that the program curriculum includes the stated learning outcomes for the program to maintain accreditation. But not all programs have accrediting bodies, making it challenging for institutions to ensure that the program has learning outcomes that are reflective of what might be necessary for graduates in their future occupations. Working with industry partners to develop learning outcomes that match associated career fields is essential in preparing students for the workforce. In addition to integrating industry-specific standards into the curriculum, using the

National Association of Colleges and Employers' nationwide study of what employers look for in college graduates can be a resource for institutions in establishing learning outcomes and designing curriculum to help with career preparation[11]

Integrate a Socially Conscious Curriculum

Knowing what this generation cares about could be useful as colleges develop both curricular and cocurricular programs. To generate interest, engagement, and excitement with this cohort of students, bring in speakers on particular social issues, use case studies of social issues of interest, and consider designing academic programs to be problem-based learning experiences using social issues as the context. Generation Z students want to learn not just for learning's sake, but because they can then use that learning to create social change. Give them the tools and experiences in a context that matters to them and they will likely do big things.

Help Students Effectively Research

Children learn to read and comprehend at a young age. And with mobile devices in their hands early on, they have access to a plethora of content online, much of it user created. This presents a double-edged sword: access to useful and relevant information as well as access to false and noncredible information. As educators and parents teach students how to use the Internet, they must also teach them information literacy. Putting such powerful devices in the hands of students also means having the responsibility to help them understand how to sift through the barrage of information to determine its accuracy.

With nearly infinite amounts of information available to them, how can Generation Z students learn to critically evaluate what information is credible, useful, and appropriate? Although some K-12 schools may integrate information literacy into the curriculum, some first-year students will not have had any exposure by the time they arrive at college. Requiring library training or a college course outside of Writing or English 101 that focuses on effectively researching and properly citing information can help ensure all students have a foundational knowledge of information literacy. These courses and trainings should not be the only experiences students have to learn about information literacy, though. Educators should revisit strategies for effectively researching credible information as it relates to each of their class assignments. This continued focus accentuates the importance of information literacy as both an academic skill and a life skill.

Teach With, Not At

Generation Z students like being consulted by others, and the classroom is no exception. These students want to be involved in the learning process with the instructor and not just be recipients of knowledge. This calls for a more facilitative than authoritative approach to teaching. Instructors who serve as facilitators of learning help students connect their foundational knowledge to applicable situations. Although lecturing may still have a presence in the classroom, instructors will do well to capitalize on the social learning nature of Generation Z students to learn from each other. While this concept is certainly not new, it will be extremely important with this generation of students.

Flip Your Classroom

Traditional classrooms are generally lecture based and incorporate homework as follow-up, whereas flipped classrooms have students do the homework first and then focus only on the application of the content and not a rehashing of it in class. Generation Z has no difficulty finding the knowledge they need; therefore, a lecture that covers introductory information may not be the most effective pedagogy for these students. By flipping a classroom, students learn foundational material on their own before class. They may read an article, watch a video, complete an online module, or do independent research to prepare them for class. When they come to class, they can participate in discussions and activities that help them apply the content they learned before class.[12] By combining the intrapersonal learning approach of individual preclass homework and social learning approach of interactive in-class discussions and activities, flipped classrooms can provide Generation Z students with a pedagogy that aligns seamlessly with how they prefer to learn.

Offer Options for Hybrid Learning

There are ample options for online learning and digital degrees for Generation Z students, and certainly in-person classes are still in abundance. But what about something in between? Institutions can realize cost savings for both instructors and students in meeting less frequently in person. Some students might want to meet face-to-face but at the same time drive their own learning more independently. Similar to the flipped classroom, the concept of hybrid courses opens up the option for students to do some learning on their own through multimedia and then meet periodically in person with the rest of the class, giving them the best of both worlds.

Like flipped classrooms, this method could fit well with Generation Z students' interest in intrapersonal learning because they could independently learn content on their own while also tending to their desire for social learning by meeting face-to-face periodically with their peers. Given that Generation Z students are keeping up on news and social issues, engaging in learning from online video platforms, and seeking out information as they need it simply out of their own personal interest, they would likely enjoy this method of learning, especially if they could earn college credit.

Curb Assignment Binging

Although assignment procrastination well preceded Generation Z, the culture of binge-watching television may exacerbate this old college practice. If a student can stay up all night to watch a season of a television show, then staying up all night to write a twenty-five-page paper due the next day seems possible. The potential overconfidence in being able to effectively complete an assignment in one sitting compounds the procrastination effect because that one sitting is usually just hours before it is due. This is certainly not what an instructor had in mind for intentional learning. Instead of having a paper due at the end of the semester, make a portion of the paper due each week, even if it is only one page, to serve as a milestone. This approach will allow Generation Z students to slow down the bingeing mentality. Maybe they still wait until the night before to complete the last section, but one page versus twenty-five at the end likely will be more manageable and result in higher-quality work.

Reconsider Group Work Expectations

This is a generation of students that likes to work independently yet collaborate, but on their own terms. A pedagogy of lecture followed by discussion might not be the best fit for them. Instead of having a large group discussion or partner discussion following the learning of particular content, consider using think-pair-share,[13] in which the students journal, reflect, or engage in some type of independent work prior to discussing it with others. The idea of having them think without the added discussion piece could work well with Generation Z students because they can make meaning of the content at their own pace and in their own ways.

In addition, reformatting group projects to fit Generation Z could yield more student engagement. Because there are always groans about doing group assignments (even from people in other generations), perhaps reconsidering the design of these types of projects could make them more effective learning experiences. For example, instead of assigning a project and then collecting the final version on the due date, it might be beneficial to require students to separate the assignment into relatively equal portions and each be responsible for a portion. This may mean each person writes two pages of a group paper, or it may be more of a strengths-based approach in which one person is responsible for doing the research, whereas the other two engage in more of the writing. Whatever the expectations are, they should be established in an agreement for all group members to sign and then provided to the instructor.

After the initial draft of the assignment is complete, perhaps have a preset list of group roles such as copyeditor, weaver, and citation checker. Each group member would take on a role and edit and refine the project. This method provides some level of autonomy and independence and allows students to collaborate while using their strengths. This focused attention on the process of group work might lead to better work.

Integrate Modern Learning in the Cocurriculum

Learning takes place in the cocurriculum as well as in the classroom. Consider the many noncredit leadership, service, student success, wellness, and recreational programs offered for students on campus. These programs often require students to attend a series of events, complete required activities or achieve specific milestones. Some programs last one day, whereas others can extend across multiple years. As Generation Z students enter higher education and have different expectations for their college experience, the way that cocurricular programs have been traditionally structured and offered might not align with their interests.

The idea of freestanding in-person workshops and trainings may be the pedagogy of the past. Generation Z students are looking to engage in just-in-time learning where if they want to know about something now, they do not wait until the next workshop to learn it.[14] They can watch TED Talks[15] and YouTube videos, as well as read forums, blogs, and even simple static web pages instead. Therefore, using MOOCs (massive open online courses) rather than planned workshops or trainings might work better with this generation as they can learn on their own time but with campus-created content.

Second, consider bringing technology into the cocurriculum. Instead of personal journals, use blogs and replace workbooks with apps. Finally, because earning credit toward a larger achievement motivates this generation, consider gamification tools like badges. These students do not want another certificate; they want an electronic badge in which they can monitor their progress toward completion, put in their badge collection, and share with others on social media.[16] Many students already earned badges prior to college through their involvement in 4-H, YMCA, and even their schools.[17] Offering badges would be a familiar practice for them.

Programmatic Strategies: Creating Real-World Learning Experiences

Real-world experience can be critical for students to develop essential career skills and build networks in their prospective occupational fields. Most colleges already offer experiential learning for their students in the form of internships, study abroad, and community engagement. These experiences are often not centralized and not guaranteed for any student, meaning that many will not have the chance to participate because of too few opportunities or the challenge in knowing about them. But Generation Z students who question the value of a college education as it relates to getting a good job after graduation will likely find experiential learning one aspect that is a draw to participate in higher education. How can these experiences be expanded to involve more, if not all, students on campus? And are there other forms of experiential learning that could be offered that fit Generation Z's interests?

Expand the Reach of Leadership Development

Many college campuses offer leadership training for students through a retreat, workshop series, cohort program, or conference, for example. These initiatives are excellent ways to integrate leadership development into the college experience. Leadership opportunities are usually housed in a unit in student affairs and are optional for student participation. Those who seek out these experiences, such as former high school student leaders, are arguably not the ones most in need because they have had previous training in leadership. Students who have had no previous exposure to leadership development may not see themselves as leaders and thus opt out of participation when they hear the word *leadership*. To reach these students, consider creating a marketing plan that highlights benefits of participation without using the word *leadership*. And have peer mentors, faculty members, and other student affairs staff recommend students who might otherwise be overlooked by offering a personal invitation to participate.

Engaging students in these experiences is more than just a marketing challenge. With the rising cost of tuition, Generation Z students may skip participating in leadership development, instead choosing to fill their time with paid employment. This may be especially true for students who have the most financial need. Leadership development should not be just an add-on to the college experience, accessible only to those who can afford the cost or time that might be necessary to participate. Because leadership competencies are required of every academic accrediting organization in higher education,[18] it is essential to work leadership development into the framework of the institution. Requiring a general education course on leadership or participation in a menu of leadership opportunities as a graduation requirement for all majors that earn them credit can ensure widespread participation and demonstrate an institutional commitment to develop leaders.

Offer Leadership Experiences That Reflect Reality

Our findings indicate that Generation Z students are highly motivated by their own desire to make a difference for others, not let others down, and advocate for something they believe in. This means they will expect that any meaningful leadership development opportunity they participate in must be connected to something that they care about. For example, to get Generation Z students to attend a conflict negotiation training might mean sharing how this training will help them improve communication with their friends, family, and coworkers to build better relationships.

Everything has to have meaning beyond the surface for these students. Role-plays, simulations, and case studies with fictitious characters and unrealistic circumstances will likely not fare well with them. They have witnessed real-life leadership crises and want to learn leadership in a real-life context, not one made up by educators. Pulling stories from the news, tapping into social issues in real time, and having students reflect on personal issues they face connect better with these students' expectations of learning leadership.

Shift Service-Learning to Social Change

Many campuses have volunteer or community service offices where service-learning takes place. Some are called just that, while others may be referred to as *civic engagement, community involvement,* or *community engagement.* Regardless of the campus, these offices have similarities in that they often offer short-term service projects like a day of service or longer-term connections with community partners, often embedded in a course. Yet Generation Z students are more interested in initiatives that foster sustainable and long-term social change than addressing immediate needs symptomatic of larger societal issues. This means that institutions need to consider offering programs that connect students to experiences that help them address social change. This may be through policy work, entrepreneurial initiatives, and technological innovation. Higher education professionals also must broaden their thinking about what constitutes service and not bind themselves by the image of serving food at a soup kitchen as the only way to make a difference. These students certainly do not.

Offer Student-Selected Community Engagement Experiences

Community engagement experiences can have immense value for student learning and real-world application. Generation Z students, however, are coming into college with ideas about issues they are passionate about and ways they like to engage. If a preset service experience offered through the institution does not resonate with them in terms of the social issue or the method of engagement, gaining their commitment and full participation may be challenging. Consider having students select issues that are important to them rather than being assigned an issue. Even for those who are not clear about an issue they care about, the process of selecting one can be empowering and engaging. And, giving students a choice as to how they want to address that issue, as long as it is helpful to any cause or agency they are working with, might elicit more engagement from them.

In cases in which preset experiences need to be offered, such as pre-planned service trips or volunteer days, it is critical to consider what is important to the students before setting up these experiences. Survey past participants or the whole student body to learn what they are interested in and how they like to engage. In addition, because these students want to turn their passions into careers, getting Generation Z students connected to community engagement opportunities around their interest areas could be a meaningful form of career preparation for them.

Rethink Mandatory Volunteer Requirements

Voluntold is a slang word used when someone is required to volunteer. The philosophy of being voluntold can be seen in high schools and colleges that require students to complete community service for graduation or in the workplace as an employment expectation. This practice is often employed with the good intention of increasing community impact and the goal of encouraging people to continue volunteering on their own after completing requirements.

Given Generation Z students' lack of interest in volunteerism to begin with, these students will likely not take well to strict parameters that reflect being voluntold to serve the community in a particular way or for a particular cause. Opening up the definition of community service or volunteerism to include entrepreneurism, invention, and other engagement opportunities might overcome the reluctance of Generation Z's participation. And since the overarching goal of having these requirements is to help students contribute to their communities, involving them in deciding how that might look could be an empowering and sustainable way for them to continue their engagement beyond the requirements.

Connect Their Passions to Their Practices

Generation Z students are passionate about many social issues but may not know how to adopt lifestyle practices around issues they care deeply about. For example, students concerned about issues of equality and social justice might not know the meaning behind some of the words they use. Providing education on inclusive language might be enlightening for these students. Or a student may be willing to not use a particular product any longer if given more information about where that product comes from. Generation Z students are eager to learn information—they are glued to their phones, after all, for latest updates—so providing more information for them may be exactly what they want. And because these students have a knack for looking at issues and identifying large-scale solutions, they might not readily think of solutions at the individual level. Offering campaigns and programs that help these students make educated decisions about their own behaviors could prove to be beneficial for them in adopting practices that align with their values.

Guarantee Internship Opportunities Early On

Highly concerned about gaining meaningful employment after graduation, Generation Z comes to college focused on getting a job. They are not seeking just any job, but one they are passionate about. Internships provide an opportunity for students to get real-life experience and build important networks to prepare them for their future careers. Yet internships are often aimed at juniors or seniors, which might be too late from a career planning perspective. Helping students get involved in internships in their first year can help them connect to what they are passionate about early on as well as get experience to better prepare them for postcollege employment.

Getting internships is a tricky process, and without a formalized program, more senior students might snatch up available internships. One possibility would be to offer a program that matches first-year and transfer students with career-related internships so they can continue building on that experience throughout college.

Require Experiential Learning

Internships are only one way for students to engage in experiential learning. As Generation Z students blend their passion for particular social issues with their conceptualization of work, many types of engagement experiences could be beneficial for them to gain real-world learning. And if experiential learning is so essential in preparing students for their future careers, then why not make it a requirement? Taking from the cautionary tale of being voluntold, however, the key would be to allow flexibility so that students engage in experiential learning that is meaningful for them. The requirement could include engaging in an experiential learning project of the student's choosing for a minimum number of hours or selecting from a menu of predetermined experiences. Both options could be required for graduation or be offered for academic credit.

Consider the versatility of this approach. For example, a student on a technology innovation team would be able to use this experience to meet the requirement, just as a student who starts up a nonprofit or raises money for a global initiative would. It is critical for higher education to understand that Generation Z students will likely engage in these activities anyway. Having colleges and universities give these students guidance, resources, and credit for doing so can be a win-win for everyone.

Increase Accessibility for Global Experiences

Study abroad offers another type of experiential learning, one in which students experience another culture and make meaning from that experience for themselves. Most campuses offer study-abroad options in which students can spend anywhere from a week to a semester or longer in another country while taking classes. Generation Z's open-mindedness and thirst for diversity has primed them for this opportunity, which is why it is not surprising that more than one-third of them believe there is a "very good chance that they will study abroad"[19] and 55 percent want to study or live abroad during their lifetimes.[20] Keep in mind, however, that students who indicate a likelihood of studying abroad are more likely to come from more affluent backgrounds.[21] Therefore, it is critical for institutions to find ways to make these experiences financially accessible for all students (e.g., through scholarships and exchanges instead of study abroad). For campuses that have financial assistance available, disseminating information about it is important, because many lower-income students may have written off study abroad as being only for wealthier students.

Offer Social Entrepreneurship Courses
for Nonbusiness Majors

Nearly two-thirds of Generation Z students believe that colleges should offer courses on how to start a business.[22] But these types of courses are often offered exclusively to students in business schools. What about students in other academic programs who might want to start their own businesses—for example, the dance major who plans to open a studio or the environmental science major who wants to start a nonprofit? Generation Z students are interested in working for themselves and combining their desire to do so with their passion for social issues can lead to a fulfilling career.

Colleges need to better equip these students to be successful entrepreneurs regardless of their major as these students may end up attempting to start their own businesses whether colleges offer courses or not. They would certainly be better prepared if they could learn effective entrepreneurial strategies as a part of their college education.

Create Opportunities for Real-Life Problem Solving

Generation Z students crave solving problems[23] and see themselves as inventors[24] and entrepreneurs.[25] Why not provide a pool of funds for students to pitch their ideas for campus improvement initiatives? Think of it as an empowering, nonaggressive version of *Shark Tank*.[26] Students could get funding to start up and run a coffee stop at a busy corner on campus, create an app for incoming students, or develop a first-year-retention program. With support from the institution, students could engage in real-world learning on campus and potentially solve institutional issues in the process.

In addition, institutions could fare well by bringing Generation Z students into serious conversations on such topics as budget cuts and campus policies. If there are formal ways to include them as voting members of governance and decision-making groups beyond the one token representative, administrators may find that Generation Z students can offer fresh perspectives and creative ideas.

Help Students Engage in Microfinancing

Generation Z students have passion and want to make a profound difference, so providing them with opportunities to engage in microfinancing could prove to be a good investment. Online microfinancing platforms make it easy for students to connect with real entrepreneurs to provide short-term start-up loans.

Consider creating a program or course that teaches students fundraising strategies and then have them raise money to fund real entrepreneurial initiatives around the world. As they consider which entrepreneurs they want to fund, they can gain a better understanding of what they care about and what makes a strong entrepreneurial initiative.

Developmental Strategies: Building Student Capacity

The Association of American Colleges & Universities, in its support of a liberal education in college, emphasizes that students should engage in learning that prepares them to apply knowledge and skills to deal with the complexity of the real world.[27]

The desire for real-world preparation is echoed by more than one-third of business leaders who believe that higher education does not adequately help students develop critical skills necessary for the workplace.[28] Thus, it is imperative that colleges focus on more than developing students' technical competencies in an academic discipline, but also prepare them to be effective members of the workforce and contributing members of society. To do this, students need to develop their professional competencies through learning and engagement opportunities. What strategies might help Generation Z students in their capacity development and professional preparation?

Help Students Create Value-Based Goals

It is hard to imagine a student success class, leadership program, or academic workshop that does not somehow integrate goal setting. Students are taught how to create goals, and they usually end up developing goals during these sessions. But do the students remember their goals one year out, six weeks out, or even two weeks out? And if they cannot recall them, they likely are not working toward achieving them.

Goal setting with Generation Z students provides a unique opportunity, especially when it comes to setting career-related goals. Remember that most Generation Z students want to have a positive impact on the world through their careers.[29] So instead of asking these students to select their future career field and then set goals, consider having them create destiny statements that help them do deep reflection on their values, passions, beliefs, and life calling.[30] In addition to providing an opportunity for meaning making for students, having them explore their destinies can help them determine a powerful vision for their futures. Armed with their destiny statements and ultimately their visions, Generation Z students can develop goals that they are likely to remember and even enact because they tie directly to what they believe they are called to do.

Cultivate Informed Opinions and Educated Actions

This generation cares about a number of social issues and certainly keeps up with national and world news. But if Generation Z students lack information literacy, then what information are they consuming in these news stories? Are they drawing their opinions from blogs and forums or are they accessing legitimate research? Helping Generation Z students turn their passions and beliefs into informed opinions will help them be able to engage in educated actions. This may involve sharing with them a variety of news media sites, some of which are more conservative and others that are more liberal to showcase multiple sides of an issue. It is also critical to help them access sources that are research based, like articles on Google Scholar[31] or their library journal search engines, as well as having them challenge the legitimacy of all sources they gather to interpret any underlying biases. These might be great topics to include in an information literacy course. Not only can being information literate help with their academic performance, they can use these skills to better understand social issues, empowering them to stand behind their informed and educated opinions.

Provide Education on Financial Literacy

Consider the many credit card offers students receive once in college and opportunities to use a meal plan to purchase just about anything without noticing the price. Although we found that Generation Z students are financially conservative, their saver mentality does not necessarily mean they are financially literate.[32] Students may not know how to put together a budget, manage a bank account, or wisely use credit. Offering personal financial management sessions can provide students access to the knowledge they need to manage their money effectively.

Focus on Intentional Leadership Competency Development

Leadership development opportunities are often optional cocurricular experiences not held to the same institutional standards of having explicit measurable learning outcomes like an accredited academic program might have. These experiences can also be perceived as, and sometimes are, feel-good experiences that have a smattering of leadership learning that does not follow an intentional and cohesive larger curriculum. Consider designing cocurricular leadership development opportunities to mirror the higher education trend of competency-based learning.[33] To do this, each leadership experience would be designed to intentionally foster the development of specific leadership competencies reflective of a theoretical framework, academic accrediting agency,[34] or the institutional strategic plan. In addition, each experience would employ measurement strategies to effectively evaluate competency development in students who participate. This intentional approach can prepare students as leaders and help them better articulate and quantify for future employers the specific leadership competencies they have developed.

Technological Strategies: Using the Right Social Media

With so many social media platforms available and new ones being added every day, it is hard to keep up. So when is it best to use Twitter rather than Facebook? How about Instagram or YouTube?

Face It and Embrace It

Generation Z students are knowledgeable, skilled, and reliant on technology.[35] Ninety percent said they would be upset if they had to give up their access to the Internet in general, and three in four said they would be upset if they could not use their phone or text their friends.[36] To Generation Z, social media and technology are tools to get things accomplished. They come to class with their laptops and phones searching the Internet and trying not to disconnect even for the short time they may be in class.

Instead of viewing this constant technology use as a distraction, as many individuals in older generations may, try to embrace it as a learning tool and avenue for accomplishment. This has the potential to build a relationship between educators and students reflective of trust ("we learn together") rather than one that is conferred through power alone ("I am the expert").[37] Consider incorporating technology use into class time by offering a topic and asking everyone to search online to find out as much information as they can to report out. This approach guides students' use of technology during class toward an intentional and meaningful learning experience and helps them develop information literacy skills rather than trying to compete for their attention. As much as higher education must face it and embrace it with technology, so must Generation Z students in knowing when to turn it off.

Be Wary of the "Do Not Enter" Sign

Social media is changing how Generation Z students manage their familial and peer relationships. This brings up important questions in regard to using social media with these students. The term *creepy tree house* has been used to describe what happens when adults and authority figures enter the social networking space that was previously used for peers to connect with each other.[38] Should higher education professionals enter the adult-free zones of Generation Z students as a way to connect? Probably not: the last thing Generation Z students want is the dean of students following them on Twitter. In this situation, students will likely move to different platforms to maintain sacred space free from adults.

Do Not Be All Platforms to All People

For older generations that have had to adapt to the digital world, trying to stay up-to-date in understanding how to use different social media platforms creates another level of difficulty in an already tricky game. When connecting with Generation Z, it may be helpful to choose one or two platforms that will align most with the purpose in using social media in the first place. Is it to help connect with students? Facebook might be a better option than e-mail for ongoing individual messaging and group announcements. Twitter might be ideal to connect only throughout the duration of one distinct event (e.g., "Follow us on Twitter during the conference"). Want to use social media to provide information? Consider a YouTube channel for your program, office, or department. Want to attract students to your programs and services? Instagram might be a good choice. Attempting to be active on all platforms will take a great deal of time and effort, whereas focusing on one or two platforms based on specific outcomes can lead to more effective and engaging content creation.

Conclusion

Generation Z students are in many ways like every other generation before and yet vastly different at the same time. Nevertheless, there are clues to help uncover how to best engage these students in higher education. And one day in the future, they will be writing books about "kids these days."

Notes

1. Apple. (2015a). *FaceTime*. Retrieved from https://www.apple.com/ios/facetime/

2. Somers, P., & Settle, J. (2010). The helicopter parent: Research toward a typology. *College and University: The Journal of the American Association of Collegiate Registrars, 86*(1), 18–27.

3. Eagan, K., Stolzenberg, E. B., Ramirez, J. J., Aragon, M. C., Suchard, M. R., & Hurtado, S. (2014*). The American freshman: National norms fall 2014*. Los Angeles: Higher Education Research Institute.

4. Pachal, P. (2014). *How the #YesAllWomen hashtag began.* Retrieved from http://mashable.com/2014/05/26/yesallwomen-hashtag/

5. Bain, S. F. (2014). Making the most of available resources within a college counseling center. *Journal of Behavioral Studies in Business, 7,* 1–7.

6. Eagan et al. (2014).

7. Bundy, A. P., & Benshoff, J. M. (2000). Research: Students' perceptions of need for personal counseling services in community colleges. *Journal of College Counseling, 3*(2), 92–99.

8. Bain, S. F. (2014).

9. Eagan et al. (2014).

10. For more information about leadership competencies required of accredited academic programs, go to the Jossey-Bass Student Leadership Competencies website: http://www.wiley.com/WileyCDA/Section/id-818224.html

11. National Association of Colleges and Employers. (2014). *The skills/qualities employers want in new college graduate hires.* Retrieved from http://www.naceweb.org/about-us/press/class-2015-skills-qualities-employers-want.aspx

12. Knewton. (2015). *The flipped classroom infographic.* Retrieved from http://www.knewton.com/flipped-classroom/

13. Lyman, F. T. (1981). The responsive classroom discussion: The inclusion of all students. In A. Anderson (Ed.), *Mainstreaming digest* (pp. 109–113). College Park: University of Maryland Press.

14. Kapil, Y., & Roy, A. (2014). A critical evaluation of Generation Z at workplaces. *International Journal of Social Relevance and Concern, 2*(1), 10–14.

15. Ted. (2015). *Our organization*. Retrieved from https://www.ted.com/about/our-organization

16. Mozilla. (2015a). *Get recognition for skills you learn anywhere*. Retrieved from http://openbadges.org/

17. Mozilla. (2015b). *Participating issuers*. Retrieved from http://openbadges.org/participating-issuers/

18. Seemiller, C. (2013). *The student leadership competencies guidebook*. San Francisco: Jossey-Bass.

19. Eagan et al. (2014).

20. Northeastern University. (2014). *Innovation survey*. Retrieved from www.northeastern.edu/news/2014/11/innovation-imperative-meet-generation-z/

21. Northeastern University. (2014).

22. Northeastern University. (2014).

23. Anatole, E. (2013). *Generation Z: Rebels with a cause*. Retrieved from http://www.forbes.com/sites/onmarketing/2013/05/28/generation-z-rebels-with-a-cause/

24. Gallup & Operation Hope. (2013). *The 2013 Gallup-Hope Index*. Retrieved from www.operationhope.org/images/uploads/Files/2013galluphopereport.pdf

25. Northeastern University. (2014).

26. ABC. (2015). *About Shark Tank*. Retrieved from http://abc.go.com/shows/shark-tank/about-the-show

27. Association of American Colleges and Universities. (2015). *What is 21st century liberal education?* Retrieved from http://www.aacu.org

28. Sidhu, P., & Calderon, V. J. (2014). *Many business leaders doubt U.S. colleges prepare students*. Retrieved from http://www.gallup.com/poll/167630/business-leaders-doubt-colleges-prepare-students.aspx

29. Sparks & Honey. (2014). *Meet Gen Z: Forget everything you learned about Millennials*. Retrieved from www.slideshare.net/sparksandhoney/generation-z-final-june-17

30. Secretan, L. (2004). *Inspire! What great leaders do*. San Francisco: Wiley.

31. Google Scholar. (2015). *About*. Retrieved from https://scholar.google.com/intl/en-US/scholar/about.html

32. Intelligence Group. (2013). *Cassandra report*. Retrieved from www.cassandra.co/report/

33. Kamenetz, A. (2015). *Competency-based degree programs on the rise*. Retrieved from http://www.npr.org/blogs/ed/2015/01/26/379387136/competency-based-degree-programs-on-the-rise

34. Seemiller, C. (2013).

35. JWT Intelligence. (2012). *Gen Z: Digital in their DNA study*. Retrieved from www.jwtintelligence.com/wp-content/uploads/2012/04/F_INTERNAL_Gen_Z_0418122.pdf

36. JWT Intelligence. (2012).

37. Koulopoulos, T., & Keldsen, D. (2014). *The Gen Z effect: The six forces shaping the future of business.* Brookline, MA: Bibliomotion.

38. O'Shea, K. (2009). *Creepy treehouse effect-How do we social network in higher ed?* Retrieved from https://www.purdue.edu/learning/blog/?p=210

REFERENCES

Abbruzzese, J. (2014). *The rise and fall of AIM, the breakthrough AOL never wanted*. Retrieved from http://mashable.com/2014/04/15/aim-history/

ABC. (2015). *About Shark Tank*. Retrieved from http://abc.go.com/shows/shark-tank/about-the-show

Abrams, R. (2014). *Short-lived science line from Lego for girls*. Retrieved from http://www.nytimes.com/2014/08/22/business/short-lived-science-line-from-lego-for-girls.html?_r=0

Accion. (2015). *What we do*. Retrieved from https://www.accion.org/what-we-do

Achieve. (2013). *The 2013 Millennial impact report*. Retrieved from http://casefoundation.org/wp-content/uploads/2014/11/MillennialImpactReport-2013.pdf

Adecco Staffing USA. (2015). *Generation Z vs. Millennials*. Retrieved from http://pages.adeccousa.com/rs/107-IXF-539/images/generation-z-vs-millennials.pdf

Aghaei, S., Nematbakhsh, M. A., & Farsani, H. K. (2012). Evolution of the World Wide Web: From Web 1.0 to Web

4.0. *International Journal of Web and Semantic Technology*, 3(1), 1–10.

Airbnb. (2015). *About us.* Retrieved from https://www.airbnb .com/about/about-us

Alex's Lemonade Stand Foundation. (2015). *Alex's lemonade stand.* Retrieved from http://www.alexslemonade.org/

Almasy, S. (2014). *Michael Phelps suspended by USA Swimming for six months.* Retrieved from http://edition.cnn.com/2014/10/ 06/sport/michael-phelps-suspended/

Amazon. (2015). *About Amazon.* Retrieved from http://www .amazonfulfillmentcareers.com/about-amazon/

America Online. (2015). *About AOL.* Retrieved from http:// corp.aol.com/about-aol

Anatole, E. (2013). *Generation Z: Rebels with a cause.* Retrieved from http://www.forbes.com/sites/onmarketing/2013/05/28/ generation-z-rebels-with-a-cause/

Anderson, W. (2014). Taking their ball and going home. *Wake Up Quarterly: A Strategic Intelligence Report: Generation Z, 25–26.* Retrieved from http://issuu.com/thisisomelet/docs/ omelet_intelligence_report_genz/27

Anti-Defamation League. (2014). *What is the DREAM Act and who are the DREAMers?* Retrieved from http://www.adl.org/ assets/pdf/education-outreach/what-is-the-dream-act-and- who-are-the-dreamers.pdf

Apple. (2015a). *About SIRI*. Retrieved from https://support
.apple.com/en-us/HT204389

Apple. (2015b). *FaceTime*. Retrieved from https://www.apple
.com/ios/facetime/

Apple. (2015b). *Maps*. Retrieved from https://www.apple.com/
ios/maps/

Arnett, J. J., & Schwab, J. (2013). *The Clark University poll of
parents of emerging adults*. Retrieved from http://www.clarku
.edu/clark-poll-emerging-adults/pdfs/clark-university-poll-
parents-emerging-adults.pdf

ASHOKA. (2015). *About us*. Retrieved from https://www
.ashoka.org/about

Association of American Colleges and Universities. (2015).
What is 21st century liberal education? Retrieved from http://
www.aacu.org

Bain, S. F. (2014). Making the most of available resources within
a college counseling center. *Journal of Behavioral Studies in Business, 7,* 1–7.

Barbash, F. (2014, August 9). Chick-fil-A founder dies. Built
chain from one small restaurant. Provoked controversy on gay-
marriage. *Washington Post*. Retrieved from http://www
.washingtonpost.com/news/morning-mix/wp/2014/09/
08/chick-fil-a-founder-dies-built-chain-from-one-small-
restaurant-provoked-controversy-on-gay-marriage/

Bell, S. (2010). Project-based learning for the 21st century: Skills
for the future. *Clearing House, 83,* 39–43.

Beres, D. (2014). *Half of all adult Americans now admit to binge-watching TV.* Retrieved from http://www.huffingtonpost.com/2014/12/11/binge-watching_n_6310056.html

Berk, R. A. (2009). Multimedia teaching with video clips: TV, movies, YouTube, and mtvU in the college classroom. *International Journal of Technology in Teaching and Learning,* 5(1), 1–21.

Berland, E. (2013). *Barriers to creativity in education: Educators and parents grade the system.* Retrieved from http://www.adobe.com/content/dam/Adobe/en/education/pdfs/barriers-to-creativity-in-education-study.pdf

Bixler, B. A. (N.d.). *A multiple intelligences primer.* Retrieved from http://www.personal.psu.edu/bxb11/MI/MultipleIntelligences_print.html

Blizzard Entertainment. (2015). *What is World of Warcraft?* Retrieved from http://us.battle.net/wow/en/game/guide/

Blogger. (2015). *The story of Blogger.* Retrieved from https://www.blogger.com/about

Board of Governors of the Federal Reserve System. (2013). *Survey of consumer finances.* Retrieved from http://www.federalreserve.gov/econresdata/scf/scfindex.htm

Bronson, P., & Merryman, A. (2010). *The creativity crisis.* Retrieved from http://www.newsweek.com/creativity-crisis-74665

Bruzzese, A. (2013). *On the job: New generation is arriving in the workplace*. Retrieved from www.usatoday.com/story/money/columnist/bruzzese/2013/10/20/on-the-job-generation-z/2999689/

Buahene, A., & Kovary, G. (2003). *The road to performance success: Understanding and managing the generational divide*. Toronto, ON: n-gen People Performance.

Buchanan, L., Fessenden, F., Lai, K.K.R., Park, H., Parlapiano, A., Tse, A., ... Yourish, K. (2014, August 13). What happened in Ferguson? *New York Times*. Retrieved from http://www.nytimes.com/interactive/2014/08/13/us/ferguson-missouri-town-under-siege-after-police-shooting.html

Buckingham, M., & Clifton, D. (2001). *Now, discover your strengths*. New York: Free Press.

Bundy, A. P., & Benshoff, J. M. (2000). Research: Students' perceptions of need for personal counseling services in community colleges. *Journal of College Counseling, 3*(2), 92–99.

Burkus, D. (2011). Building the strong organization: Exploring the role of organizational design in strengths-based leadership. *Journal of Strategic Leadership, 3*(1), 54–66.

Businessballs.com. (N.d.). *Kolb learning styles*. Retrieved from http://www.businessballs.com/kolblearningstyles.htm

Buzzfeed. (2015). *About*. Retrieved from http://www.buzzfeed.com/about

Centers for Disease Control and Prevention. (2013a). *Cigarette smoking among US high school students at lowest level in 22 years*. Retrieved from www.cdc.gov/media/releases/2014/ p0612-YRBS.html

Centers for Disease Control and Prevention. (2013b). *Hispanic or Latino populations*. Retrieved from http://www.cdc .gov/minorityhealth/populations/REMP/hispanic.html

Chick-fil-A. (2015). *Company fact sheet*. Retrieved from http:// www.chick-fil-a.com/Company/Highlights-Fact-Sheets

Ciulla, J. B. (2004). Ethics and leadership effectiveness. In J. Antonakis, A. T. Cianciolo, & R. J. Sternberg (Eds.), *The nature of leadership* (pp. 302–312). Thousand Oaks, CA: Sage.

CNN. (2015). *About CNN.com*. Retrieved from http://www.cnn .com/about

College Board. (2014). *Trends in college pricing 2014*. Retrieved from http://trends.collegeboard.org/sites/default/files/2014- trends-college-pricing-final-web.pdf

Collins, S. (2008). *The hunger games*. New York: Scholastic Press.

Cornell University Law School. (2015). *First Amendment*. Retrieved from www.law.cornell.edu/constitution/first_ amendment

Craigslist. (2015). *Factsheet*. Retrieved from https://www .craigslist.org/about/factsheet

Davidson, P. (2014). US economy regains all jobs lost in recession. Retrieved from http://www.usatoday.com/story/money/business/2014/06/06/may-jobs-report/10037173/

Dawson, A. (2014). *Generation Z (or is that Edge?) shows a fluid sense of style.* Retrieved from http://www.latimes.com/fashion/la-ig-edge-generation-20141102-story.html#page=1

Dickey, M. R. (2013). *The 22 key turning points in the history of YouTube.* Retrieved from http://www.businessinsider.com/key-turning-points-history-of-youtube-2013-2?op=1

Digital History. (2015). *Overview of the post-war era.* Retrieved from http://www.digitalhistory.uh.edu/era.cfm?eraID=16

Digital Information World. (2014). *#SocialMedia 2014: User demographics for Facebook, Twitter, Instagram, and Pinterest -#infographic.* Retrieved from www.digitalinformationworld.com/2014/10/social-media-user-demographics-linkedin-tumblr-facebook-and-more-infographic.html

Duggan, M. & Smith, A. (2013). *Social media update 2013.* Retrieved from http://www.pewinternet.org/2013/12/30/social-media-update-2013/

Duggan, M., Ellison, N. B., Lampfe, C., Lenhart, A., & Madden, M. (2015). *Social media update 2014.* Retrieved from http://www.pewinternet.org/2015/01/09/social-media-update-2014/

Dutta, S., & Fraser, M. (2008). *Barack Obama and the Facebook election.* Retrieved from http://www.usnews.com/opinion/articles/2008/11/19/barack-obama-and-the-facebook-election

E! (2015). *Keeping up with the Kardashians.* Retrieved from http://www.eonline.com/shows/kardashians

Eagan, K., Stolzenberg, E. B., Ramirez, J. J., Aragon, M. C., Suchard, M. R., & Hurtado, S. (2014). *The American freshman: National norms fall 2014.* Los Angeles: Higher Education Research Institute.

eBay. (2015). *Who we are.* Retrieved from http://www.ebayinc .com/who_we_are/one_company

eBay Classifieds. (2015). *About us.* Retrieved from http://www .ebayclassifieds.com/m/About

Educause. (2015). *What is a MOOC?* Retrieved from http:// www.educause.edu/library/massive-open-online-course-mooc

Ekins, E. (2014). *65% of Americans say Millennials are "entitled," 58% of Millennials agree.* Retrieved from http://reason.com/ poll/2014/08/19/65-of-americans-say-millennials-are-enti

Elam, C., Stratton, T., & Gibson, D. D. (2007). Welcoming a new generation to college: The Millennial students. *Journal of College Admission, 195,* 20–25.

Elfman, L. (2012). *Flexible workplace is great for employees—and the companies they work for?* Retrieved from http:// www.huffingtonpost.com/2012/11/20/flexible-workplace-employees-companies_n_2165727.html

eMarketer. (2014). *How elusive is Generation Z after all?* Retrieved from http://www.emarketer.com/Article/How-

Elusive-Generation-Z-After-All/1011466#sthash.ex9GqfVz
.dpuf

Encyclopaedia Britannica. (2015a). *Dewey Decimal Classification*. Retrieved from http://www.britannica.com/science/Dewey-Decimal-Classification

Encyclopaedia Brittanica. (2015b). Don't ask, don't tell (DADT). Retrieved from http://www.britannica.com/event/Dont-Ask-Dont-Tell

Ennis, S. R., Rios-Vargas, M., & Albert, N. G. (2010). *The Hispanic population: 2010*. Retrieved from http://www.census.gov/prod/cen2010/briefs/c2010br-04.pdf

Etsy. (2015). *About Etsy*. Retrieved from https://www.etsy.com/about/?ref=ftr

Euromonitor International. (2011). *Make way for generation Z: Marketing for today's teens and tweens*. Retrieved from http://oaltabo2012.files.wordpress.com/2012/03/make-way-for-generation-z1.pdf

Evangelista, B. (2009). *Attention loss feared as high-tech rewires brains*. Retrieved from http://www.sfgate.com/business/article/Attention-loss-feared-as-high-tech-rewires-brain-3281030.php

Facebook. (2012). *Form S-1 registration statement: Letter from Mark Zuckerberg*. Washington DC: Facebook.

Facebook. (2015a). *About Facebook*. Retrieved from https://www.facebook.com/facebook/info?tab=page_info

Facebook. (2015b). *Company history*. Retrieved from http://newsroom.fb.com/company-info/

Facebook. (2015c). *Games overview*. Retrieved from developers.facebook.com/docs/games/overview

Farsides, T., & Pettman, D. (2013). Inspiring altruism: Reflecting on the personal relevance of emotionally evocative prosocial media characters. *Journal of Applied Social Psychology*, 43(11), 2251–2258.

Fiegerman, S. (2014). *Instagram tops 300 million active users, likely bigger than Twitter*. Retrieved from http://mashable.com/2014/12/10/instagram-300-million-users/

FindLaw. (2015). *States that have stand your ground laws*. Retrieved from http://criminal.findlaw.com/criminal-law-basics/states-that-have-stand-your-ground-laws.html

Fitterman, S. (2013). *The ultimate debate: Online shopping vs. brick and mortar shopping*. Retrieved from http://insights.wired.com/profiles/blogs/the-ultimate-debate-online-shopping-vs-brick-and-mortar-shopping#axzz3eSZsFwHC

Fitzpatrick, L. (2010, May 31). *Brief history YouTube*. Retrieved from http://content.time.com/time/magazine/article/0,9171,1990787,00.html.

Flipboard. (2015). *About us*. Retrieved from https://about.flipboard.com/about-us/

Freelancers Union and Elance oDesk. (2014). *Freelancing in America: A national survey of the new workforce*. Retrieved from http://fu-web-storage-prod.s3.amazonaws.com/content/ filer_public/c2/06/c2065a8a-7f00-46db-915a-2122965df7d9/ fu_freelancinginamericareport_v3-rgb.pdf

Frosch, D. & Johnson, K. (2012, July 21). Gunman kills 12 in Colorado, reviving gun debate. *New York Times*. Retrieved from http://www.nytimes.com/2012/07/21/us/shooting-at-colorado-theater-showing-batman-movie.html?_r=0

Fry, R. (2015). *This year, Millennials will overtake Baby Boomers*. Retrieved from http://www.pewresearch.org/fact-tank/2015/01/16/this-year-millennials-will-overtake-baby-boomers/

Furham, A., & Bradley, A. (1997). Music while you work: The differential distraction of background music on the cognitive test performance of introverts and extroverts. *Applied Cognitive Psychology*, 11(5), 445–455.

Galley, L. (2014). *Generation Z: A world gone cyber*. Retrieved from www.huffingtonpost.com/lauren-galley/generation-z-a-world-gone_b_6349074.html

Gallup & Operation Hope. (2013). *The 2013 Gallup-Hope Index*. Retrieved from www.operationhope.org/images/uploads/Files/2013galluphopereport.pdf

Gallup. (2015a). *Gallup strengths center*. Retrieved from https://www.gallupstrengthscenter.com/

Gallup. (2015b). *StrengthsQuest*. Retrieved from http://www.strengthsquest.com/content/141728/index.aspx

Gardner, H. (1993). *Multiple intelligences: The theory in practice*. New York: Basic Books.

Gargis, J., & Gray, B. (2014). *Two people shot at midtown movie theater*. Retrieved from http://www.ajc.com/news/news/local/2-people-shot-at-midtown-movie-theater/njZYQ/

Garrett, R. S. (2013). *Super PACs in federal elections: Overview and issues for Congress*. Retrieved from https://www.fas.org/sgp/crs/misc/R42042.pdf

Gaudiosi, J. (2012). *New reports forecast global video game industry will reach $82 billion by 2017*. Retrieved from www.forbes.com/sites/johngaudiosi/2012/07/18/new-reports-forecasts-global-video-game-industry-will-reach-82-billion-by-2017/

Giuliano, K. (2015). *YouTube turns 10 today*. Retrieved from http://www.cnbc.com/id/102611949

Glass, A. (2013). *Occupy Wall Street began, Sept. 17, 2011*. Retrieved from http://www.politico.com/story/2013/09/this-day-in-politics-96859.html

Glassner, B. (2010). *The culture of fear*. New York: Basic Books.

Glenn, H. (2013). *Losing our religion: The growth of the "nones."* Retrieved from http://www.npr.org/blogs/thetwo-way/2013/01/14/169164840/losing-our-religion-the-growth-of-the-nones

GoFundMe. (2015). *How it works*. Retrieved from http://www.gofundme.com/tour/

Goodbread, C. (2014). *Michael Sam, NFL draft prospect, announces he's gay*. Retrieved from http://www.nfl.com/news/story/0ap2000000324603/article/michael-sam-nfl-draft-prospect-announces-hes-gay

Google. (2015a). *About Google*. Retrieved from http://www.google.com/about/

Google. (2015b). *Docs*. Retrieved from https://www.google.com/docs/about/

Google Maps. (2015). *About*. Retrieved from http://www.google.com/maps/about/

Google Scholar. (2015). *About*. Retrieved from https://scholar.google.com/intl/en-US/scholar/about.html

Gordon, T. (2012). *State and local budgets and the Great Recession*. Retrieved from http://www.brookings.edu/research/articles/2012/12/state-local-budgets-gordon

Gore, A. (2006). *An inconvenient truth*. New York: Rodale Books.

Grail Research (2011). *Consumers of tomorrow*. Retrieved from www.grailresearch.com/pdf/ContenPodsPdf/Consumers_of_Tomorrow_Insights_and_Observations_About_Generation_Z.pdf

Grohol, J. M. (2011). *FOMO addiction: The fear of missing out*. Retrieved from http://psychcentral.com/blog/archives/2011/04/14/fomo-addiction-the-fear-of-missing-out/

Gross, G. (2014). *How boys and girls learn differently*. Retrieved from http://www.huffingtonpost.com/dr-gail-gross/how-boys-and-girls-learn-differently_b_5339567.html

HackerLab. (2015). *About*. Retrieved from http://hackerlab.org/about/

Harris, D. (2009). *Young Americans losing their religion*. Retrieved from http://abcnews.go.com/Politics/story?id=7513343

Harry Potter Alliance. (2015a). *Chapters*. Retrieved from thehpalliance.org

Harry Potter Alliance. (2015b). *Home*. Retrieved from thehpalliance.org

Hayghe, H. (1981). *Husbands and wives as earners: An analysis of family data*. Retrieved from http://www.bls.gov/opub/mlr/1981/02/art5full.pdf

Heifetz, R., Linsky, M., & Grashow, A. (2009). *The practice of adaptive leadership: Tools and tactics for changing your organization and the world*. Boston: Harvard Business Press.

Hempel, J. (2013). *Are teens fleeing Facebook or not?* Retrieved from http://fortune.com/2013/07/31/are-teens-fleeing-facebook-or-not/

Heneghan, T. (2012). *"No Religion" is world's third-largest religious group after Christians, Muslims according to Pew study*. Retrieved from http://www.huffingtonpost.com/2012/12/18/

unaffiliated-third-largest-religious-group-after-christians-muslims_n_2323664.html

Henseler, C. (2014). *Generation X: What's in the label?* Retrieved from http://www.huffingtonpost.com/christine-henseler/generation-x-whats-in-the_b_5390568.html

Hersey, P., Blanchard, K. H., & Johnson, D. E. (2012). *Management of organizational behavior: Leading human resources.* Upper Saddle River, NJ: Prentice Hall.

Hill, K. (2013). *Vine, Instagram and the appeal of apps that turn us into artists.* Retrieved from www.forbes.com/sites/kashmirhill/2013/01/25/vine-instagram-and-the-appeal-of-apps-that-turn-us-into-artists

History.com. (2010). *Baby Boomers.* Retrieved from http://www.history.com/topics/baby-boomers

History.com. (2015). *Boston Marathon bombings.* Retrieved from http://www.history.com/topics/boston-marathon-bombings

Hixon, L., Hepler, B. B., & Kim, M. O. (2011). *The white population: 2010.* Retrieved from http://www.census.gov/prod/cen2010/briefs/c2010br-05.pdf

Hsaio, A. (2015). *How did eBay start?* Retrieved from http://ebay.about.com/od/ebaylifestyle/a/el_history.htm

Hulu. (2015). *About.* Retrieved from http://www.hulu.com/about

IBM. (2015). *What is big data?* Retrieved from http://www-01
.ibm.com/software/data/bigdata/what-is-big-data.html

IMDB. (1957). *Leave It to Beaver plot summary.* Retrieved from
http://www.imdb.com/title/tt0050032/plotsummary

IMDB. (1995). *Toy Story plot summary.* Retrieved from http://
www.imdb.com/title/tt0114709/plotsummary

IMDB. (2006). *An Inconvenient Truth plot summary.* Retrieved
from http://www.imdb.com/title/tt0497116/plotsummary

IMDB. (2008). *Food, Inc. plot summary.* Retrieved from http://
www.imdb.com/title/tt1286537/plotsummary

IMDB. (2012). *21 Jump Street plot summary.* Retrieved from
http://www.imdb.com/title/tt1232829/plotsummary

IMDB. (2012). *The Hunger Games plot summary.* Retrieved
from http://www.imdb.com/title/tt1392170/plotsummary

IMDB. (1999). *Law & Order: Special Victims Unit plot summary.* Retrieved from http://www.imdb.com/title/tt0203259/
plotsummary

Instagram. (2015). *About us.* Retrieved from https://instagram
.com/about/us/?hl=en

Institute of Medicine. (2013). *Educating the student body: Taking
physical activity and physical education to school.* Retrieved from
http://www.iom.edu/~/media/Files/Report%20Files/2013/
Educating-the-Student-Body/EducatingTheStudentBody_rb
.pdf

Intelligence Group. (2013). *Cassandra report*. Retrieved from www.cassandra.co/report/

International Health, Racquet, and Sportsclub Association. (2011). *US health club membership exceeds 50 million*. Retrieved from www.ihrsa.org/news/2011/4/5/us-health-club-membership-exceeds-50-million-up-108-industry.html

Investopedia. (N.d.). *Sharing economy*. Retrieved from http://www.investopedia.com/terms/s/sharing-economy.asp

Ipsos MediaCT. (2013). *Generation Z: A look at the technology and media habits of today's teens*. Retrieved from http://www.wikia.com/Generation_Z:_A_Look_at_the_Technology_and_Media_Habits_of_Today%E2%80%99s_Teens

Jackson, J., & Gouseti, I. (2014). Fear of crime and the psychology of risk. In G. Bruinsma & D. Weisburd (Eds.), *Encyclopedia of criminology and criminal justice* (pp. 1594–1603). New York: Springer.

Jacques, A. (2012). *Parlaying Pinterest: What you need to know about virtual pinboards*. Retrieved from www.prsa.org/Intelligence/Tactics/Articles/view/9744/1048/Parlaying_Pinterest_What_you_need_to_know_about_vi#.VSRyUfnF-4Y

Jones, A. M. *Historical divorce rate statistics*. Retrieved from http://divorce.lovetoknow.com/Historical_Divorce_Rate_Statistics

Jones, N. A., & Bullock, J. (2012). *The two or more races population: 2010*. Retrieved from https://www.census.gov/prod/cen2010/briefs/c2010br-13.pdf

JWT Intelligence. (2012). *Gen Z: Digital in their DNA.* Retrieved from http://www.jwtintelligence.com/wp-content/uploads/2012/04/F_INTERNAL_Gen_Z_0418122.pdf

Kamenetz, A. (2014). *School testing: How much is too much?* Retrieved from http://www.cgcs.org/cms/lib/DC00001581/Centricity/Domain/31/National%20Public%20Radio.pdf

Kamenetz, A. (2015). *Competency-based degree programs on the rise.* Retrieved from http://www.npr.org/blogs/ed/2015/01/26/379387136/competency-based-degree-programs-on-the-rise

Kapil, Y. & Roy, A. (2014). A critical evaluation of Generation Z at workplaces. *International Journal of Social Relevance and Concern,* 2(1), 10–14.

Kendzior, S. (2014). *Only Baby Boomers could afford to be helicopter parents.* Retrieved from http://finance.yahoo.com/news/only-baby-boomers-could-afford-161109070.html

Khan Academy. (2015). *A personalized learning service for all ages.* Retrieved from https://www.khanacademy.org/about

Kickstarter. (2015). *Seven things to know about Kickstarter.* Retrieved from www.kickstarter.com

Kiefer, A. (2013). *The learning environment sweet spot: Elevating the educational paradigm.* Retrieved from https://www.ki.com/uploadedFiles/Docs/literature-samples/white-papers/Learning-Sweet-Spot-White-Paper.pdf

Kingston, A. (2014). *Get ready for Generation Z.* Retrieved from http://www.macleans.ca/society/life/get-ready-for-generation-z/

Kiss, G. (2008). Tactics for removing cultural barriers: A practical approach to effective communication. *AARMS,* 7(3), 425–433.

Kiva. (2015). *About us.* Retrieved from http://www.kiva.org/about

Knewton. (2015). *The flipped classroom infographic.* [Graph Illustration from Knewton] Retrieved from http://www.knewton.com/flipped-classroom/

Knoll. (2014). *What comes after Y? Generation Z: Arriving to the office soon.* Retrieved from www.knoll.com/knollnewsdetail/what-comes-after-y-generation-z-arriving-to-the-office-soon

Kolb, A. Y., & Kolb, D. A. (2005). Learning styles and learning spaces: Enhancing experiential learning in higher education. *Academy of Management Learning and Education,* 4, 193–212.

Koulopoulos, T., & Keldsen, D. (2014). *The Gen Z effect: The six forces shaping the future of business.* Brookline, MA: Bibliomotionc.

Kurtzleben, D. (2013, October 23). CHARTS: Just how fast has college tuition grown? *U.S. News & World Report.* Retrieved from http://www.usnews.com/news/articles/2013/10/23/charts-just-how-fast-has-college-tuition-grown

Lawless, J. L., & Fox, R. L. (2015). *Running from office*. New York: Oxford University Press.

Leckart, S. (2012). *The hackathon is on: Pitching and programming the next killer app*. Retrieved from http://www.wired.com/2012/02/ff_hackathons/

Lenhart, A., Ling, R., Campbell, S., & Purcell, K. (2010a). *Attitudes towards cell phones*. Retrieved from www.pewinternet.org/2010/04/20/chapter-three-attitudes-towards-cell-phones

Lenhart, A., Ling, R., Campbell, S., & Purcell, K. (2010b). *How phones are used with friends: What they can do and how teens use them*. Retrieved from www.pewinternet.org/2010/04/20/chapter-two-how-phones-are-used-with-friends-what-they-can-do-and-how-teens-use-them/

Lenhart, A., Ling, R., Campbell, S., & Purcell, K. (2010c). *Teens and mobile phones*. Retrieved from www.pewinternet.org/2010/04/20/teens-and-mobile-phones

Levine, A., & Dean, D. R. (2012). *Generation on a tightrope: A portrait of today's college student*. San Francisco: Wiley.

Lewin, T. (2012, November 2). Digital natives and their customs. *New York Times*. Retrieved from http://www.nytimes.com/2012/11/04/education/edlife/arthur-levine-discusses-the-new-generation-of-college-students.html?_r=0

Lewis, T. (2013). *Hurricane Sandy impacts: How the superstorm changed the public's view of weather threats*. Retrieved from http://www.huffingtonpost.com/2013/08/12/hurricane-sandy-impacts_n_3743902.html

Lewis, V., Rollo, J., Devitt, S. Egbert, J., Strawn, M., & Nagasaka, M. (2012). *Social gambling: Click here to play.* Retrieved from http://linkback.morganstanley.com/web/sendlink/webapp/f/u4a8mcp4-3ohe-g001-b7cd-002655210101?store=0&d=UwBSZXNlYXJjaAA0NzE3NTY%3D&user=2t7a7p40q5buy-2365&__gda__=1479106416_6a55cefa848830ece67e9f0e40d5607a

Lipman-Blumen, J. (1996). *Connective leadership.* New York: Oxford University Press.

Liptak, A. (2010, January 22). Justices, 5-4, reject corporate spending limit. *New York Times.* Retrieved from http://www.nytimes.com/2010/01/22/us/politics/22scotus.html?pagewanted=all

Liptak, A. (2015, June 27). Supreme Court ruling makes same-sex marriage a right nationwide. *New York Times.* Retrieved from http://www.nytimes.com/2015/06/27/us/supreme-court-same-sex-marriage.html

Lorin, J. (2014, November 13). College tuition in the US again rises faster than inflation. *Bloomberg News.* Retrieved from http://www.bloomberg.com/news/articles/2014-11-13/college-tuition-in-the-u-s-again-rises-faster-than-inflation

Lyman, F. T. (1981). The responsive classroom discussion: The inclusion of all students. In A. Anderson (Ed.), *Mainstreaming digest* (pp. 109–113). College Park: University of Maryland Press.

Madden, M., Lenhart, A., Duggan, M., Cortesi, S., & Gasser, U. (2013). *Teens and technology*. Retrieved from http://www .pewinternet.org/2013/03/13/teens-and-technology-2013/

Magid Generational Strategies. (2014). *The first generation of the twenty-first century: An introduction to the pluralist generation*. Retrieved from http://magid.com/sites/default/files/pdf/ MagidPluralistGenerationWhitepaper.pdf

Marchetti, T. J. (2014). *Three fundamental ways Generation Z differs from Millennials*. Retrieved from www.imediaconnection .com/content/37005.asp

Martinez, O., & Pentchoukova, K. (2014). *Sixteen admirable celebrities who are actively changing the world for the better*. Retrieved from http://www.epochinspired.com/ inspired/1117982-16-admirable-celebrities-who-are-actively- changing-the-world-for-the-better/

Matthew's Place. (2015). *Matthew's story*. Retrieved from http:// www.matthewsplace.com/matthews-story/

McElroy, J. (2015). *Saanich teen's newest invention can use hot coffee to power devices*. Retrieved from http://globalnews.ca/news/1933356/saanich-teens- newest-invention-uses-hot-coffee-to-power-devices/? hootPostID=3a43918d6c03e0dab48395972ac64f32

MetLife Mature Market Institute. (2013). *The MetLife study of Gen X: The MTV generation moves into mid-life*. Retrieved from https://www.metlife.com/assets/cao/mmi/publications/ studies/2013/mmi-gen-x.pdf

Millennial Branding. (2014). *Gen Y and Gen Z global work-place expectations study*. Retrieved from millennialbranding.com/tag/gen-z/

Mobile Statistics. (2012). *Phone calls are dead says Generation Z*. Retrieved from www.mobilestatistics.com/mobile-news/phone-calls-are-dead-say-generation-z.aspx

Mortensen, T. G. (2012). *State funding: A race to the bottom*. Retrieved from http://www.acenet.edu/the-presidency/columns-and-features/Pages/state-funding-a-race-to-the-bottom.aspx

Mozilla. (2015a). *Get recognition for skills you learn anywhere*. Retrieved from http://openbadges.org/

Mozilla. (2015b). *Participating issuers*. Retrieved from http://openbadges.org/participating-issuers/

Murray, N. (2015). *"From the home office … "*: *Ten David Letterman top 10 lists*. Retrieved from http://www.avclub.com/article/home-office-10-david-letterman-top-ten-lists-219375

Myers, K. K., & Sadaghiani, K. (2010). Millennials in the workplace: A communication perspective on Millennials' organizational relationships and performance. *Journal of Business and Psychology*, 25(2), 225–238.

National Association of Colleges and Employers (2014). The skills/qualities employers want in new college graduate hires. Retrieved from http://www.naceweb.org/about-us/press/class-2015-skills-qualities-employers-want.aspx

National Center for Health Statistics. (2011). *Health, United States, 2011: With special features on socioeconomic status and health.* Retrieved from www.cdc.gov/nchs/data/hus/hus11.pdf

National Conference of State Legislatures. (2015). *Arizona's immigration enforcement laws.* Retrieved from http://www.ncsl .org/research/immigration/analysis-of-arizonas-immigration-law.aspx

NBC. (2015). *About the show.* Retrieved from http://www.nbc .com/the-voice/about

Neal, R. (2013). *WhatsApp, SnapChat, and LINE: Why mobile messaging apps are taking teens away from Facebook.* Retrieved from www.ibtimes.com/whatsapp-snapchat-line-why-mobile-messaging-apps-are-taking-teens-away-facebook-1464804.

Netflix. (2015). *Company overview.* Retrieved from https://pr .netflix.com/WebClient/loginPageSalesNetWorksAction.do? contentGroupId=10476

New Strategist Publications. (2010). *American generations: Who they are and how they live.* Ithaca, NY: New Strategist Publications.

Ng, E.S.W., Schweitzer, L., & Lyons, S. T. (2010). New generation, great expectations: A field study of the Millennial generation. *Journal of Business and Psychology,* 25(2), 281–292.

Nielsen Company. (2015). *We are what we eat.* Retrieved from http://www.nielsen.com/content/dam/nielsenglobal/eu/ nielseninsights/pdfs/Nielsen%20Global%20Health%20and %20Wellness%20Report%20-%20January%202015.pdf

North Carolina State University. (2015). *About Hunt Library*. Retrieved from http://www.lib.ncsu.edu/huntlibrary/about

Northeastern University. (2014). *Innovation survey*. Retrieved from www.northeastern.edu/news/2014/11/innovation-imperative-meet-generation-z/

NYC Health. (2015). *Sugary drinks*. Retrieved from http://www.nyc.gov/html/doh/html/living/cdp_pan_pop.shtml

O'Leary, H. (2014). *Recruiting Gen Z: No more business as usual*. Retrieved from http://www.eduventures.com/2014/09/recruiting-gen-z/

O'Shea, K. (2009). *Creepy treehouse effect: How do we social network in higher ed?* Retrieved from https://www.purdue.edu/learning/blog/?p=210

Orsini, L. (2010). *History of social games*. Retrieved from http://kotaku.com/5548105/history-of-social-games#

Pachal, P. (2014). *How the #YesAllWomen hashtag began*. Retrieved from http://mashable.com/2014/05/26/yesallwomen-hashtag/

Parents Television Council. (2013). *An examination of violence, graphic violence, and gun violence in the media*. Retrieved from http://w2.parentstv.org/main/Research/Studies/CableViolence/vstudy_dec2013.pdf

Parker, K., Czech, D. R., Burdette, T., Stewart, J., Biber, D., Easton, L. E., … McDaniel, T. (2012). The preferred coaching styles of Generation Z athletes: A qualitative study. *International Sport Coaching Journal,* 5(2), 5–23.

Parsad, B., Splegelman, M., & Coopersmith, J. (2012). *Arts education in public elementary and secondary schools 1999-2000 and 2009-2010.* Retrieved from http://nces.ed.gov/pubs2012/2012014.pdf

Passel, J. S., & Cohn, D., (2011). *Unauthorized immigrant population: National and state trends, 2010.* Pew-Research Hispanic Trends Project. Retrieved from www.pewhispanic.org/2011/02/01/unauthorized-immigrant-population-brnational-and-state-trends-2010/

Patterson, M. M., Pahlke, E., & Bigler, R. S. (2013). Witnesses to history: Children's views of race and the 2008 United States presidential election. *Analyses of Social Issues and Public Policy,* 13(1), 186–210.

Pew Research Center. (2010a). *Religion among the Millennials.* Retrieved from http://www.pewforum.org/2010/02/17/religion-among-the-millennials/

Pew Research Center. (2010b). *Religion and the issues.* Retrieved from http://www.pewforum.org/files/2010/09/immigration-environment-views-fullreport.pdf

Pew Research Center. (2013). *Teens, social media, and privacy.* Retrieved from http://www.pewinternet.org/2013/05/21/teens-social-media-and-privacy-3/

Pew Research Center. (2014). *Mobile technology fact sheet.* Retrieved from http://www.pewinternet.org/fact-sheets/mobile-technology-fact-sheet/

Physical Activity Council. (2014). *2014 participation report.* Retrieved from http://www.physicalactivitycouncil.com/pdfs/current.pdf

Pinterest. (2015). *About Pinterest.* Retrieved from https://about.pinterest.com/en

Plumer, B. (2012). *Everything you need to know about the assault weapons ban, in one post.* Retrieved from http://www.washingtonpost.com/blogs/wonkblog/wp/2012/12/17/everything-you-need-to-know-about-banning-assault-weapons-in-one-post/

Pofeldt, E. (2014). *Obama: Is the job of the future a freelance one?* CNBC. Retrieved from www.cnbc.com/id/101371164#

Portillo, C. M. (2014). *Only 14 percent of CEOs on this year's Inc. 5000 list are female-and that's a major improvement.* Retrieved from http://www.bizjournals.com/bizwomen/news/latest-news/2014/08/only-14-percent-of-ceos-on-this-years-inc-5000.html

Prelude Consulting Limited. (2014). *Generation Z and learning.* Retrieved from http://www.prelude-team.com/articles/generation-z-and-learning.

Prensky, M. (2001). Digital natives, digital immigrants. *On the Horizon, 9,* 5. Retrieved from http://www.marcprensky

.com/writing/Prensky%20-%20Digital%20Natives,%20Digital %20Immigrants%20‐%20Part1.pdf

Prescott, S. (2014). *World of Warcraft subscriber count spikes following release of Draenor release*. Retrieved from www .pcgamer.com/world-of-warcraft-subscriber-count-spikes-following-draenor-release/

President's Committee on the Arts and the Humanities. (2011). *Re-investing in arts education: Winning America's future through creative schools*. Retrieved from http://www.pcah.gov/sites/ default/files/photos/PCAH_Reinvesting_4web.pdf

Price-Mitchell, M. (2015). *Youth protests: A positive sign of the times?* Retrieved from https://www.psychologytoday.com/ blog/the-moment-youth/201501/youth-protests-positive-sign-the-times

Purcell, K., Rainie, L., Heaps, A., Buchanan, J., Friedrich, L., Jacklin, A., … Zickuhr, K. (2012). *How teens do research in the digital world*. Retrieved from http://www.pewinternet.org/ 2012/11/01/how-teens-do-research-in-the-digital-world/

Raphelson, S. (2014). *Amid the stereotypes, some facts about Millennials*. Retrieved from http://www.npr.org/2014/11/ 18/354196302/amid-the-stereotypes-some-facts-about-millennials.

Rath, T. (2007). *StrengthsFinder 2.0*. New York: Gallup Press.

Reckmeyer, M. (2015). *Strengths based parenting: Making the most of your children's innate talents*. New York: Gallup Press.

Regus. (2013). *Boomers struggle to find their balance-Regus work:life balance report 2013*. Retrieved from http://press .regus.com/united-states/boomers-struggle-to-find-their-balance---regus-worklife-balance-report-2013

Roose, R. (2014). *Pinterest is sneaking up on Twitter, Facebook, and Google*. Retrieved from http://nymag.com/daily/intelligencer/2014/05/pinterest-is-sneaking-up-on-twitter-and-facebook.html

Ross, W. G. (2013). *Environmental challenges facing Generation Z*. Retrieved from http://iei.ncsu.edu/wp-content/uploads/2013/01/Environmental-Response.pdf

Rowling, J. K. (2009). *Harry Potter and the deathly hallows*. New York: Scholastic.

Salt Communications. (2014). *Generation Z*. Retrieved from www.salt-communications.com/generation-z/

Schawbel, D. (2013). *Millennial Branding and Internships.com release study on the future of education*. Retrieved from http://millennialbranding.com/2013/the-future-of-education/

Schawbel, D. (2014a). *Gen Y and Gen Z global workplace expectations study*. Retrieved from http://millennialbranding.com/2014/geny-genz-global-workplace-expectations-study/

Schawbel, D. (2014b). *Why "Gen Z" may be more entrepreneurial than "Gen Y."* Retrieved from http://www.entrepreneur.com/article/231048

Scheier, M. F., Carver, C. S., & Bridges, M. W. (1994). Distinguishing optimism from neuroticism (and trait anxiety, self-mastery, and self-esteem): A re-evaluation of the Life Orientation Test. *Journal of Personality and School Psychology*, 67(7), 1063–1078.

Schulman, M. (2013, January 10). Generation LGBTQIA. *New York Times*. Retrieved from http://www.nytimes.com/2013/01/10/fashion/generation-lgbtqia.html?_r=0

Secretan, L. (2004). *Inspire! What great leaders do*. San Francisco: Wiley.

Seemiller, C. (2013). *The student leadership competencies guidebook*. San Francisco: Jossey-Bass.

Selinger, E. (2013). *We're turning digital natives into etiquette sociopaths*. Retrieved from www.wired.com/2013/03/digital-natives-etiquette-be-damned

Shin, P. H. B. (2015). *Lance Armstrong on doping: "I would probably do it again."* Retrieved from http://abcnews.go.com/Sports/lance-armstrong-doping/story?id=28491316

Sidhu, P., & Calderon, V. J. (2014). *Many business leaders doubt US colleges prepare students*. Retrieved from http://www.gallup.com/poll/167630/business-leaders-doubt-colleges-prepare-students.aspx

Skocpol, T. (1997). The Tocqueville problem: Civic engagement in American democracy. *Social Science History*, 21(4), 455–479.

Smith, A., & Duggan, M. (2013). *Online dating and relationships*. Retrieved from www.pewinternet.org/2013/10/21/online-dating-relationships/

Smith, C. (2015a). *90+ amazing Pinterest statistics*. Retrieved from http://expandedramblings.com/index.php/pinterest-stats/

Smith, C. (2015b). *By the numbers: 40+ amazing Reddit statistics*. Retrieved from www.expandedramblings.com/index.php/reddit-stats

Smith, C. (2015c). *By the numbers: 60+ interesting Pinterest pin and board statistics*. Retrieved from http://expandedramblings.com/index.php/pinterest-pinand-board-statistics/

Snapchat. (2015). *3V Advertising*. Retrieved from https://www.snapchat.com/ads

Somers, P., & Settle, J. (2010). The helicopter parent: Research toward a typology. *College and University: Journal of the American Association of Collegiate Registrars, 86*(1), 18–27.

Sparks & Honey. (2014). *Meet Gen Z: Forget everything you learned about Millennials*. Retrieved from www.slideshare.net/sparksandhoney/generation-z-final-june-17

Spotify. (2015). *About us*. Retrieved from https://www.spotify.com/us/about-us/contact/

Stein, J. (2013, May 20). Millennials: The me me me generation. *Time*, 26–34.

Steinmetz, K. (2015). *States battle over bathroom access for transgender people.* Retrieved from http://time.com/3734714/transgender-bathroom-bills-lgbt-discrimination/

Strauss, W., & Howe, N. (1990). *Generations: The history of America's future.* New York: Morrow.

Tamir, D., & Mitchell, J. (2012). Disclosing information about the self is intrinsically rewarding. *Proceedings of the National Academy of Sciences,* 109, 8038–8043. Retrieved from http://www.pnas.org/content/109/21/8038.full

Taskrabbit. (2015). How Taskrabbit works. Retrieved from https://www.taskrabbit.com/how-it-works

Taylor, P., & Gao, G. (2014). *Generation X: America's neglected 'middle child.'* Retrieved from www.pewresearch.org/fact-tank/2014/06/05/generation-x-americas-neglected-middle-child/

Tecca, C. B. (2012). *Four pros and cons of e-readers vs. textbooks.* Retrieved from http://www.today.com/parents/4-pros-cons-e-readers-vs-textbooks-2D80556082

Techopedia. (N.d.). *Massively multiplayer online role-playing game (MMORPG).* Retrieved from http://www.techopedia.com/definition/1919/massively-multiplayer-online-role-playing-game-mmorpg

Ted. (2015). *Our organization.* Retrieved from https://www.ted.com/about/our-organization

Thompson, C. (2015). *A timeline of the history of blogging: The early years*. Retrieved from www.nymag.com/news/media/15971

Thompson, C. (2015). *How the "Uber Effect" is changing work*. Retrieved from http://www.cnbc.com/id/102503684

Tiller, C. (2011). Philanthro-teens: the next generation changing the world. *Media Planet*, 2 (USA Today). Retrieved from http://doc.mediaplanet.com/all_projects/6574.pdf

Tolbize, A. (2008). *Generational differences in the workplace*. Retrieved from http://rtc3.umn.edu/docs/2_18_Gen_diff_workplace.pdf

Tulgan, B. (2013). *Meet Generation Z: The second generation within the giant "Millennial" cohort*. Retrieved from http://rainmakerthinking.com/assets/uploads/2013/10/Gen-Z-Whitepaper.pdf

Tumblr. (2015). *About*. Retrieved from https://www.tumblr.com/about

Twitter. (2015). *About*. Retrieved from https://about.twitter.com/

Uber. (2015a). *Uber*. Retrieved from https://www.uber.com/

Uber. (2015b). *Sign up to drive with Uber*. Retrieved from https://get.uber.com/drive/

Uhl-Bien, M., Marion, R., & McKelvey, B. (2007). Complexity leadership theory: Shifting leadership from the industrial age to the knowledge era. *Leadership Quarterly, 18*(4), 298–318.

UN Joint Staff Pension Fund. (2007). *Overcoming generational gap in the workplace.* Retrieved from http://www.un.org/staffdevelopment/pdf/Designing%20Recruitment,%20Selection%20&%20Talent%20Management%20Model%20tailored%20to%20meet%20UNJSPF%27s%20Business%20Development%20Needs.pdf

UN. (2015). *Status of ratification of the Kyoto Protocol.* Retrieved from http://unfccc.int/kyoto_protocol/status_of_ratification/items/2613.php

US Bureau of Labor Statistics. (2015). *Labor force statistics from the current population survey.* Retrieved from http://data.bls.gov/timeseries/LNS14000000

US Census Bureau. (2009). *Voter turnout increases by 5 million in 2008 presidential election, U.S. Census Bureau reports.* Retrieved from https://www.census.gov/newsroom/releases/archives/voting/cb09-110.html

US Department of Agriculture. (2014). Number of U.S. *farmers' markets continue to rise.* Retrieved from http://ers.usda.gov/data-products/chart-gallery/detail.aspx?chartId=48561&ref=collection&embed=True&widgetId=37373

US Department of Health and Human Services. (2014). *About the law.* Retrieved from http://www.hhs.gov/healthcare/rights/

US Department of Justice. (2015a). *The USA Patriot Act: Preserving life and liberty*. Retrieved from http://www.justice.gov/archive/ll/highlights.htm

US Department of Justice. (2015b). *Information and technical assistance on the Americans with Disabilities Act*. Retrieved from http://www.ada.gov/

US House of Representatives. (2015). *Constitutional amendments and major civil rights acts of Congress reference in Black Americans in Congress*. Retrieved from http://history.house.gov/Exhibitions-and-Publications/BAIC/Historical-Data/Constitutional-Amendments-and-Legislation/

Van Riper, T. (2013). *Tim Tebow tops Forbes' 2013 list of America's most influential athletes*. Retrieved from http://www.forbes.com/sites/tomvanriper/2013/05/06/americas-most-influential-athletes-2/

Viacom. (2012). *Consumer insights: Nickelodeon's "International GPS: Kids' influence."* Retrieved from http://blog.viacom.com/2012/08/consumer-insights-nickelodeons-international-gps-kids-influence/

Vidyarthyi, N. (2011). *Attention spans have dropped from 12 to 5 minutes-How social media is ruining our minds*. Retrieved from http://www.adweek.com/socialtimes/attention-spans-have-dropped-from-12-minutes-to-5-seconds-how-social-media-is-ruining-our-minds-infographic/87484

ViralGains. (2014). *The history of viral video*. Retrieved from https://www.youtube.com/watch?v=snHey-snTb8

Wald, J. (2014). *What the rise of the freelance economy really means for business.* Retrieved from http://www.forbes.com/sites/waldleventhal/2014/07/01/a-modern-human-capital-talent-strategy-using-freelancers/

Wallerson, R. (2014). *Youth participation weakens in basketball, football, baseball, soccer: Fewer children play team sports.* Retrieved from http://www.wsj.com/articles/SB10001424052702303519404579350892629229918

Washington Post Editorial Board. (2015). *Indiana's religious freedom law can have real discriminatory effects.* Retrieved from http://www.washingtonpost.com/opinions/indianas-religious-freedom-law-can-have-real-discriminatory-effects/2015/03/30/f7470520-d71f-11e4-b3f2-607bd612aeac_story.html

WhatsApp. (2015). *About WhatsApp.* Retrieved from https://www.whatsapp.com/about/

White, G. B. (2015). *In the sharing economy, no one's an employee.* Retrieved from http://www.theatlantic.com/business/archive/2015/06/in-the-sharing-economy-no-ones-an-employee/395027/

White, S. (2014). *Generation Z: The kids who'll save the world.* Retrieved from http://www.theglobeandmail.com/life/giving/generation-z-the-kids-wholl-save-the-world/article20790237/

Wikipedia. (2015). *Wikipedia: About.* Retrieved from https://en.wikipedia.org/wiki/Wikipedia:About

WordPress. (2015). *About WordPress*. Retrieved from https://wordpress.org/about/

World Wide Web Foundation. (2015). *History of the web*. Retrieved from http://webfoundation.org/about/vision/history-of-the-web/

YouTube. (2015a). *About YouTube*. Retrieved from https://www.youtube.com/yt/about/

YouTube. (2015b). *Press room*. Retrieved from https://www.youtube.com/yt/press/

Yukl, G. (2006). *Leadership in organizations* (6th ed.). Upper Saddle River, NJ: Pearson-Prentice Hall.

Zak, E. (2013). *How Twitter's hashtag came to be*. Retrieved from http://blogs.wsj.com/digits/2013/10/03/how-twitters-hashtag-came-to-be/

INDEX

A

Aboujaoude, Elias, 180
Accion, 140
Adult-free social media sites,
  79–80, 223
Advanced Placement (AP) teacher
  survey, 27
Advocating activities, 142–143
Affordable housing concerns, 106
AIDS crisis (1980s), 34
Airbnb, 30, 31
Airport terrorism fears, 35
Albus Dumbledore (*Harry Potter
  and the Deathly Hallows*
  character), 159
Alex's Lemonade Stand's 5Ks, 141
Alibaba, 31
Amazon shopping experience, 28
American dream, 39–40
Americans with Disabilities Act,
  38
AOL Instant Messenger,
  60–61
Apple Maps, 26
Armstrong, Lance, 162
ASHOKA, 135
Assignment binging, 206–207
Association of American Colleges &
  Universities, 218

Attention difficulties: how
  multitasking reinforces lack of
  focus and, 180–181; smart
  phones and the Internet
  contribution to, 180–181
Avatar identity: Massive multiplayer
  online role-playing games
  (MMORPGs), 72; sharing
  expertise or opinion using an,
  77–78; social gaming with their
  Facebook, 72

B

Baby Boomers (born 1946 to 1964):
  description of the, 2–3; as parents
  of Generation X and Generation
  Y, 3, 5; reliance on the Dewey
  Decimal System to find resources
  by, 173; Vietnam War and social
  upheaval influencing the, 2, 97
Beliefs: about education, 98, 99*t*;
  creative entrepreneurship, 30–34;
  diversity and social justice,
  37–40; on future employment,
  102*t*; how context shapes beliefs
  and, 25–26; how disasters and
  tragedies have shaped Generation
  Z, 34–37; immediate information
  availability shaping Generation Z,

26–27; impact of educational budget cuts and increased debt burdens on, 40–41; political, 44–46*t*; on racial equality, 104–105*t*; religious, 42–44
Bell, Alexander Graham, 59
Bisexuals, 116–117
Blog sites: description and widespread use of, 70; sharing and forwarding the news through, 132
Blogger, 70
Body Bijou, 144
Border debate/immigration, 117–118
Bosses. *See* Employers
Boston Marathon bombing (2013), 36
Bronies (My Little Pony), 112
Budget cuts/debt burdens: Generation Z growing up in an environment of, 40–41; Generation Z's conservative approach to financial matters and, 41–42, 105–106
Bullying, 110
Businesses with social mission, 134–135
Buzzfeed, 131

C

Candidates: campaigning for, 139; Generation Z's distaste for politics and lack of interest in voting for, 137–139
Celebrities, 162
Cell phone ownership, 29
Challenger explosion, 3–4
Chick-fil-A, 136

Citizens United, 115
Civic engagement. *See* Service-learning
Civil Rights Act, 38
Civil rights movement, 2
Clifton, Don, 153
Climate change: Generation Z's concerns over, 119–120; Kyoto Protocol effort to reduce, 155
CNN news site, 131
Coach role models, 158
Cocurricular experiences: focusing on intentional leadership competency development through, 221; integrating modern learning in, 208–209. *See also* College curriculum
College campuses: cultivate Generation Z donors, 200–201; enhance safety of, 195–196; ensure an inclusive and affirming environment, 196; help students access funding and scholarships, 197–198; make healthy food options the norm on, 199; offer expanded services for students on, 199–200; operational strategies for designing ones that fit Generation Z, 192, 195–201; reconsider housing requirements, 198; support mental health and provide personal counseling on, 196–197
College curriculum: align industry standards with learning outcomes of, 202–203; help students engage in microfinancing, 218; integrating a socially conscious, 203; offer options for hybrid

learning, 205–206; offer social entrepreneurship courses for nonbusiness majors, 217. *See also* Cocurricular experiences; Learning environments

College to career transition: developmental strategies for building student capacity, 192, 218–221; instructional strategies for designing learning environments, 192, 201–209; operational strategies for designing a campus that fits, 192, 195–201; programmatic strategies creating real-world learning experiences, 192, 209–218; relational strategies for connecting with Generation Z students, 192–194; technological strategies for using the right social media, 192, 222–224

Colleges: community service requirements by, 141–142; concerns over rising costs of, 98, 100–101, 106; concerns over school shootings at high schools and, 36, 109–110; debate over DREAMers and DREAM Act, 117–118; designing a campus that best fits Generation Z students, 192, 195–201; Generation Z's beliefs on importance of education and, 97–98, 101–102t; helping Generation Z to make the transition to careers from, 192–224; how Generation Z's approach decisions about, 185.

See also Educational issues; High schools; Learning

Collins, Suzanne, 159

Communication: concerns over Generation Z's face-to-face, 57; emotion icons used to add layer to text messaging, 59; face-to-face, 57, 61, 193; multiple channels used by Generation Z for, 58–61. *See also* Social media

Communication channels: e-mail, 60; face-to-face over Facebook, 61; instant messaging, 60–61; social media, 61, 65–80; text or iMessage, 58–60

Community engagement activities: campaigning for candidates, 139; leading 5Ks and PTAs, 139–140; making a lifestyle change, 136–137; raising money, 140; voting, 137–139

Community engagement practices: activities that work for some but not for all, 135–141; advocating and protesting, 142–143; creating a business with a social mission, 134–135; finding new solutions for new needs, 143–144; how Generation Z have embraced, 129–130; how technology has created new opportunities for, 130; inventing the next big thing or project, 133–134; spreading news and views, 130–133; volunteering or being voluntold, 141–142. *See also* Politics; Social change

Community service: offer student-selected experiences for,

212–213; shift focus to social change, 211–212; social change through, 141; volunteering vs. being voluntold, 141–142, 213–214

Compassion: influencing their relational aspect of motivation, 15; as self-described Generation Z characteristic, 8–9

Conservatism ideology: description of, 45; Generation Z political leanings toward, 45–46*t*

Corporate social mission, 134–135

Craigslist, 30, 32

Creativity: how standardized tests have negatively impacted the development of, 177–178; imagination learning methods that foster, 177–178; as quality most sought after by employers, 177

Creepy tree house (adult-free social media zones), 79–80, 223

Crowdfunding sites: cultivate Generation Z donors for college fundraising on, 200–201; GodFundMe, 134; Kickstarter, 133, 201

Curriculum. *See* College curriculum

D

Danger perspective: fear of terrorism during post-9/11 era, 34–36; Generation Z's, 36–37

DaVanzo, Sarah, 111

DeGeneres, Ellen, 116

Determination trait, 11–12

Developmental strategies: building student capacity using, 192, 218–221; cultivate informed opinions and education actions, 220; focus on intentional leadership competency development, 221; help students create value-based goals, 219–220; provide education on financial literacy, 220–221

Diary of a Wimpy Kid (Kinney), 159

DiCaprio, Leonardo, 162

Disasters and tragedies: feeling unsafe due to, 36–37; Great Recession (2007–2009), 7, 35, 40; impact of September 11th on Generation Z, 34–36; the world perceived as a scary place, 35–36

Diversity: Generation Z's beliefs in importance of equality for all, 40; Generation Z's beliefs shaped by exposure to, 37–38; Generation Z's open-mindedness about, 39

Divorce rates, 3, 4

Doing (executing a task) leadership style, 164

Domestic terrorism fears, 36

Don't Ask, Don't Tell, 116

dot-com bust (2000), 7

DREAMers, 117–118

Duke University, 120

Dumbledore (*Harry Potter and the Deathly Hallows* character), 159

E

eBay, 30

eBay Classifieds, 33

Ebola, 35

Economic inequality, 113–114

Educational budget cuts: financially conservative approach by Generation Z to, 41–42; Generation Z experience of growing up with, 40–41

Educational decision making: by Generation Z on their choice of colleges, 185; "helicopter parenting" control of Generation X, 158, 196; providing more flexibility in their programs of study, 185; role of parents in Generation Z's, 194

Educational issues: budgets cuts, 40–42; bullying in schools, 110; fear of school shootings issue of, 36, 109–110; Generation Z's on importance of education to their future, 97–98, 101–102t; how standardized tests has negatively impacted the development of creativity, 177–178; reality of higher costs for education, 98, 100–101; strategies for Generation Z transition from colleges to careers, 192–224. *See also* Colleges; Learning

The Elks, 130

E-mail communication, 60

Emotion icons, 59

Employers: aligning learning outcomes to industry standards expected by, 202–203; bosses as not being Generation Z role models, 161; creativity as quality most sought after by, 177; the leadership skills desired in employees by, 152–153; offering internship opportunities with future, 214–215

Employment: concerns about unemployment, 103; financial compensation as not a motivator of Generation Z, 16–17; Generation Z concerns over future, 101–102t; Generation Z interest in self-employment and non-traditional, 103–104; Generation Z on importance of education to future, 97–98, 101–102t; helping Generation Z to make the transition from colleges to career, 192–224. *See also* Work

Enron scandal, 7

Entrepreneurship: ASHOKA network providing resources on, 135; creating a business with a social mission, 134–135; Generation Z beliefs and perceptions on, 30–34; HackerLab resources to education and inspire, 176; offer social entrepreneurship courses for nonbusiness majors, 217

Entrepreneurship beliefs/perceptions: comparing Generation Z and Millennials' use of online sites for selling, 32; creative environment shaping Generation Z, 30–31; freelancing to be your own boss, 33–34; selling is not just for business, 32–33; sharing can be revenue generating, 31–32

Environmental movement, 119–120

Equality: economic inequality and, 113–114; Generation Z concerns about gender, 112–113; Generation Z's beliefs on social justice and, 40, 104–105*t*; Generation Z's beliefs shaped by exposure to diversity, 37–38; laws protecting, 38
ESPN Twitter feed, 73
Etsy, 32–33
Everdeen, Katniss (*Hunger Game* character), 159
Experiential learning, 175–176, 215–216
Expertise/opinion sharing, 77–78

F
Facebook: face-to-face communication through, 61; gender differences in use of, 78; Generation Z's high use of Twitter and, 72–73; how Generation Z friendships are played out on, 89; how Generation Z manages their familial and peer relationships on, 79–80; Instagram acquired by, 66, 67; Mark Zuckerberg on the original social mission of, 66; personal information shared on, 76–77; primarily used for family and close friends, 79–80; sharing expertise or opinions using, 77–78; social gaming with their avatar, 71–72; as social network, 66–67; used for keeping up with others, 74–75; users older than age sixty–five using, 79
Face-to-communication: to build relationship with Generation Z, 193; concerns over Generation Z's abilities for, 57; using Facebook for, 61
Facilitated learning approach, 179–180
Factory farming, 120–121
Fair Housing Act, 38
Familial relationships: Generation Z's high regard for parents and, 4, 89–90, 157–158; Generation Z's use of adult-free zones of social media free from, 79–80, 223; how Generation Z use social media to manage their, 78–80; understanding Generation Z's, 194; valued by Millennials, 90
Fears: how disasters and tragedies have shaped Generation Z, 34–37; of terrorism, 34–36
Fictional character role models, 159–160
Financial aid services, 197–198
Financial crisis (2008), 7, 35, 40, 106, 113
Financial issues: compensation as not Generation Z motivator, 16–17; concerns over affordable housing, 106; concerns over rising costs of college, 98, 100–101, 106; economic inequality, 113–114; Financial crisis (2008) and Great Recession (2007–2009) impact on Generation Z, 7, 35, 40, 106, 114; Generation Z's conservative approach to, 41–42, 105–106; help students provide education on financial literacy, 220–221
Financial literacy, 220–221

5Ks: Alex's Lemonade Stand, 141; community engagement by leading, 139–140

Flipboard, 131

Flipped classrooms, 205, 206

Follower–leader relationship, 165

FOMO (fear of missing out), 29

Food, Inc. (movie), 120

Food production concerns, 120–121

14 Reasons Why People Still Have Landlines, 131

Free the Children, 130

Freelancing/self-employment, 33–34

Friendships: social media role in Generation Z, 88–89; what matters to Generation Z students in, 88

Fundraising: cultivate Generation Z donors to colleges, 200–201; GoFundMe site for, 134; help students engage in microfinancing, 218; Kickstarter site for, 133, 201

G

Gallup's StrengthsFinder, StrengthsQuest, and StrengthsExplorer program, 153, 154

Garage sales, 32

Gay rights, 115–117, 196

Gay/Straight Alliance, 116

Gender differences: Generation Z as the gender-bending generation, 112–113; in Generation Z learning preferences, 182; social media use and, 78

Gender identity: Gay and LGBTQIA rights movement and, 116–117, 196; politics and practices related to, 112–113

Gender-neutral bathrooms, 112

Generation X (born 1965 and 1980): active parenting of Generation Zs by, 4, 89, 166; comparing Generation Z's belief in the American dream and, 39–40; comparing Generation Z's religious participation and, 43; description of the, 3; as original "latchkey kids," 3; percentage naming their parents as their heroes, 157–158; transitioning from typewriters to computers, 173

Generation Y and Generation Z comparisons: on issues of economic inequality to, 113–114; their optimism about the future, 36; their religious participation, 43, 45; of their role models, 157; their selling activities on online sites, 32; their volunteerism, 142; their workplace type preferences, 30

Generation Y (Millennials) [born 1980s to early 1990s]: Baby Boomers parents of the, 3, 5; description of the, 4–6; "helicopter parents" of, 157, 194; percentage naming their parents as their heroes, 157–158; September 11th influencing both Generation Z and, 34–36, 97; technological learning resources available to, 173; valuing their close family relationships, 90; workplace generation clash often experienced by, 5–6

Generation Z (born 1995 to 2010): compared to other generations, 7; description of the, 6–7; Generation X's active parenting of, 4, 89, 166; helping them to make the transition form college to careers, 192–224; as less physically active than other generations, 14–15; motivators and unmotivators of, 15–17; personality characteristics of, 7–13; strategies for making the transition from colleges to careers, 192–224; 21 Jump Street (TV show) as a profile of today's, 87

Generation Z personality characteristics: compassionate, 8–9, 15; determined, 11–12; historic events shaping the, 7–8; loyal, 8, 15; open-minded, 10; responsible, 11; self-described ones that they don't have, 12–13; self-descriptions of themselves but not others in same generation, 13; thoughtful, 9, 15

Generation Z students: curbing assignment binging by, 206–207; developmental strategies for building capacity of, 192, 218–221; instructional strategies for designing learning environments for, 192, 201–209; operational strategies for designing a campus that fits, 192, 195–201; programmatic strategies creating real-world learning experiences, 192, 209–218; reconsider group work expectations of, 207–208; relational strategies for connecting with, 192–194; technological strategies for using the right social media for, 192, 222–224

Get-it-when-you-want-it mentality, 28

Global experiences accessibility, 216

Global warming, 119–120

Goal setting: helping students to create value-based goals, 219–220; unique opportunities with Generation Z students,' 219

Goodwin, Tom, 31

Google accounts, 69

Google Doc, 181

Google Maps, 26

Gore, Al, 119

Government regulations: concerns over limitations on personal freedom due to, 106–107; debate over DREAMers and DREAM Act, 117–118; marijuana legalization debate, 121; passage of same-sex marriage, 116, 136; Patriot Act, 107

Great Recession (2007–2009), 7, 35, 40, 105, 113

Grohol, John M., 29

Group work learning approach: benefits to Generation Z of the, 179, 181; reconsider group work expectations, 207–208

H

Hackathons, 134

HackerLab, 176

Harry Potter Alliance, 160

Harry Potter and the Deathly Hallows (Rowling), 159

Harry Potter series, 159, 160

Hashtags: description of a, 68; Generation Z as the "hashtag generation," 67–68; #YesAllWomen movement, 196

Havas Media, 31

Healthy food choices, 199

"Helicopter parents," 157, 194

High schools: concerns over school shootings at colleges and, 36, 109–110; Gay/Straight Alliance in, 116. *See also* Colleges

Hispanic US population, 37

The Hobbit (Tolkien), 159

Housing: concerns over affordable, 106; housing bubble burst, 35, 113

Hulu, 28

Human rights: economic inequality, 113–114; gay rights and LGBTQIA rights movement, 116–117, 196; gender quality and concerns over sexism, 112; Generation Z awareness of, 111; immigration and the border debate, 117–118; making lifestyle changes in relation to, 137; political dysfunction, 114

Hunger Games (Collins), 159

The Hunger Games (movie), 108

Hunt Library (North Carolina State University), 184

Hurricane Katrina, 35

Hybrid learning approach, 205–206

I

Identity theft, 110

Imagination-based learning approach, 177–178

iMessaging, 58–60

Immigration/border debate, 117–118

Impulse Control Disorders Clinic (Stanford University), 180

An Inconvenient Truth (documentary), 119

Independent contractors/freelancers, 33–34

Information: helping Generation Z students to effectively research and evaluate, 203–204; how technology has shaped Generation Z's perceptions about, 27–30; as instantaneous, accessible, and abundant to Generation Z learners, 173–174; the Internet used for gaining knowledge and learning new, 75; social media used for sharing personal, 76–77. *See also* Knowledge; The news

Information beliefs/perceptions: constant connection with others, 29; fluidity of time and space, 30; FOMO (fear of missing out), 29; get-it-when-you-want-it mentality, 28; poor information literacy, 27

Information literacy: cultivate students' informed opinions and educated actions on social issues through, 220; help students to effectively research and develop, 203–204; using technology to develop students,' 222–223

Information overload, 27

Innovation/inventing new ideas: for a complex world needing a complex definition of leadership, 154–156; creating a business with a social mission, 134–135; crowdfunding sites for fundraising, 133–134; Generation Z's finding new solutions for new needs, 143–144; Hackathons competitions for, 134; HackerLab's mission to spark, 176

Instagram: description of, 67; gender differences in use of, 78; Generation Z's flocking to, 80; "like" a picture on, 66; personal information shared on, 76–77; sharing expertise or opinions using, 77–78; used for keeping up with others, 74–75

Instant messaging, 60–61

Instructional strategies: align learning outcomes with industry standards, 202–203; curb assignment binging, 206–207; designing learning environments for Generation Z, 192, 201–209; flipped classrooms, 205, 206; help students effectively research, 203–204; integrate a socially conscious curriculum, 203; integrate modern learning in the cocurriculum, 208–209; offer options for hybrid learning,

205–206; reconsider group work expectations, 207–208; teach with and not at Generation Z, 204

Internet: availability of the news on the, 130–131; concerns over identity theft and security of, 110; contributing to attention difficulties, 181; how it has shaped Generation Z's perceptions and beliefs, 27–30; romance and romantic relationships on the, 90–93; as tool for school and learning, 184; used for gaining knowledge, 75. *See also* Social media; Technology

Internship opportunities, 214–215

Interpersonal skills: concerns over Generation Z's lack of, 57; face-to-face over Facebook use of, 61. *See also* Relationships

Intrapersonal learning approach: flipped classrooms used for, 205, 206; gender preferences in, 182; generally preferred by Generation Z, 178–179

Inventing. *See* Innovation/inventing new ideas

J

Just-in-time learning, 200

K

Katniss Everdeen (*Hunger Game* character), 159

Kennedy, John F., 162

Khan Academy, 174–175

Kickstarter (crowdfunding site), 133, 201

Kielburger, Craig, 130

Kiva, 140

Klinenberg, Eric, 34

Knowledge: Generation Z's poor information literacy that may compromise their, 27; social media used for gaining new, 75, 174. *See also* Information; Learning

Kyoto Protocol (1997), 155

L

"Latchkey kids," 3

Leader role models: bosses as not being, 161; coaches as, 158; fictional characters as, 159–160; parents as, 157–158; peers as, 158–159; political leaders as not being, 162–163; professional athletes and celebrities as not being, 162; religious leaders as not being, 161–162; teachers as, 158; those who are Generation Z, 156–160; those who are not Generation Z, 160–163

Leader–follower relationship, 165

Leadership: Generation Z and the act of following, 165; Generation Z and the act of leading, 164–165; Generation Z's value of honesty and transparency, 166; Generation Z's view of effective political, 163; how the definition has changed between the 1920s and 2000s, 151–152; our modern and complex worlds needs a complex definition of, 154–156; the skills employers want, 152–153; strengths-based, 153–154

Leadership development: expanding the reach of, 210–211; focus on intentional, 221; offer leadership experiences that reflect reality for, 211

Leadership styles: Doing (executing a task), 164; Leading (taking initiative), 164, 165; Relating (building the team), 164, 165; Thinking (strategizing a plan), 164–165

Leading (taking initiative) leadership style, 164, 165

Learners: desire for facilitated learning approach by Generation Z, 179–180; gender preferences in learning by Generation Z, 182; how standardized tests has negatively impacted the development of creativity in, 177–178; imagination as least preferred learning approach by Generation Z, 177–178; intrapersonal learning preference by Generation Z, 178–179, 182, 205; logic-based approaches and experiential learning forms sought by Generation Z, 175–176, 215–216; multitasking and inability to focus by Generation Z, 180–181; social learning or group work by Generation Z, 179, 181, 207–208

Learning: aligning industry standards to outcomes of, 202–203; Generation Z as learners, 175–182; just-in-time, 200; resources available to Generation Z for, 173–175;

unique learning environments available to Generation Z for, 182–184. *See also* Educational issues; Knowledge

Learning approaches: creating real-world learning experiences, 192, 209–218; facilitated, 179–180; gender preferences in, 182; hybrid, 205–206; imaginative, 177–178; intrapersonal, 178–179, 182, 205; social or group work, 179, 181, 207–208

Learning environments: facilitating Generation Z's college to careers transition through design of, 192, 201–209; flipping classrooms, 205, 206; Generation Z students' description of their ideal, 182–184; helping Generation Z students to effectively research and evaluation information, 203–204; learning spaces, 183; modern libraries, 183–184; teaching with and not at Generation Z students, 204; tools for school, 184. *See also* College curriculum

Learning resources: instantaneous, accessible, abundant information, 173–174; virtual student support, 174–175; YouTube as a, 75, 174

Learning space physicality, 183

Leave It to Beaver (TV show), 3

Lesbian rights, 116–117

Letterman's David, 130

LGBTQIA rights movement, 117, 196

Liberal ideology: description of, 44–45; Generation Z political leanings toward, 45–46*t*

Library learning environment, 183–184

Lifestyle changes, 136–137

Lincoln, Abraham, 162

Logic-based learning approaches, 175–176

Low and Order: Special Victims Unit (TV show), 108

Loyalty: influencing their relational aspect of motivation, 15; as self-described Generation Z characteristics, 8

M

Manziaris, Linda, 144

Marijuana legalization debate, 121

The Masons, 130

Massive multiplayer online role-playing games (MMORPGs), 72

Massive open online courses (MOOCs), 134, 208

Mental health services, 196–197

Microfinancing, 218

Millennials. *See* Generation Y (Millennials) [born 1980s to early 1990s]

MMORPGs (massive multiplayer online role-playing games), 72

Modern libraries learning environment, 183–184

MOOCs (massive open online courses), 134, 208

Motivation: Generation Z motivators driving their, 15–16;

Generation Z unmotivators that influence their, 16–17
Movie theater shootings, 36
Multitasking myth, 180–181
Music (as learning space background), 183
My Little Pony, 112

N

National Association of Colleges and Employers, 152, 203
National Writing Project (NWP) teacher survey, 27
Netflix, 28
New ideas. See Innovation/inventing new ideas
The news: availability on the Internet, 130–131; Generation Z's consumption of, 131–132; Generation Z's sharing and forwarding, 132–133. See also Information; Social media
NextGen Learning Commons, 184
No Child Left Behind Act (2001), 40–41, 177–178
North Carolina State University's Hunt Library, 184
Now, Discover Your Strengths (Clifton), 153

O

Obama, Barack, 39
Occupy Movement, 113
Older generations: as creating the environments that younger ones are raised in, 2; traditionally having disdain for the new generations, 1–2
On-demand work, 33–34

Online Forums, 71
Online petitions, 133
Open-mindedness trait, 10
Operational strategies: cultivate Generation Z donors, 200–201; designing a campus that fits, 192, 195–201; enhance campus safety, 195–196; ensure an inclusive and affirming campus environment, 196; help students access funding, 197–198; make healthy food options the norm, 199; offer expanded services for students, 199–200; reconsider housing requirements, 198; support mental health and offer personal counseling, 196–197
Opinion/expertise sharing, 77–78
Orwell, George, 1

P

Parents: Generation Z's high regard for their Generation X, 4, 89–90, 166; Generation Z's using social media sites private from their, 79–80, 223; "helicopter," 157, 194; as role models of Generation Z, 157–158
Patriot Act, 107
Peanuts cartoons, 179
Peer relationships: creating and sustaining, 87–89; how Generation Z use social media to manage their, 79–80; as motivator for Generation Z, 15–17; romance in a digital world, 90–93
Peer role models, 158–159
Peer-to peer-rental market, 31

Perceptions: about education, 98, 99t; creative entrepreneurship, 30–34; diversity and social justice, 37–40; on future employment, 102t; how context shapes beliefs and, 25–26; how disasters and tragedies have shaped Generation Z, 34–37; immediate information availability shaping Generation Z, 26–27; impact of educational budget cuts and increased debt burdens on, 40–41; political beliefs and, 44–46t; on racial equality, 104–105t; religious beliefs and, 42–44

Personal freedom limitations, 106–107

Personal information sharing, 76–77

Phelps, Michael, 162

"Philanthro-teens," 140

Physical activity levels, 14–15

Pinterest, 70–71

Political leaders: Generation Z's view of effective, 163; as not being Generation Z role models, 162–163

Politics: campaigning for candidates, 139; concerns over political dysfunction, 114–116; Generation Z political leanings, 45–46t; Generation Z's distaste of, 138–139; ideologies identified with liberals vs. conservatives, 44–45. See also Community engagement practices

Post-9/11 era: concerns over limitations on personal freedom during, 106–107; Generation Z shaped by fear and insecurity of the, 34–36, 97

Price-Mitchell, Marilyn, 144

Privacy: concerns over identity theft and Internet security, 110–111; online romance and Generation Z's desire for, 92; using social networking sites that are adult-free zones for, 79–80, 223

Problem solving: creating opportunities for real-life, 217–218; our complex world needs complex leadership for complex, 154–155

Problems: climate change, 119–120; creating a business with a social mission to tackle social, 134–135; immigration and the border debate, 117–118; our complex world needs complex leadership to solve complex, 154–155. See also Social change

Professional athletes, 162

Programmatic strategies: connecting students' passions to their practices, 214; create opportunities for real-life problem solving, 217–218; creating real-work learning experiences, 192, 209–218; expand the reach of leadership development, 210–211; guarantee internship opportunities early on, 214–215; help students engage in microfinancing, 218; increase accessibility for global experiences, 216; offer leadership experiences that reflect reality, 211; offer social entrepreneurship courses for nonbusiness majors, 217; offer student-selected community engagement experiences, 212–213; require experiential learning, 215–216; rethinking mandatory volunteer requirements, 213–214; shift service-learning to social change, 211–212

Protesting activities, 142–143

PTAs (Parent Teacher Associations): community engagement by volunteering for, 130; driving social change by leading, 139–140

R

Racial equality: Generation Z beliefs about, 104–105t; Generation Z's beliefs on social justice and, 40, 104–105t; Generation Z's beliefs shaped by exposure to diversity, 37–38; laws protecting, 38

Real-world learning experiences: connect Generation Z passions to their practices, 214; create opportunities for real-life problem solving, 217–218; expand the research of leadership development with, 210–211; guarantee internship opportunities early on, 214–215; help students engage in microfinancing, 218; increase accessibility for global experiences, 216; offer leadership experiences that reflect reality,

211; offer social entrepreneurship courses for nonbusiness majors, 217; offer student-selected community engagement experiences for, 212–213; providing Generation Z students with, 192, 209–218; require experiential learning, 215–216; rethink mandatory volunteer requirements, 213–214; shift service-learning to social change, 211–212

Reddit, 71, 131, 133

Relating (building the team) leadership style, 164, 165

Relational strategies: be transparent, 193–194; for connecting with Generation Z, 192–194; make time for face time, 193; understand family roles, 194

Relationships: creating and sustaining peer, 87–89; Facebook versus Twitter for managing friends and family, 79–80; Generation Z's high regard for parents and familial, 4, 89–90, 157–158; leader–follower, 165; as a motivator for Generation Z, 15–17; romance and romantic, 90–94. See also Interpersonal skills

Religion: Generation Z's trend away toward spirituality and away from organized, 44; participation and nonparticipation of Generation Z in, 43–44; religious leaders as not being Generation Z role models, 161–162; US embrace of freedom of religion and diversity of, 42

Research skills: helping Generation Z students effectively use, 203–204; on using the Internet for gaining knowledge, 75

Responsible trait: as self-described Generation Z characteristic, 11; shared by both Generation Z and Generation X parents, 7

Role models: bosses as not being, 161; coaches as, 158; fictional characters as, 159–160; parents as, 157–158; peers as, 158–159; political leaders as not being, 162–163; professional athletes and celebrities as not being, 162; religious leaders as not being, 161–162; teachers as, 158; those who are Generation Z, 156–160; those who are not Generation Z, 160–163

Romantic relationships: dating sites and meeting "the one," 90–91; how technology can create drama and trust issues, 92–93; impact of social media and technology on, 91–93; social media role in starting up and breaking up, 93–94

Roots of Action (Price-Mitchell), 144

Ross, William G., Jr., 120

Rotary Club, 130

Rowling, J. K., 159

S

Safe sex talks, 157

Sam, Michael, 162

Same-sex marriage, 116, 136

SARS (Severe Acute Respiratory Syndrome), 35

Scholarship resources, 197–198

Schools. *See* Colleges; High schools

Schulz, Charles, 179

Self-employment/freelancing, 33–34

September 11th: concerns over limitations on personal freedom after, 106–107; Generation Z shaped by fear and insecurity of the, 34–36, 97

Service-learning: offer student-selected experiences for, 212–213; shift focus to social change, 211–212; social change through, 141; volunteering vs. being voluntold, 141–142, 213–214

Sexism concerns, 112–113

Sexual harassment: enhancing campus safety free of violence and, 195–196; #YesAllWomen movement empowering women to share concerns about, 196

Sexual stereotypes, 112–113

Sharing: expertise or opinion through social media, 77–78; personal information through social media, 76–77

Sharing economy: description of, 31; Generation Z's engagement with the, 32

Shark Tank (TV show), 217

Shepard, Matthew, 116

Smart phones: contributing to attention difficulties, 181; multiple communication channels available on, 58; negative influence on focus by, 180; texting using, 58–60

Social change: advocating and protesting for, 142–143; campaigning for candidates for, 139; creating a business with a social mission for, 134–135; crowdfunding sites to raise money for, 133–134; Generation Z's finding new solutions for new needs, 143–144; leading 5Ks and PTAs, 139–140; making a lifestyle change for, 136–137; sharing and forwarding news for, 132–133; shift service-learning to, 211–212; spreading news and views for, 130–133; volunteering vs. being "voluntold" for, 141–142; voting to promote, 137–139. *See also* Community engagement practices; Problems

Social gaming, 71–72

Social issues: beliefs about employment conditions and security, 101–104; climate change, 119–120; concerns over political dysfunction, 114–115; concerns over violence and endless wars, 108–109; connecting Generation Z practices to the passions they have about specific, 214; cultivate students' informed opinions and educated actions on, 220; financial security issues for Generation Z, 105–107; gay rights and LGBTQIA rights movement, 116–117, 196; Generation Z beliefs on racial equality as important, 40, 104–105*t*; Generation Z concerns over education, 97–101; human rights importance to Generation Z, 111–114; immigration and the border debate, 117–118; Internet security, 110–111; legalization of marijuana, 121; school shootings and safety, 36, 109–110; unhealthy food production and factory farming, 120–121

Social justice: designing a socially conscious college curriculum tied to, 203; Generation Z's beliefs shaped by exposure to diversity, 37–38; Generation Z's open-mindedness about diversity and, 39; human rights and, 111–114; immigration and the border debate, 117–118; racial equality, 40, 104–105*t*; realistic view of the American dream and, 39–40

Social learning approach (group work), 179, 181, 207–208

Social media: be aware of *creepy tree house* and adult-free zones of, 79–80, 223; building a social network through, 66–73; connectivity through, 65–66; deciding when specific platform is best for student connections, 223–224; drama and trust issues created through, 92–93; gender differences in use of, 78; Generation Z applications of, 73–80; impact on romantic relationships by, 91–94; as learning resource, 75, 174; role in Generation Z friendships, 88–89.

See also Communication;
Internet; The news; Technology
Social media applications: be aware
of *creepy tree house* and adult-free
zones, 223; deciding when
specific platforms are best for
specific, 223–224; to develop
students' information literacy,
222–223; for gaining new
knowledge and information, 75;
gender differences in use of social
media, 78; keeping up with others
through Facebook and
Instagram, 74–75; sharing and
forwarding news, 132–133;
sharing expertise or opinion,
77–78; for sharing personal
information, 76–77
Social networking sites: avatar
identity used on, 72, 77–78; be
aware of *creepy tree house* and
adult-free zones of, 79–80, 223;
blog sites, 70, 132; Buzzfeed, 131;
creating an online, 66–67;
crowdfunding, 133–134;
deciding when specific platform
is best for student connections,
223–224; Facebook, 61, 66–67,
72–80, 89; Instagram, 66, 67,
74–77, 80; online forums, 71;
Pinterest, 70–71; Reddit, 71, 131,
133; Tumblr, 70, 133; Twitter,
66–68, 72–73, 78–80, 132;
YouTube, 69–70, 75, 77
Space and time fluidity perception,
30
Spirituality: Generation Z's
self-identification with religion
and, 43; Generation Z's trend
away from organized religion and
toward, 43
Standardized testing, 177–178
Stanford University's Impulse
Control Disorders Clinic, 180
Startup Canada Awards, 144
Strengths-based leadership,
153–154
StrengthsFinder 2.0 (Clifton), 153
StrengthsFinder, StrengthsQuest,
and StrengthsExplorer program
(Gallup), 153, 154
Students with disabilities, 196
Study abroad opportunities, 216
Super-PACS, 115
Superstorm Sandy, 35

T

Taskrabbit, 34
Teachers: Generation Z's preference
for facilitated learning with,
179–180; as role models of
Generation Z, 158; teaching with
and not at Generation Z students,
204
Tebow, Tim, 162
Technological strategies: be wary of
creepy tree house and adult-free
social media zones, 79–80, 223;
deciding on when a specific
platform is best to use for student
connections, 223–224;
embracing the fact that
Generation Z students know and
rely on technology, 222–223; for
using the right social media for
students, 192, 222–224
Technology: bringing into the
cocurriculum for Generation Z

students, 209; communication channels through use of, 58–61; creating new opportunities for community engagement, 130; evolution of online gaming due to, 71–72; how it has shaped Generation Z's perceptions about information, 27–30; identity theft and Internet security concerns of, 110; romance in the digital world of, 90–94; as tool for school and learning, 184. *See also* Internet; Social media

TED Talks, 208

Telephone: 14 Reasons Why People Still Have Landlines, 131; Generation Z dislike for making voice calls over the, 59–60; smart phones, 58–60, 180

Terrorism: concerns over limitations on personal freedom due to fears of, 106–107; fears of airport, 35; September 11th and post/11 era and increase fears of, 34–36, 97

Texting, 58–60

Thinking (strategizing a plan) leadership style, 164–165

Thoughtfulness trait: influencing their relational aspect of motivation, 15; as self-described Generation Z characteristic, 9

Time and space fluidity perception, 30

Time magazine, 8

Top 10 Cartoon Characters' That Look Like a Political Figure, 130–131

Top Ten lists (David Letterman), 130

Tragedies and disasters: feeling unsafe due to, 36–37; Great Recession (2007–2009), 7, 35, 40; impact of September 11th on Generation Z, 34–36; the world perceived as a scary place, 35–36

Transparency: to build relationship with Generation Z, 193–194; Generation Z's value of leadership with honesty and, 166

Tumblr, 70, 133

TV binge-watching, 28

21 Jump Street (TV show), 87

Twilight (Meyer), 159

Twitter: gender differences in use of, 78; Generation Z's high use of Facebook and, 72–73, 79–80; getting the news through, 132; the hashtag generation of, 67–68; how Generation Z manages their familial and peer relationships on, 79–80; kept private from Generation Z's familial relationships, 80; primarily used for friends, 79–80; sending out "tweets" from, 66–68; when it is most appropriate to use for student connections, 223; #YesAllWomen movement empowering women to share concerns through, 196

U

Uber, 30, 31, 34

Unhealthy food production, 120–121

United States racial composition, 37
U.S. Census (2010), 37

V

Value-based goals, 219–220
Veteran students, 196
Vietnam War, 2, 97
Violence: bullying, 110; concerns
   over real and depicted, 108; of
   endless wars, 108–109;
   enhancing campus safety that is
   free of potential, 195–196; school
   shootings, 36, 109–110
Virtual pinboarding, 70–71
Virtual student support, 174–175
Volunteering: being "voluntold" vs.,
   141–142, 213–214; comparing
   Generation Z and Millennials
   students,' 142
Voting: Generation Z's distaste of
   politics and lack of, 138–139;
   power of the youth in the 2008
   election, 137
Voting Right Act, 38

W

WhatsApp, 80
Wi-Fi accessibility, 59, 180
Wikipedia, 26, 174

Wordpress, 70
Work: comparing Millennials and
   Generation Z preferences for
   workplace type and, 30;
   Generation Z's engagement in
   meaningful, 144; helping
   Generation Z to make the
   transition from colleges to careers
   and, 192–224; importance of
   providing Generation Z with
   learning experiences transferable
   to, 185; offer internship
   opportunities for realistic
   experience with future career,
   214–215. See also Employment

Y

#YesAllWomen movement, 196
YouTube: capturing experience
   through videos of, 69–70;
   gaining new knowledge through,
   75, 174; sharing expertise or
   opinions using, 77; used as part
   of college curriculum, 208; when
   it is most appropriate to use for
   student connections, 224

Z

Zuckerberg, Mark, 66